THE THEORY AND PRACTICE OF TEXT-EDITING

THE THEORY AND PRACTICE OF TEXT-EDITING

Essays in Honour of James T. Boulton

EDITED BY

IAN SMALL AND MARCUS WALSH

Senior Lecturers, School of English, University of Birmingham

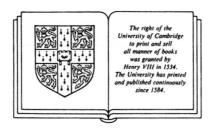

*The right of the
University of Cambridge
to print and sell
all manner of books
was granted by
Henry VIII in 1534.
The University has printed
and published continuously
since 1584.*

CAMBRIDGE UNIVERSITY PRESS

Cambridge
New York   Port Chester
Melbourne   Sydney

CAMBRIDGE UNIVERSITY PRESS
Cambridge, New York, Melbourne, Madrid, Cape Town, Singapore, São Paulo

Cambridge University Press
The Edinburgh Building, Cambridge CB2 2RU, UK

Published in the United States of America by Cambridge University Press, New York

www.cambridge.org
Information on this title: www.cambridge.org/9780521401463

First published 1991
This digitally printed first paperback version 2006

A catalogue record for this publication is available from the British Library

Library of Congress Cataloguing in Publication data
The Theory and practice of text editing: essays in honour of James T.
Boulton/edited by Ian Small and Marcus Walsh.
p.   cm.
Includes index.
ISBN 0 521 40146 1 (hardcover)
1. Editing. 2. Criticism. Textual. I. Boulton, James T.
II. Small, Ian. III. Walsh, Marcus.
PN162.T47 1992
801'.959–dc20 91-9690   CIP

ISBN-13 978-0-521-40146-3 hardback
ISBN-10 0-521-40146-1 hardback

ISBN-13 978-0-521-02705-2 paperback
ISBN-10 0-521-02705-5 paperback

Contents

Notes on contributors   *page* viii

Acknowledgements   x

Introduction: the theory and practice of text-editing   1
Ian Small and Marcus Walsh

1   D.H. Lawrence: problems with multiple texts   14
    John Worthen

2   Editing Johnson's *Dictionary*: some editorial and
    textual considerations   35
    Anne McDermott and Marcus Walsh

3   'Creeping into print': editing the letters of John
    Clare   62
    Mark Storey

4   Towards a mobile text   90
    Philip Brockbank

5   Rectifying Shakespeare's *Errors*: romance and
    farce in bardeditry   107
    Charles Whitworth

6   Victorian editors of *As You Like It* and the
    purposes of editing   142
    Russell Jackson

7   Bentley our contemporary; or, editors, ancient
    and modern   157
    Marcus Walsh

8   The editor as annotator as ideal reader   186
    Ian Small

James T. Boulton: publications 1951–1991   210

Index   216

vii

Notes on contributors

Philip Brockbank was Director of the Shakespeare Institute and Professor of English at the University of Birmingham. He was formerly Professor of English at the University of York, and was general editor of the New Cambridge Shakespeare. His publications include editions of *Coriolanus* (Arden Shakespeare), and of Ben Jonson's *Volpone* (New Mermaids). Philip Brockbank died while this book was in preparation.

Russell Jackson is a Fellow of the Shakespeare Institute at the University of Birmingham. He has edited Oscar Wilde's *The Importance of Being Earnest* (New Mermaids) and *Plays* by Henry Arthur Jones (Cambridge University Press). He is joint editor of *Theatre Notebook*, and, with Ian Small, is general editor of the Oxford English Texts edition of the *Complete Works of Oscar Wilde*. He is currently working on an edition of *As You Like It* for the New Cambridge Shakespeare.

Ann McDermott is Leverhulme Fellow on the Birmingham School of English Johnson *Dictionary* Project. She is currently completing a book on the thought of Samuel Johnson.

Ian Small is Senior Lecturer in English at the University of Birmingham. He has edited works by Oscar Wilde and Walter Pater. With Russell Jackson he is general editor of the Oxford English Texts edition of the *Complete Works of Oscar Wilde*.

Mark Storey is Professor of English at the University of Birmingham. His numerous publications include the Oxford

English Texts edition of the *Letters* of John Clare, *Poetry and Ireland since 1880: A Source-Book* (Routledge), and an edition of Gissing's *The Private Papers of Henry Ryecroft* (World's Classics).

Marcus Walsh is Senior Lecturer in English at the University of Birmingham. With Karina Williamson, he is editor of the Oxford English Texts edition of the *Poetical Works of Christopher Smart*, and of the Penguin *Christopher Smart: Selected Poems*. With Nigel Wood, he is Co-Director of the Birmingham School of English Johnson *Dictionary* Project.

Charles Whitworth is Lecturer in English at the University of Birmingham. He has edited *Three Sixteenth-Century Comedies* (New Mermaids), and is currently working on the Oxford edition of *The Comedy of Errors*.

John Worthen is Professor of English at University College, Swansea. He has edited *The Lost Girl*, *The Prussian Officer and Other Stories*, *Love Among the Haystacks and Other Stories*, and (with David Farmer and Lindeth Vasey) *Women in Love*, in the Cambridge edition of the works of D.H. Lawrence. He has also edited *The Rainbow* (Penguin).

Acknowledgements

The editors are grateful for the assistance of the Vice-Chancellor and the Registrar of the University of Birmingham, and for the help and support of Helen and Allan Wilcox, Doreen and Jonathan Brockbank, Kelsey Thornton, Geoff Barnbrook, Michael Black and Anne Buckley in the preparation of this book.

Introduction: the theory and practice of text-editing

Ian Small and Marcus Walsh

This collection of essays attempts to address some of the problems which its contributors have encountered in their work as practising textual editors. The practice of textual editing throws into sharp relief some of the crucial issues recently isolated by literary theorists. Simply in order to carry out their work – to produce editions for contemporary readers, that is – modern editors have to engage with, and make decisions about, some of the most contested of these issues. The questions of authorial intention, authority, the relationship between 'literary' and non-literary works, and hence the concept of literature itself, all affect the ways in which modern textual scholars set about their tasks.

Most of the contributors to this volume are members of the School of English at the University of Birmingham; all have been, in one or more capacities, associated with James T. Boulton. Together they have been involved in editing a considerable number and diversity of works, in the main undertaken over the thirteen years when James T. Boulton was head of the Department, later the School, of English at the University of Birmingham. These works include the Oxford and the Cambridge editions of Shakespeare; the Cambridge edition of the works and letters of D.H. Lawrence; the Oxford editions of the letters of John Clare, and of the *Poetical Works* of Christopher Smart; and the forthcoming Oxford edition of the *Complete Works* of Oscar Wilde. The essays which follow reflect this wide experience in the hard (and often tedious and undervalued) practice of editing, and draw attention especially to three related groups of editorial problems: those produced

by the variety of the physical embodiments in which texts
present themselves; those produced by the generic diversity of
the works we edit; and those produced by the different
purposes for which works are edited. Each of these issues
involves, in some form or other, larger theoretical problems in
English studies. They might best be approached under the
rubric of a general question, namely, what is the relationship of
the theory to the practice of editing?

Generally speaking, the relationship between theory and
practice in the whole field of literary studies has become
increasingly strained. Of course, literary studies have enjoyed
or endured a surfeit of theorizing over the past two decades.
Theories such as formalism, structuralism, postmodernism, and
cultural materialism have waxed and waned with a remarkable
regularity, so much so that the advent and demise of a new
theory within the space of a few years is not unusual. In the
general impetus to institute the study of theory as an end in
itself, to create what some have called a 'theory industry', the
relationship of theory to practice has been lost sight of. In most
other disciplines of knowledge theory is related to practice in a
rather different way: there are the practices used to carry out
the study of a discipline; and there is a theory of those practices
– that is, the explicit elaboration both of the principles which
underlie practices, and of the appropriateness of explanations
thus produced. Moreover, within any discipline there is usually
agreement about the adequacy of the theories used. In this
sense, the essays contained in this volume represent – to adapt
a phrase of Hans-Robert Jauss – the challenge of a practice to
theory. The large question which they attempt to answer is
whether any single theory of editing can encompass the
diversity of the texts we edit, or the purposes for which we edit
them.

The first issue, addressed by many essays in this volume, is
that of the variety of the physical embodiments in which texts
present themselves. Some works were realized in a variety of
different textual forms. Oscar Wilde's *The Picture of Dorian Gray*,
for example, was published first in *Lippincott's Monthly Magazine*,
and then extensively revised for its first book publication. Some
texts have a different or special status, such as working

performance texts of Shakespeare's plays (as discussed here by Philip Brockbank and Charles Whitworth), or poems which appear in autograph letters. Some texts have a history of extended and continuous revision. In this volume John Worthen discusses the problems which D.H. Lawrence's habits of extensive revision pose for the editor of his novels and poems. A different but related problem is presented by the discrete, fragmented, and extended revisions made by Samuel Johnson to the text of his *Dictionary* over two decades. Cases such as these all undermine the case for any unified theory of literary editing. The general question here is, in what senses is it possible to talk of a theory of editing which will encompass the diversity of textual forms in which works appear? The evidence offered by the contributors to this volume corroborates what has been suggested by many recent theorists: that textual editing is an inevitably pragmatic activity whose many practices can only with difficulty be subsumed under any single overarching theory.

The second significant issue which this volume addresses is that produced by disagreements about what could constitute a precise taxonomy of different kinds of writing. How, for example, can we define works as candidates for literary editing? Should editors treat literary and documentary or historical texts in the same manner, and why? What relationships do literary and non-literary texts have to each other? For some of the contributors to this volume this question has figured in a very precise way: in the possible justifications of, and the problems raised by, editing documents as varied as letters and dictionaries. Here the question is, on what grounds can such texts be considered literary? In general terms, the debate about editing literary and non-literary documents has mirrored a larger argument about the nature of literariness. Some recent theorists, particularly cultural materialists, have wished to disable the whole category of literary works, and subsume under some all-embracing concept of 'text' many hitherto distinct categories of writing. Indeed, the question of how to edit diverse texts was a topic which engaged a good deal of the attention of some textual scholars during the 1980s. In 1981, G. Thomas Tanselle made a distinction which at first sight seemed to go some way towards generating a theory of editing which could encompass literary and non-literary works. Tanselle suggested that the distinction between editing literary and non-literary texts should not be based on what an editor does with a text, but on what Tanselle calls 'the kinds of documents that editors ... have to deal with':

Two broad classes of documents, calling for different editorial treatment, do exist: documents preserving writings of the kind normally intended for publication and those preserving writings of the kind not normally intended for publication. Historians more often find themselves editing the latter kind of writing, and as a result they have not had as much experience editing the former as have literary scholars; and literary scholars, in turn, have had somewhat less occasion for editing private documents.[1]

Such a taxonomy has undoubtedly been adopted by many editors, but once more the practice of editing outruns the theory. Some classes of documents, particularly letters (with which some of the contributors to this volume have been concerned), show the inadequacy of Tanselle's distinction. The 'two broad classes' which he proposes are in fact not so clear-cut as he leads us to believe. The main drawback to Tanselle's proposition has to do with what the term 'publication' in this context means. For medieval authors, publication meant something quite different from what later writers might have understood by the term. Indeed the medieval relationship between author, authority, text, and reader, as Alastair Minnis notably has pointed out,[2] tests the assumptions of traditional editorial rationales most usually identified with the names of W.W. Greg and Fredson Bowers, and invariably posited upon the belief that the replication of a text by an agent other than the author is a process of inevitable textual corruption. But the problematic nature of publication also manifests itself with many more recent texts. Indeed, on closer examination, the term 'publication' seems to refer to such a wide variety of circumstances that any distinction based upon it loses most of its force.

    As we have indicated, the problems inherent in editing letters provide a good example of the complexity of the notion of 'publication', and therefore its unreliability as a practical guide for editing. It is possible to locate the letters of many literary figures on scales ranging from the intensely personal to the intentionally public, from the practical and quotidian to the more or less self-consciously literary. At one point would be the letters of Alexander Pope, written in some sense with publication in view; at another is the correspondence, private and often practical, of writers such as Christopher Smart and Walter Pater. At other points would be writers such as Lord Chesterfield, whose letters to his son are effectively a kind of *paedia*, and writers such as D.H. Lawrence and John Clare, some of whose letters form a narrative sequence. At some other point would have to be Oscar Wilde's long letter to Lord Alfred Douglas, *Epistola: In Carcere et Vinculis* (better known as *De Profundis*),[3] which, on his release from prison, Wilde gave to Robert Ross, together with instructions to have copies made and extracts of the letter circulated to friends.[4] Taken collectively, these distinctions in the status of letters make Tanselle's private/published opposition a difficult one to sustain, and suggest that other issues are involved. Indeed James T. Boulton's *Prospectus and Notes for Volume Editors of The Letters of D.H. Lawrence* is nicely aware of the complexity of the issues, asserting that Lawrence's letters 'are obviously documents of primary importance for any biographical study of Lawrence or critical assessment of his writings', yet pointing out that they have certain literary qualities similar to those found in his published 'literary' work; the *Prospectus* goes so far as to insist that readers will find in Lawrence's letters 'much of the creative vitality and brilliance which... [they] associate with his published writings' (pp. 1–2).

Such a comment suggests that the appropriate editorial criteria for editing documents such as letters are constituted primarily by their value, and only secondarily, despite Tanselle's insistence, by their nature. The work of contributors to this volume on the rationales for editing dictionaries and letters broadly endorses such a proposition. Proposals for the use of a criterion of value in editorial judgements have been made explicit by Claire Badaracco in an essay which is in part a reply to Tanselle. Indeed, she claims that the distinction between literary and historical editorial approaches is best understood in terms of a concept of value, although Badaracco uses the term 'value' in a special sense to distinguish between the relationships each kind of editor has with her 'text' or her document: 'How an editor approaches the problem of value precedes questions of principle, and it is upon the basis of the solution to the problem of value that principles and procedures are enacted.'[5] Badaracco's argument, simply put, is that questions of a text's value predetermine, and are anterior to, questions of its function; and that a text's function determines its status. It follows that, for a documentary editor, the relationship between value, function and status is not a problem, in the sense that questions of value (insofar as they affect historical or other documents) are determined by the community: they are not editorial decisions. Badaracco argues that the documentary (that is, historical) editor's audience is 'contemporaneous with the document'. For this reason 'the editor acts as a scribe, reporter, cultural archaeologist, and does not interpret or introduce the editorial persona in the edition'; for such an editor 'the business of editing is the art of evidentiary reporting' (pp. 42–3). The literary editor, however, does have a role in assigning value and function; indeed the very act of editing does itself assign value to a text. In these senses, the editor is a mediator, for the audience of a literary edition is contemporaneous with the editor rather than with the text:

The textual editor relates the authorial time to the present. Because the editor and hypothetical audience are contemporary, sharing cultural assumptions about the overall myth or general Story within which the edited text occupies a proportionate position like plot, the textual editor's work can be described as canonical. The editor relates the plot (or text) to the overall Story, acting as talebearer within the culture, by virtue of having presented the text. Both author and texts are other to editor and audience, and this admits the necessity for interpretation, elevating the role of the editor to that of a critic. (p. 42)

The specific experiences of contributors to this collection give such a distinction some force. The letters of D.H. Lawrence or

John Clare, for example, considered in relation to other individuals in their lives, are documents. To edit them as literary texts involves interpreting them in a way which was manifestly unnecessary and impossible for the original recipients; moreover it involves – as Badaracco once more indicates – assigning to them a place in a narrative sequence. Such an act of mediation is both a necessary precondition for their being considered literary texts, and a necessary consequence of such a consideration. The same issue arises in the case of Johnson's *Dictionary*; Anne McDermott and Marcus Walsh argue in their essay in this volume that to edit a dictionary as a literary work involves seeing it first in aesthetic categories.

Badaracco's use of the term 'textual editor' where most would use 'critical editor' suggests a Barthesian connection; editor and reader make the text 'readerly'. Fredson Bowers, in the same conference and in the same periodical, resisted wholesale such a proposal and argued instead that the critical editor must communicate the text in its historical particularity:

I cannot see that our present rigorous theories of editing the humanities have been affected by any other *Zeitgeist* than that the works of the past should be presented to today's readers – textually – as much as possible in terms of the age in which they were written, whether this was three or three hundred years ago.[6]

The argument that texts written at an earlier historical moment may be and should be presented to modern readers 'in terms of the age in which they were written' has been fundamental for modern humanist editors. It was implicit in the work of some of the earliest scholarly editors of secular scriptures in the early eighteenth century, and was explicitly formulated at least as early as the rise of German biblical–textual scholarship in the late eighteenth century. It is predicated on the assumption that any text that we edit has determinate meaning, and that meaning is produced by an author within the linguistic and cultural assumptions of his own historical time and place. If we are to understand the nature of the twin texts of Genesis, argued Eichhorn, we must read them 'as two historical works of high antiquity', and become intimately acquainted with 'the manner of thinking and imagining among uncultivated peoples gained through study of the ancient world'.[7]

The belief that texts are to be constituted and understood in their own historical terms has a bearing upon the last of the large issues which this volume seeks to address: the purposes for which works are edited, and the ways in which they are annotated. The contextual information that an editor must provide in order to enable the text to be understood is determined by the particularity of the text, by the specific connections and appeals it makes to its own world. The editor who brings a text from the past to the present must assess what now-lost information is necessary to an understanding of the text which would be equivalent to its original understanding, and provide that information in the commentary. This editorial practice is intimately related to what M.H. Abrams has called 'the traditional, or humanistic paradigm of the writing and reading of literature':

> Literature... is a transaction between a human author and his human reader. By his command of linguistic and literary possibilities, the author actualizes and records in words what he undertakes to signify of human beings and actions and about matters of human concern, addressing himself to those readers who are competent to understand what he has written. The reader sets himself to make out what the author has designed and signified, through putting into play a linguistic and literary expertise that he shares with the author. By approximating what the author undertook to signify the reader understands what the language of the work means.[8]

The aim of the editor is to enable the modern reader to become as 'competent' as the original intended readership, by making available again a once-shared 'linguistic and literary expertise'. It is precisely because a modern readership knows not less than, but differently from, a seventeenth-century one, precisely because past texts (as McGann as well as Badaracco has argued[9]) are other, that annotation becomes necessary. The editor must, for example, tell an eighteenth-century audience what was generally understood about bees in Milton's time, or a late twentieth-century audience what Wilde means by a Tantalus frame, or why D.H. Lawrence should associate pink pills with pale people.[10]

Annotation must thus be partly determined by the nature of the modern audience for whom the edition is intended. Here once again the apparently uncontentious practice of editors turns out to involve theoretical complexities. In the context of an argument against the New Critical assumption that our main source of information about a poem is the poem itself, Gerald Graff insists that 'there is no telling how much a poem or any other text "can tell us about itself"', since that will be relative to how much requisite background information its reader already possesses. It is impossible to specify in advance the extent to which any text is independent of contextual information, since this will depend on who reads the text, when, and in what circumstances.'[11] Some editions of course are produced only with a restricted scholarly audience in mind; one of the writers of this Introduction was once advised to annotate imagining that Helen Gardner was the model reader. Other editions however are aimed at the undergraduate or school-age reader, whose reading experience might differ from that of Dame Helen. Some editions of English literary works may seek an audience among non-English users, who require quite different, and much fuller, kinds of annotation. In any case the theoretical assumptions of the annotating editor are inevitably not those of the New Criticism. Speaking with Richards's *Practical Criticism* in mind, and with the experience of a university teacher, Graff credibly asserts that a coherent and sympathetic understanding of past writings is not likely to be inculcated by 'bare, unmediated contact with the work itself'.[12]

Much larger questions are begged here. To what extent, for example, is it desirable to understand the work in its past context? And to what extent is it possible to re-make the context of understanding? To what extent is meaning dependent on reference? Indeed Stanley Fish has argued that the different explanatory hypotheses presented in the *Variorum Milton* of, for example, the 'two-handed engine' in 'Lycidas' are evidence that such problems 'cannot be solved, at least not by the methods traditionally brought to bear on them', and has concluded 'that the commentators and editors have been asking the wrong questions'.[13] Most annotating editors work on the assumption that such interpretative problems are in principle always soluble by the advancing of a convincing hypothesis based upon referential evidence; that such cruces are, in George Steiner's words, 'contingent, always susceptible to the bringing to bear of relevant information'.[14] Ultimately this disagreement about the methods and possibilities of annotation turns on the answers to quite fundamental questions about textual determinacy, and about the nature of explanatory hypotheses.

Humanist editing has indeed been predicated on the assumption, often unspoken, that it is possible to distinguish between, on the one hand, genuinely explicatory annotation which brings to bear upon the text those forms of contextual knowledge which are essential to the understanding of its determinate meaning, and, on the other hand, more subjective modes of commentary founded on assumptions of the indeterminacy of the text and of its meaning. That non-humanist tradition has a long history, in allegorizing Greek and Roman interpretations of Homer, in the gemara, in the cabbala, in fourfold medieval exegesis of the Bible. Most recently it has been manifested in the works of (to use Abrams's term) 'Newreaders' of a variety of persuasions, including Derrida, Bloom, and Fish. Few modern editors are Newreaders. Within the relatively recent history of the editing of secular and vernacular 'literary' texts, an extreme form of an editor's insistence on his rights to evaluate and criticize his text is to be found in Richard Bentley, the reception of whose edition of Milton suggests that he was not readily accepted as 'talebearer' within his own culture. In that debate between Bentley and his eighteenth-century opponents we see theory arising out of attempts to characterize and defend conflicting editorial practices. Increasingly notoriously, Shakespeare has been a locus of the imposition of a normative cultural stance, in schools as well as in the playhouse and the cinema. Russell Jackson demonstrates the (to modern eyes) astonishing conviction and consistency with which Victorian editors of Shakespeare present the Bard's plays as works in which may be seen, and from which may be learned, the desirable shared values of

Victorian culture. This may not be wholly contemptible, but it is clearly a 'talebearing', a nineteenth-century version of Shakespeare Our Contemporary, rather than a re-presentation of an objectively knowable past.

Even if it is agreed that editing and editorial annotation may reasonably be thought to re-present a knowable past, it remains inescapably true that editing must be an act of mediation for the benefit of the modern audience who, as Badaracco insists, are the editor's contemporaries. Robert Halsband has remarked, in words quoted by James T. Boulton in the *Prospectus* for the Cambridge Lawrence, that letters must be printed by editors 'in such a form as to allow them to be read as widely as possible, and with ease and pleasure'; otherwise, 'we are in danger of creating a coterie scholarship, when we will only read each other's footnotes' (p. 2). No editor can afford to be unaware of those who will use the eventual text, and this must affect the editing of the text itself as well as any accompanying annotations.

A particularly fraught aspect of the editor's task of textual mediation is the question of modernization. Modernization is viewed by many theorists as 'always unscholarly',[15] and this not merely for reasons of taste but because it raises crucial questions about our attitude to the historical orientation of the text. According to Philip Gaskell, 'the deliberate modernization of the spelling, punctuation, etc. of an early text is undesirable because it suggests that the modern meaning of the words of the text is what the author meant by them; because it conceals puns and rhymes; because it causes the editor to choose where the author was ambiguous; and because it deprives the work of the quality of belonging to its own period'.[16] Partial modernization has been subjected to a particularly severe questioning by theorists of the stature of Bowers and Hershel Parker.[17] There is no doubt at all that modernization is inevitably interpretation or translation, as is clear from the writings of those who would defend, as well as those who would attack it.[18] However, editors who would themselves have serious doubts about modernization in editions for a scholarly market may not infrequently find themselves constrained by the requirement for full or partial modernization, in editions intended, often as part of a publisher's series, for a larger market. It may be possible to argue for a consistent and coherent approach to partial modernization on the basis of the essential distinction between author's intention and printing house practice.[19]

There are identifiable revolutions in the history of textual editing associated for example with Erasmus, with Bentley, with Lachmann, with Greg. There is no doubt that the last ten or fifteen years have seen as active, as wide-ranging, and, in most respects, as open-minded a debate amongst editors as at almost any moment in the past. Recent writers have insisted on and explored flexible ideas about the uses of copy-text. Questions of value and subjectivity in editorial judgement and procedure have been widely debated. The nature of textual production, with reference to both authorial and non-authorial determinants, has been closely analysed and extensively theorized. In the whole field of English studies some of the most powerful and distinguished writers of our time are practising and theorizing editors – George Kane, Jerome McGann, G. Thomas Tanselle. The theoretical debate is set to become yet more lively, compelling, and central as technological changes revolutionize attitudes to editing and book production, as standardized text encoding systems and computational analysis become increasingly commonplace, and as the edition in the form of the printed book is joined by the edition in electronic forms. This collection of essays is intended as a contribution to this continuing discussion.

NOTES

1 G. Thomas Tanselle, 'Literary Editing', in *Literary and Historical Editing*, ed. George L. Vogt and John Bush Jones (Kansas, 1981), p. 37.
2 See A.J. Minnis, *Medieval Theory of Authorship* (London, 1984).
3 The letter now known as *De Profundis* is reprinted in *Letters of Oscar Wilde*, ed. Rupert Hart-Davis (London, 1962), pp. 423–511.
4 For details of Wilde's instructions, see *ibid.*, pp. 512–13.
5 Claire Badaracco, 'The Editor and the Question of Value: Proposal', *TEXT*, 1 (1984), p. 42.

6 Fredson Bowers, 'The Editor and the Question of Value: Another View', *TEXT*, 1 (1984), 59.

7 Quoted by Jerome McGann, *The Beauty of Inflections* (Oxford, 1985), pp. 98–9.

8 M.H. Abrams, 'How to do Things with Texts', in his *Doing Things with Texts: Essays in Criticism and Critical Theory* (New York, 1989), pp. 269–70.

9 McGann, *The Beauty of Inflections*, p. 107.

10 Pearce's reference to Butler's *Feminine Monarchie*, in his note on *Paradise Lost*, VII, 490, referred to in Marcus Walsh's essay on Bentley in this volume; the stage directions to Act III of Oscar Wilde, *Lady Windermere's Fan*, ed. Ian Small (London, 1980), p. 52; James T. Boulton's note on Lawrence's letter to Blanche Jennings of 6 March 1909, *The Letters of D.H. Lawrence*, I (1979), 119.

11 Gerald Graff, *Professing Literature: An Institutional History* (Chicago, 1987), p. 190.

12 *Ibid.*, p. 255.

13 Stanley Fish, *Is There a Text in this Class?* (Cambridge, Mass., 1980), p. 149.

14 George Steiner, 'On Difficulty', in *On Difficulty and Other Essays* (Oxford, 1972), pp. 26–7.

15 Bowers, 'The Editor and the Question of Value: Another View', p. 54.

16 Gaskell, *From Writer to Reader* (Oxford, 1978), p. 8.

17 See Bowers, 'The Text of Johnson', *Modern Philology*, 61 (1964), 298–309; Hershel Parker, 'Regularizing Accidentals: The Latest Form of Infidelity', *Proof*, 3 (1973), 1–20.

18 See, for example, Gary Taylor and Stanley Wells, *Modernizing Shakespeare's Spelling* (Oxford, 1979); *Re-Editing Shakespeare for the Modern Reader* (Oxford, 1984), especially pp. 5–31.

19 Such an argument is offered by Karina Williamson and Marcus Walsh in the Preface to their Penguin Classics edition of Christopher Smart's *Selected Poems* (Harmondsworth, 1990). For a key theoretical statement on the importance of the distinction between author's practice and printer's practice, see Tom Davis, 'The CEAA and Modern Textual Editing', *Library*, 32 (1977), 61–74.

CHAPTER I

D.H. Lawrence: problems with multiple texts

John Worthen

Textual editors in our tradition have been educated to believe that it is their normal job to produce the single, superior text which marks an advance on all previous versions and texts. Charles L. Ross, for example, maintains, in his Introduction to the Penguin edition of *Women in Love* (1982), that 'this edition corrects all major substantive errors in Seltzer. As a result it has the...distinction of being the most accurate text yet published' (p. 47). The General Editors' Preface to the Oxford *Dombey and Son* (1974) tells us that 'in this edition a critical text is established, a text free from the numerous corruptions that disfigure modern reprints' (p. v). The recent Garland editor of *Ulysses*, Hans Walter Gabler, goes so far as to describe his job as 'beyond correction to establish the text', and to assert that 'this critical edition endeavours to conserve intact Joyce's text for *Ulysses*' (p. vii). It is probably inevitable that textual editors should not only use language such as 'the most accurate text' and 'the text', but should also be tempted to the hubristic extreme of claiming to have established the text 'beyond correction'. Gabler is simply being bold enough to articulate what many editors believe about their texts, but would hesitate to assert. For it is as something single, and ideally final, that we have come to conceive of 'the text'. Even if we recognize that such an object may at least in some details have to be an ideal construct of the editor, all the same, usually – if idealistically – we continue to believe in such 'accurate', 'intact', or 'critical' texts as our appropriate, common goal.

It is, however, unfortunately the case that fairly often the works of the authors we are editing turn out to be resistant to the very idea of the single, appropriate text. Almost every editor will at some stage realize a problem of that kind; most editors, however, will bury or suppress their unease. And that is because, as editors, we remain extremely suspicious of goals other than that of 'the text'. The idea, for example, that there might be different editions, which properly serve different kinds of readers, which yet are equally valid, is still one which raises eyebrows. I wish, however, to present an argument which not only suggests that, sometimes, editions are appropriately multiple, but that, on occasion, texts are too; because, either in significant details, or even (in some cases) throughout, there exists no 'single text'. Such ideas have been outlined by others before me, of course. The very idea of the synchronous text as argued by Gabler and others (and presented in the Gabler edition of *Ulysses*) is a way of asserting that a text may be called multiple when, as edited, it provides the full evidence of its creation; any other version of the same work would fall a long way short of being 'the text'.

But I am not concerned with such an idea of the 'multiple text', any more than I shall be arguing (except by implication) for the validity of multiple editions of the same work, or (for that matter) be discussing editions stressing the primacy of the author and his or her intention, as opposed to what might be called cultural-primacy editing. Those schools of editing (if they acknowledged each other's existence) might indeed claim to be concerned with the multiplicity of appropriate texts.[1] I shall, instead, restrict myself to evidence emerging from the recent editing of the work of D.H. Lawrence; and I shall simply be suggesting that, on occasion at least, no such thing as 'the text' of his work can be said to exist.

At one extreme, as an obvious if very simple example of how extensive the problem of multiple text may become, it has long been recognized that a number of Lawrence's poems exist in versions so utterly different from each other as to constitute, not just different versions of one text, but actually different poems: genuinely multiple texts, of an even more sharply defined kind than those created by Henry James's notorious revisions in the 1907–8 New York edition of his work. The poem 'Virgin

Youth', for example, which first appears in one of Lawrence's Nottingham University poetry notebooks,[2] probably dating from 1910 at latest, and which reappears in the notebook he used in 1916 to prepare the poems for his volume *Amores*,[3] suffered an extraordinary revision in 1928, when Lawrence was putting together his *Collected Poems*. Only five lines of the original twenty-two-line poem (lines 1, 4, 8, 10, 11) are even similarly phrased, out of a text finally totalling fifty-six lines: only the very first line, of three words – 'Now and again' – is identical in both poems. As editors or critics of Lawrence's work, we need to choose which poem to edit, or to discuss: in no sense is there a single poem entitled 'Virgin Youth'. The same point could be made, if a little less strikingly, about a number of the poems revised for Lawrence's 1928 collection. These versions could not be editorially conflated with their forerunners, any more than James's revisions to some of his texts. The case for the multiplicity of versions of a number of Shakespeare's texts (in particular those of *King Lear*) has of course also been widely discussed during the past decade.[4] To edit versions, rather than conflate texts, is of course the decision of Shakespearean editors who believe that the two versions of *King Lear* represent two chronologically distinct and possibly distant versions, created in and for different theatrical and publishing situations. But I am here more interested in examining cases where the editor of Lawrence actually has a problem, rather than in cases like 'Virgin Youth', where strictly speaking he has not.

Every editor, however, will be aware of more problematic multiple texts occurring when the question of one text's priority over another is not only unclear, but possibly cannot be clarified. A choice, for example, fairly often has to be made between the reading of a surviving authorial manuscript, and that of a subsequent printed text; and that choice can sometimes turn into a simple decision about whether the change in question was introduced by the author, either in a manuscript later than any now surviving, or in proof. The text has, for that word, phrase, or sentence, become multiple: which is to say that there are two possible readings, both potentially authorial, but only one of them certainly so. And the certainly authorial reading is equally certainly early, and possibly superseded. If no proofs (or only uncorrected proofs) survive, then the final editorial decision about the appropriate text to print may become as arbitrary as 'following copy-text' sometimes inevitably is. Such cases are known to every editor, and they will be solved as they always have been, by a combination of knowledge of the author's habits of revision, knowledge of the printer's or typist's habits of textual transmission, a decision about the relative importance of the author in the process of textual transmission, and critical judgement.

The second sort of multiple text in Lawrence which I wish to examine is of just that kind, and occurs in very precise and local forms: where, for a sentence or phrase, there is arguably no such thing as a single text. My four examples, of rather different kinds, are taken from *Women in Love* as it has recently been edited.[5]

(1) At some point between August and October 1916, while engaged in extensive revision of the typescripts he himself had made of the first three-fifths of the novel, Lawrence inserted an ink revision into one of the two copies of the typescript, to create the phrase 'wry, satiric face' (TS1a, p. 259). When his wife Frieda copied this into the other copy of the typescript (TS1b) – she was assisting him in the very considerable task of transferring the revisions – she produced 'dry satiric face'. This phrase was perpetuated when TS1b was retyped (not by Lawrence) as TS11 early in 1917; but in TS11, sometime between 1917 and 1919, Lawrence himself revised the phrase to 'dry, sly face' (p. 338). What, one may ask, is 'the text' at such a point? One might argue that the revised reading of TS11, representing Lawrence's final thoughts on the matter, should be adopted as the text; but one might argue with equal point that his revision was prompted by an error: he attempted to recover his original reading (and did manage to restore the omitted comma), but failed to recover it completely (he no longer had either TS1a or TS1b in his possession to consult). An editor, however, can recover it for him. Against that, it could

be argued that Lawrence, according to his own practice evident elsewhere, would have been most unlikely to have checked TS1a or TS1b even if they had been in his possession; his concept of text was always that of a work developing to its own final shape, and he would probably not have objected if his wife participated in that process. This, again, is a useful example of a case where the degree of an editor's commitment to the traditional idea of 'the author' is crucial; the more one believes in such an author's solitary responsibility for his text, the more likely one is to evade Frieda Lawrence's influence if possible; the more one believes in the creation of text as a collaborative activity, the more likely one is to accept her contribution and not evade her. That, however, simply reinforces my argument that, at such a point, the text is multiple; it is possible for an editor to adopt either text, for good and responsible reasons. Neither text (in spite of the best endeavours of editors) can be demonstrated 'correct'; yet to adopt one text means to eclipse the other. If the texts are genuinely multiple, all an editor may be able to do is choose one text and record the readings of the other in a textual apparatus. Not all editions will, however, have such an apparatus; providing that circumstances permit, nevertheless, an editor may be able to explain, in an introduction, or in a footnote or explanatory note, what has been done. In the case of the Cambridge edition, where of course we have a textual apparatus, we have decided that, on this occasion, Frieda should be evaded (Lawrence's restoration of the missing comma is for us a small but significant indication of what he was trying to do). Such a choice does not, however, indicate that we reject the idea of a text collaboratively achieved, or that we believe the author's text to be somehow unassailable. But, along with most editors, we have the problem of providing a publisher and a readership with 'a text'; that does not mean that we believe it is the only possible text, or even the 'right' text – only that, on this occasion, it is perhaps a better text. And we recognize that there might well be other editors who would disagree with us.

The whole matter, indeed, of an author's spouse being

involved in the production of a version of a work of literature raises fascinating problems. Frieda's writing appears more than once in Lawrence's manuscripts: in the holograph of his 1913 story 'New Eve and Old Adam', for example, two adjectives on the first page in Lawrence's handwriting have been crossed out and replaced by adjectives in Frieda's handwriting – both of them relating to a character she might well have seen as a portrait of herself. (It is also noticeable that her adjustments to the text of *Women in Love* occur more frequently in places where Ursula is the character whose speech or appearance is to be adjusted, as if Frieda felt that she had certain rights over the character.) In 'New Eve and Old Adam', Lawrence made Paula Moest's first remark run: '"I can't see it was so wonderful of you, to hurry home to me, if you are so tame when you do come."' Frieda replaced 'tame' with 'cross'. A few lines lower down, Paula's green eyes are described by Lawrence as having 'a curious, inhuman expression'; Frieda adjusted the phrase to 'a curious, puzzled expression'.[6] Here, as in *Women in Love*, Frieda Lawrence seems to have been using her husband's pen, as her ink and penstrokes – though not, fortunately, her handwriting – appear identical to corrections made in Lawrence's own hand. The two of them probably worked, on both occasions, in the same room, with the same pen, almost certainly discussing the work as they went along. At what stage does assistance become collaboration – or error itself become collaborative?

(2) A different kind of multiple text, not one involving Frieda Lawrence, occurs a little later in *Women in Love*. Lawrence had typed 'An access of worship came over his mind' into TS1 (p. 292) when describing how Gerald reacted to Gudrun. The typist of TS11, however, totally altered the meaning by producing 'An excess of worship came over his mind' (p. 379). While revising TS11, Lawrence changed the fourth word from 'worship' to 'appreciation'. Which, then, is the proper text of the novel for an editor to print? What, indeed, is 'the text' at all? That of TS1 or of the revision in TS11? In the case of a constantly revising author such as Lawrence, it is not surprising that *Women in Love* has a number

of equally problematic cases. An editor's job, of course, is to judge how to distinguish an appropriate course of action; but, in some cases, that action will inevitably be simply to adopt one text at the expense of the other. In this case, we decided that Lawrence's attention to the problematic reading – he was clearly thinking carefully about it, when he replaced 'worship' by 'appreciation' – is outweighed by the fact that 'appreciation' is a word which (compared with 'worship') inevitably lessens the extent of the character's feelings, whilst it was the typist's error which created the very 'excess' of feelings which 'appreciation' serves to counter. Again, however, our adoption of one reading, however much we could justify our choice of it, does not mean that the other reading is not also significant, and might well be considered to be preferable.

(3) My third example from *Women in Love* is a case rather similar to my second. In his notebook manuscript, Lawrence wrote of Gudrun's reaction to Gerald:

But she felt him quiver, and come down involuntarily nearer upon her. He could not help himself. (p. 67)

This appeared correctly in TS1, but the typist of TS11 altered the 'her' at the end of the first sentence to 'him' (p. 530). Lawrence saw that something had gone wrong when he revised TS11, but made an adjustment which in fact altered his meaning completely. He retained the erroneous 'him', and made Gudrun the one to 'come down involuntarily':

But she felt him quiver, and she came down involuntarily nearer upon him. He could not help himself. (p. 530)

Arguments could be adduced either to restore the original, or to preserve the final reading. Has Lawrence radically revised his text? Or has he, rather, confused it? He has certainly attended to it with some care, even if the sentence he did not revise – 'He could not help himself' – reads more plausibly when it is Gerald, not Gudrun, who acts 'involuntarily'. That last point weighed heavily with us when we decided to return to the reading of MS and TS1; the text is arguably more coherent when the error (and emendation) are rejected. Yet, again, while being certain that our judgement has assisted us in making an appropriate choice, we cannot say that our text is the 'right' or only one.

(4) My last example, different again, concerns the result of the typist of the last part of TSI at one point omitting an eight-word phrase. Gerald is stooping down, at Gudrun's request, to look into her handbag; in Lawrence's notebook manuscript she sees him

undoing the loosely buckled strap. She had conquered him, he was stooping down, servile. (p. 269)

TSI skipped the line of writing between 'strap' and 'servile', and produced:

undoing the loosely buckled strap, servile. (p. 557)

Lawrence revised this in TSII to read:

undoing the loosely buckled strap, inattentive. (p. 669)

Should one restore the original, omitted phrase? If one restores it, then does it follow that the revision 'inattentive' will have to be discarded? Can one, in fact, ignore such a revision, Lawrence's final comment on a particular moment in his fiction? Would it be better, perhaps, to combine both original and revision – and thus cause Lawrence, in effect, to emend a sentence which (to him, revising TSII) did not exist? I would myself be sure that to combine the two readings would be one of the few ways in which we can be certain one should *not* proceed. But my argument is that, again, there can be no 'proper' – that is, single – reading of the text. In this case we have chosen to adopt the original, manuscript, version of the text on the grounds that the word 'servile' belonged to (and was explained by) the omitted phrase; and that thus when Lawrence read the word divorced from its proper context, he naturally altered it to a more neutral one. I would argue, however, that both authorial readings, the original and the revision, are valid. Traditionally, editors would feel obliged to adduce some argument to 'prove' that one reading was demonstrably more correct or more important than the other, even if this argument were really no more than a plea in favour

of the reading which the editor preferred. I quote from Alan
Horsman justifying his procedure in just such a case in the
editing of *Dombey and Son*: he is distinguishing an occasion
'where an error in the proof prompts Dickens to correct but the
correction gives a reading inferior to that in MS. Here the
restoration of the MS reading is required, since, if it had
appeared in the proof, the correction would have been
unnecessary and this particular correction unlikely.'[7] The
phrase 'inferior to that in MS' is clearly the hinge upon which
the argument pivots. Horsman may be right that Dickens
would not have altered his text if it had not been for the error,
though, of course, not even that can be proved; he might have
altered it anyway. But since Dickens has altered it, the editor
has a problem; and I am struck by the fact that Horsman's
main reason for rejecting what Dickens has now chosen to write
is because he judges it 'inferior' to what Dickens originally
wrote. The editor has based his procedure, as editors often do,
upon a critical judgement, but Horsman's language ('the
restoration of the MS reading is required') suggests a rather less
partial procedure. It is also doubtful whether a simple and
unsupported judgement of one text's 'inferiority' is the right
kind of critical judgement for an editor to be exercising. It is
perhaps Horsman's need to define only one of the two texts as
'correct' – to see his potentially multiple texts as 'single' – that
makes him dismiss one text out of hand, and adopt a language
in which the manuscript reading is, sternly and impersonally
(as if the editor had no choice), 'required'.

If the problem of multiple texts in Lawrence were confined
to occasional phrases, however, even if Frieda's collaboration
were a factor in some cases, none of us would perhaps be very
worried. That is, unfortunately, not the position. In the cases of
the heavily (or totally) revised poetry, we can at least choose
which version we are going to edit: revised or unrevised, early
or late, unpublished or published. But on other occasions the
editor's task is much more difficult. Where, for example, we
have, as we frequently do in Lawrence, two typescript copies of
a single work, created at the same time but emended differently,
it may not be possible to determine which text should take

priority, or what, indeed, 'priority' might be in such a case. It became a habit of Lawrence, when he had two typescript copies of a single work (usually a ribbon-copy and a carbon-copy), to revise them slightly differently. He was not alone in this, of course; in a celebrated case, Fredson Bowers was confronted by the evidence of Stephen Crane correcting the two typescripts of *The Red Badge of Courage* differently, one typescript containing 'a different and more extensive set of authorial revisions'.[8] When dealing with the relatively few cases where both texts represented Crane's revisions, made with equal authority but differently, Bowers very properly admitted that 'both versions have equal authority, and the choice... by the present editor is a purely arbitrary one'.[9]

But in Lawrence's case, the problem is extensive, and arbitrary choices might not seem appropriate. The first time we find him correcting two typescripts differently was, in fact, the first time he ever had two typescripts: the typed copies of the story then called 'The Right Thing to Do/The Only Thing to be Done' (later 'The Shades of Spring'), made by Douglas Clayton early in 1912. These two typescripts must have been revised slightly differently, as the text derived from the (missing) carbon copy, reproduced in *Forum* magazine,[10] varies in detail from the text of the (surviving) ribbon-copy.[11] Lawrence did just the same with the revisions to the two surviving copies of the duplicate typescripts made of *Women in Love* in 1916, TS1a and TS1b; he did the same with the two typescripts made of *Mr Noon* in 1921.[12] He did it again with the two typescripts of *Aaron's Rod* made in the summer of 1921 (of which only one survives), with the two typescripts of *Fantasia of the Unconscious*, corrected in the autumn of 1921, with the two typescripts of *The Boy in the Bush* which he corrected in 1923–4, and with the three typescripts of *Lady Chatterley's Lover* corrected early in 1928.[13] It may be possible, in such cases, to determine which of the variant typescripts should take priority; the ribbon-copy of 'The Right Thing to Do/The Only Thing to be Done', for example, served as setting-copy for the story's publication as 'The Soiled Rose' in the *Blue Review* in 1913,[14] and Lawrence used a revised copy of the magazine text as setting-copy for the story's volume publication in *The Prussian Officer and Other Stories* in 1914; he therefore gave the ribbon-copy version of the story a kind of retrospective authority which he denied the carbon-copy. Again, he chose to send copy TS1b of the *Women in Love* typescripts to his agent J. B. Pinker in January 1917, knowing that it would be retyped and that the future text of the novel would be derived from it. TS1b therefore arguably acquired authority over TS1a and the variant readings of the latter. Of the two typescripts of *Mr Noon*, Lindeth Vasey writes that 'Lawrence sent out both typescripts, and it was pure chance which one might have appeared in print.' However, she goes on to argue that 'TCC1 contains his latest revisions and must be the base-text for this edition'.[15] In the case of *Aaron's Rod*, the sole surviving typescript was the source of Seltzer's American edition; the corrections made to the other typescript are preserved only in the English edition of the novel derived from it. The latter was, however, also subject to some unauthorized revision by its publisher, Martin Secker, so that it is mostly impossible to distinguish alternative typescript corrections from Secker's own alterations. Only in cases such as the title to Chapter 17 – 'High Up over the Cathedral Square' in the surviving typescript and in Seltzer's edition, and 'Nel Paradiso' in Secker's edition – is it possible to be certain that one is seeing the evidence of alternative typescript revision. However, it appears that it is possible to distinguish, within the two surviving typescripts of *The Boy in the Bush* (which are mixtures of ribbon and carbon pages), the pages which at any one moment contain Lawrence's later or second revisions, to which priority may reasonably be given; and the same may be possible within the two surviving typescripts of *Fantasia of the Unconscious*. In the case of *Lady Chatterley's Lover*, Lawrence had, in all, three typescripts (one for his Florentine printer, one for his American publisher Knopf, and one for the English publisher Martin Secker); only the typescript destined for Knopf still survives, but it was clearly revised differently from the typescript used as setting-copy for the Florentine edition.[16] The textual variants in the Knopf typescript belong, therefore, to a textual cul-de-sac, playing no part in the creation of the novel's final text; but as with all these variant typescripts, we certainly cannot dismiss their textual variants as unimportant. In most cases it was a matter of chance which typescript, and therefore which variants, went forward along the line of textual transmission. I would argue that, in each case, the typescript variants – though playing no part in the creation of the final text – nevertheless have a particular textual status, and provide us with a species of textual sub-culture. They are themselves, in fact, examples of multiple texts, and they have a claim on our attention perhaps rather more pressing than the layers of revision which, for Gabler, make up 'the text' of *Ulysses*. Significantly, Lindeth Vasey acknowledged the status of Lawrence's variant typescript readings in her edition of *Mr Noon*: 'because TS1 has nearly equal authority [to TCC1], all its variants are recorded in the textual apparatus'.[17]

Having offered these examples of multiple texts, in Lawrence, I would like, before concluding with a still more striking example, to suggest that in one rather celebrated case, where there might appear to be a rather large and worrying problem of multiple text, in fact there is not. Lawrence finished the final manuscript of *Sons and Lovers* on 19 November 1912, and immediately sent it to Edward Garnett, whom he counted as a friend, and who had for about a year been playing the role of his agent. Garnett had given him a great deal of help and advice about publication. But it was Garnett who, as publisher's reader for Duckworth, had encouraged Duckworth to accept the novel in July 1912, and had encouraged Lawrence to do one final draft of it. He had supplied lists of suggestions which he thought Lawrence could use. It was, therefore, to Garnett in his professional capacity as publisher's reader that Lawrence sent the manuscript. In that capacity Garnett read and judged it. By 1 December, he must have replied with the unpleasant news that, so far as he (and Duckworth) were concerned, the novel was too long and had to be cut: and that he would do the cutting, without waiting for Lawrence's approval or permission. Lawrence's response clearly indicates his feelings at this stage:

I sit in sadness and grief after your letter. I daren't say anything. All right, take out what you think is necessary – I suppose I shall see what you've done when the proofs come, at any rate. I'm sorry I've let you in for such a job – but don't scold me too hard, it makes me wither up.[18]

Lawrence had defended the novel's form and length in a very eloquent letter when he had first sent Garnett the manuscript: 'If you can't see the development – which is slow like growth – I can' (*Letters*, I, 477). But, very much in need of the money that the novel would earn him, he was in no position to protest against Garnett's strictures, and Garnett accordingly reduced the length of the novel by approximately one-tenth.

It might appear that a modern textual editor is faced with a problem in this situation. On the one hand, Lawrence had argued eloquently for his novel's integrity, was writing a new and remarkable kind of novel, and was obviously distressed by the fact that Garnett felt that the novel had to be cut. On the other, he knew that he badly needed to get his novel into print, and that Garnett's skill and experience would certainly enable him to do so; and in mid-February, when he had seen the proofs, Lawrence acknowledged the fact that Garnett 'did the pruning jolly well, and I am grateful. I hope you'll live a long long time, to barber up my novels for me before they're published'; and that Garnett 'did well in the cutting – thanks again' (*Letters*, I, 517, 520). At least two critics, Keith Sagar and Mark Schorer, have argued that the novel actually benefited from Garnett's cutting,[19] and that we (like Lawrence) should be grateful to Garnett.

Such critics have, however, ignored a number of problems. The first is that Lawrence's final draft of the novel – 'haven't I made it patiently, out of sweat as well as blood' (*Letters*, I, 476) – arguably had a coherence which either escaped Garnett, or with which he was less concerned than he was with the length and appearance of the kinds of novels Duckworth normally published. We should ask, if we think of once more publishing the text as Garnett cut it, why the publisher's standards of 1912 should dictate, today, the form in which the work of an original genius like Lawrence should take.

The second problem is that Garnett's cutting also involved a small but significant amount of bowdlerization, both on the manuscript and in the proofs. Unless we are concerned to make our edition the record of a particular historical period, most editors would not want to accept such bowdlerization.

The third problem is that many of Garnett's cuts, however judiciously carried out, damaged the novel. Without, for example, the four-page account (cut by Garnett) of Paul meeting Miriam at the library in Chapter 7 ('Lad-and-Girl Love'), and their intimate talk afterwards, the whole balance of the novel's presentation of Paul and Miriam is upset. When we come across such phrases as 'this atmosphere of subtle intimacy',[20] we are liable to think that Lawrence is fiddling the evidence of what he has shown us, when actually he has carefully and subtly prepared his way. Without the extended treatment of William in the first part of the novel, as an example of the effects of Mrs Morel's love on her sons (which Garnett cut extensively) we are losing a very great deal of the case against Mrs Morel which Lawrence is carefully con-structing. And these are only two examples out of hundreds that could be cited.

Lastly, it would not be right to accept Garnett's cuts simply on the grounds that (in the end) Lawrence was prepared to approve them; that way, we would be in danger of accepting all unauthorized changes made to a text, simply on the grounds that an author tacitly accepted them.

The problem for an editor considering what course to follow is, certainly, complicated by the fact that Lawrence did a certain amount of revision to the novel at the proof stage, when (of course) it had already been cut; and that a very small number of his revisions in proof can be attributed directly to the consequences of Garnett's cuts. But, if care is taken in the handling of such revisions, that problem can be overcome. Again, the cut passages received no final authorial revision, which they almost certainly would have had if they had appeared in the proofs. But the mixture of unrevised November 1912 writing with later proof revision is the price one must pay for restoration of the cut passages. Some small potential inconsistency of texture within one-tenth of a novel is, in itself, no reason for arguing that such a tenth should not be printed.

Accordingly, it seems correct to say that the only proper text of the novel to print today is one in which what Garnett cut has been reinstated. It seems to me that, although an editor might at some stage perhaps wonder whether the text of the novel, because of Garnett's intervention, has become multiple, both logical argument and critical judgement would strongly suggest that it has not.[21]

However, my final example is of a genuinely (and most awkwardly) multiple text in Lawrence. The origins of the short story 'Delilah and Mr. Bircumshaw' are mysterious. There is no reference to it in any of Lawrence's correspondence, there is no surviving complete manuscript in his hand, and there is no typescript on which we can be sure he worked. A manuscript fragment of an early version (hereafter, MS Fragment)[22] exists, which probably dates from the period 1909–11; the fact that it survives only from page nine onwards may indicate that Lawrence, as he sometimes did, re-used the first pages of his manuscript (doubtless with interlinear revision) in a revised version, but that by page nine his revisions had grown so extensive that he preferred to abandon the old manuscript and create an entirely new one. Whether or not that happened in this case must of course be speculation. Frieda Lawrence remembered the story dating 'from her early years with Lawrence, circa 1912–13',[23] which suggests that Lawrence may have created his revised version then. At all events, the story was not published in his lifetime. It only turned up early in 1938, when a desk belonging to the recently deceased publisher Gerald Duckworth was being cleaned out. Its only non-published form to come down to us is that of a typescript (hereafter, TS) of unknown origin, which may or may not be what was found in Duckworth's desk.[24] The story was, however, published shortly afterwards in the *Virginia Quarterly Review* (hereafter *VQR*);[25] but the magazine text does not appear to have been derived from TS, or from any manuscript which itself had been the source of TS. The punctuation of *VQR* was clearly normalized for magazine punctuation, as one would

expect, but there are fifteen occasions where the substantives of
the two texts are strikingly different. The following is a table of
these differences, with the page and line numbers of the new
Cambridge edition. It does not include every possible substantive variant.

	TS	*VQR*	
(1)	quiet	quick	143:15
(2)	protectress	protector	144:16
(3)	spanks	beats	144:40
(4)	spanking	beating	145:1
(5)	thick	strict	146:4
(6)	attentive	listening	146:11
(7)	hear –	hear – she said	146:22
(8)	splendidly,' she said.	splendidly.'	146:23
(9)	been so very considerate –'	so fussy –'	147:10
(10)	then,' declined the older woman, 'I	then. I	147:29
(11)	there's the other bed. Take the baby	You've got another bed aired – you had visitors yesterday – there's the bed – take baby	148:8
(12)	wearily	weariedly	148:10
(13)	good and gracious	fair and fussy	148:13
(14)	due. Her mind was triumphant, but her heart was pained and anxious. She could still smile. She had clipped a large lock from her Samson, and her smile rose from the depth	dues. Though her heart was pained and anxious, still she smiled: she had clipped a large lock from her Samson. Her smile rose from the deep	149:23
(15)	brow.	brow, that reminded one of the brow of a little virgin by Memling.	150:6

In the lack of any information, one would probably judge that
(1), (2), (10), (12), and (15) were errors (or deliberate
alterations) by a typist or a printer. However, it is most unlikely
that (9), (11), (13), or (15) originated from anyone except the
author himself; and if, therefore – quite apart from the evidence
of MS Fragment – we can be reasonably certain that at some
stage Lawrence revised his text, then (3), (4), and (6) can be
seen as almost certainly his as well, while (10) and (15) also
acquire the status of probable authorial revisions. Variants (7)

and (8) are a linked pair, where someone altered the position of 'she said' from the end of one line to the end of the next; that might be authorial, but might also be an intrusive typist (or even a printer). Variant (12) may be authorial, but could also easily be a printer's or, in this case, most probably a typist's error; 'weariedly' is by far the more likely reading. Variant (1) in TS, too, is almost certainly a typist's error, since at that point in the text 'quick' is possible but 'quiet' practically impossible: a typist could easily have misread Lawrence's 'ck' as 'et'. Variant (5) is also very likely an error, only this time it is TS which is correct with 'thick', and 'strict' in *VCR* is the error, again caused by the misreading of Lawrence's handwriting ('ck' read as 'ct', with the start of the word adjusted to match).

But a number of problems remain. How can we account for the differences, and the similarities, between the texts of TS and *VCR*? Would any theory of textual transmission allow us to decide which of each of these fifteen substantive variant pairs is the revision, and which the unrevised original? On the one hand, the nature and quality of the variants in *VCR* might suggest a revised, rather than an original draft; on the other, the phrase 'fair and fussy' at (13) is fairly close to the MS Fragment's reading 'so fair' (p. 11), suggesting that 'good and gracious' is the revision and not the original. Similarly, the wording of (11) in *VQR* is slightly closer to that of the MS Fragment: 'You've got another bed aired – you had your cousin till yesterday – it's aired. Take the baby' (p. 10). A variant like (15) might equally easily be Lawrence adding an extra detail, or Lawrence deleting an unnecessary detail. The problem is further complicated by the fact that, while the typist of TS reproduced some of Lawrence's characteristic punctuation habits – suggesting that he or she was working from a manuscript original – that same typist introduced one spelling for which Lawrence was almost certainly not responsible: 'Galahad' is twice spelled with two 'l's in TS. That may cast doubt on the typist's ability to reproduce the details of Lawrence's manuscript accurately.

On the other hand, as I have already pointed out, although the punctuation of *VQR* appears to be extensively normalized for publication, on one occasion at least – variant (2) – the printer of *VQR* would appear to have been working from a document in Lawrence's handwriting, or at least one directly copied from it. And that might make us look more favourably on the punctuation of *VQR*. Again, on the other hand, a magazine editor or printer capable of revising punctuation as extensively as happened on this occasion would probably not have been above altering the occasional substantive as well. It is, however, inconceivable that all the variants of substantives, particularly (11) and (14), could have been created by over-zealous magazine editors, particularly ones as keen to re-produce a genuine and unpublished Lawrence manuscript as the editors of the *VQR* were.[26]

If, however, we assume, as I think we should, that two distinct authorial states of text lie behind TS and *VQR*, then does any theory of their textual transmission assist our attempts to distinguish original text from revised text? If a manuscript original did indeed provide copy for the typist of TS, then it would seem likely that a revised typescript made from that original – probably in 1913, when Lawrence was having a number of short story manuscripts typed by Douglas Clayton[27] – was the source of *VQR*. And that of course would make *VQR*'s the later, the authorially revised, text. On the other hand, TS may have been typed from just such an authorially revised typescript (those made by Douglas Clayton in 1913–14 frequently reproduce many of the characteristics of Lawrence's own punctuation); and, in that case, *VQR* would be derived from the original manuscript, and TS would represent the revised version. Unfortunately, such speculations work equally well both ways; they offer us no way of solving our dilemma.

Which text therefore should an editor print? Which is 'the text' of the story? I hope I have done enough to show that there can be no clear or simple answer to either of those questions. It would probably be sensible for an editor to reproduce the styling and the punctuation of TS, as arguably closer to Lawrence's manuscript (except in such cases as the spelling of 'Gallahad'); and, rather than mixing versions, an editor should probably adopt only one version of the substantives, either from TS or *VQR*. All he can do apart from that is make clear his text's peculiar status; and, if possible, reproduce at least the substantive, but ideally all, the variants from the other text. This is the solution adopted in the new Cambridge edition of the story, in *Love Among the Haystacks and Other Stories*.

The story has therefore a multiple text. Both texts probably retain some elements of Lawrence's own styling and punctuation; even the styling and punctuation of *VQR*, in spite of the normalization they suffered, probably retain details from Lawrence's own manuscript. Although most of the details of TS are probably closer to Lawrence's manuscript practice, some points of styling and punctuation may well reproduce only its typist's idiosyncrasies. And, of course, either text may contain Lawrence's final revisions. I would argue therefore that, when one wishes to read 'Delilah and Mr. Bircumshaw', one must read both texts; it is, fascinatingly but perhaps unfortunately, a multiple text. Editors cannot assume that logical deduction and disciplined procedure can always solve their problems of textual priority. To embark on a search for the single text which royally stands clear of the mob of imposters and pretenders may, in fact, simply prejudge the textual situation. Some texts can only be presented in a very special kind of critical edition, precisely because they have no single existence. All we can do is to record, in one form or another, the versions that make up their multiplicity.

NOTES

I must record my debt of gratitude to the individual editors of the Cambridge edition of Lawrence's works, who have assisted me in understanding many details of manuscripts, typescripts, and variants which would otherwise have remained obscure, and for their kindness in allowing me to use their findings in advance (in some cases) of the publication of their editions. Above all, I must thank Professor James T. Boulton, one of the two General Editors of the Cambridge edition, for his advice, assistance, and encouragement over many years. Without his work, there would have been no Cambridge edition to acknowledge, nor individual editors to thank.

1 See G. Thomas Tanselle, 'Historicism and Critical Editing', *Studies in Bibliography*, 39 (1985), 1–46.

2 As 'Movements' no. 3: 'The Body Awake', MS E317 in Warren Roberts's *A Bibliography of D. H. Lawrence* (2nd edn, Cambridge, 1982) (hereafter Roberts).

3 As 'Spring-Fire (Autumn Sunshine)' no. 31: 'Virgin Youth', Roberts E320.2.

4 See in particular *The Division of the Kingdoms*, ed. Gary Taylor and Michael Warren (Oxford, 1983), and Trevor Howard-Hill's review in *The Library*, 7 (1985), 161–79.

5 D.H. Lawrence, *Women in Love*, ed. David Farmer, Lindeth Vasey, and John Worthen (Cambridge, 1987). References in the text to MS, TS1a, TS1b, and TS11 refer to Roberts E441c, E441d, E441e, and E441f respectively.

6 Roberts E268. Frieda's two revisions are accepted in the text of the story published in the Cambridge edition of *Love Among the Haystacks and Other Stories*, ed. John Worthen (Cambridge, 1987), p. 161.

7 Charles Dickens, *Dombey and Son*, ed. Alan Horsman (Oxford, 1974), p. xxxix.

8 Stephen Crane, *The Red Badge of Courage*, ed. Fredson Bowers (Charlottesville, 1975), p. 222.

9 *Ibid.*, p. 227.

10 'The Soiled Rose', *Forum*, 49 (1913), 324–40.

11 Roberts E359.4b; see D.H. Lawrence, *The Prussian Officer and Other Stories*, ed. John Worthen (Cambridge, 1983), p. xliii.

12 Roberts E240b and 240c; see D.H. Lawrence, *Mr Noon*, ed. Lindeth Vasey (Cambridge, 1984), pp. xxxviii–xxxix.

13 Roberts E2a; Roberts E125a and 125b; Roberts E55e and 55f. I am grateful for this, and for much helpful information, to Dr Mara Kalnins, Dr Paul Eggert, and Professor Michael Squires, the editors of *Aaron's Rod*, *The Boy in the Bush*, and *Lady Chatterley's Lover* for the Cambridge edition, and to Adrian Matthews for his work on *Fantasia of the Unconscious*.

14 'The Soiled Rose', *Blue Review*, 1 (1913), 6–23.

15 'Introduction', *Mr Noon*, ed. Vasey, p. xxxix.

16 Roberts E186f survives.

17 'Introduction', *Mr Noon*, ed. Vasey, p. xxxix.

18 *The Letters of D.H. Lawrence*, 1, ed. James T. Boulton (Cambridge, 1979), p. 481.

19 See Keith Sagar, *Life into Art* (Harmondsworth, 1985), pp. 94–5; and Mark Schorer, 'Introduction', *Sons and Lovers: A Facsimile of the Manuscript* (Berkeley, 1977), pp. 4, 8–9.

20 D.H. Lawrence, *Sons and Lovers* (London, 1913), p. 149.

21 I am very grateful to Dr Helen Baron and Dr Carl Baron for allowing me access to their work on the Cambridge edition of the

novel, and for convincing me that *Sons and Lovers* is not a multiple text. Michael Black also discusses the problem of the text in 'Editing a Constantly-Revising Author: The Cambridge Edition of Lawrence in Historical Context', in *D.H. Lawrence: Centenary Essays*, ed. Mara Kalnins (Bristol, 1986), p. 204.

22 Roberts E90.5a.
23 E.W. Tedlock, *The Frieda Lawrence Collection of D.H. Lawrence Manuscripts: A Descriptive Bibliography* (Albuquerque, New Mexico, 1948), p. 41.
24 Roberts E90.5b. For further details, see D.H. Lawrence, *Love Among the Haystacks and Other Stories*, ed. Worthen, p. xlvi.
25 'Delilah and Mr Bircumshaw', *Virginia Quarterly Review*, 16 (1940), 257–66.
26 See the correspondence between the managing editor, William Jay Gold, and the editor, L. Lee, with Frieda Lawrence, Carmin Jones, Ben Abramson, Edward M.L. Burchard, Norman B. Hickox, A.J. Liebmann, and E.D. McDonald during late December 1939 and January 1940, in the archives of the *Virginia Quarterly Review*.
27 See *The Prussian Officer*, ed. Worthen, pp. xxv–xxvi, xxxvi–xxxvii.

CHAPTER 2

Editing Johnson's Dictionary: *some editorial and textual considerations*

Anne McDermott and Marcus Walsh

THE EDITORIAL PROBLEM

Producing a critical edition of a dictionary is something that has never been attempted before and, because it is a radically new enterprise, it pushes at the boundaries of current editorial theory. At Birmingham we are undertaking an editorial project not only daunting in scale but also unique in character: a critical edition of one of the greatest dictionaries, Samuel Johnson's *Dictionary of the English Language* (1755). The problems associated with this task stem not just from the size but from the nature of the work. The Greg–Bowers line on textual editing, once regarded as axiomatic, has been pulled and stretched to its limits by editors attempting to apply the theory to works well outside the Renaissance period for which it was primarily devised. The result has been some interesting divergences from this line, and consequently competing editorial theories. Most of these theories have attempted to deal with the editorial problems posed by 'literary' texts. One of the major theoretical difficulties we face is that we are aiming to submit to a process of literary editing a work which belongs to a genre not normally regarded as literary. Our first task, therefore, must be to address the questions: in what sense need the editor be concerned with the literariness of the work being edited, and in what sense has it become possible to regard Johnson's *Dictionary* as a literary work?

The exact nature of the 'literariness' of literary editing has been given inadequate attention by editorial theorists, and those that have devoted any attention to this matter have tended to argue that the editor should be indifferent to the category to which the text being edited belongs. A representative version of this familiar argument is offered by Morse Peckham in 'Reflections on the Foundations of Modern Textual Editing':

> Textual editing and its assistant, analytical bibliography, are logically independent of problems of aesthetics. The fact that both are ordinarily applied to what are known as literary works of art is a matter of no importance, as the current editions of John Stuart Mill and John Dewey make perfectly evident. The textual critic and the analytical bibliographer are theoretically indifferent as to whether they are concerned with Shakespeare or with Fanny Farmer, and in practice they should be indifferent.[1]

Peckham is intolerant of what he calls the 'hagiography of literary humanism' and implies that the typical activity of textual critics and analytical bibliographers who emerge from a humanist background, centred around culturally derived notions of the 'author' and the 'work of art', cannot be rationally justified. But Peckham does not produce evidence to support the position he ascribes to 'humanists'; he merely asserts it. And his counter-argument, containing a description of the way in which text is produced, is inadequate in many respects. He claims that

> an author produces a series of utterances, the assemblage of which he judges to be a discourse; and, by making it available to another or others, proposes that they too judge it to be a discourse...A writer proceeds, then, by producing utterances until he judges that he has come to the end of a discourse...A writer produces utterances because he is a human being. It is a condition of being human. (pp. 138–9)

But what does Peckham mean when he speaks of an author judging? Authors 'judge' a series of utterances to be a discourse and further judge that they have come to the end of a discourse. What is the nature of these judgements? Are they the same kind of judgement in each case? Peckham makes no attempt to distinguish cognitive and aesthetic judgements at even the most basic level. It is also evident that he slides almost imperceptibly from discussion of an 'author' to discussion of a 'writer', and he returns to discussion of an 'author' later in the article.[2] The important distinction is that authors produce works in a creative intentional act, whereas writers produce 'utterances' which are not defined under any description. It suits Peckham's purpose to deny that there is any valid distinction between these two concepts, but he must explain why it is that we attach a value and a certain description to works (whether these are literary or not) produced by authors, while we attach a different value and a different description to utterances produced by writers; the simple accusation of hagiolatry will not do.

By denying creativity, and even individuality, to the producer of the discourse, Peckham makes the notion of intentionality as a guiding editorial principle meaningless. We are not concerned here to argue the case against Peckham on this ground (although it is difficult to see why the editor should be concerned with the perfect repetition by a compositor of a discourse if intention is a meaningless concept). What interests us is the argument Peckham puts forward denying creativity and intentionality in the author as justifications for editorial activity:

Nor can a distinction be made between authorial change and anyone else's change on the grounds that the author was engaged in an aesthetic activity, was producing a work of art. In the first place, the activity of producing an artistic discourse is no different from producing any other kind of discourse. The fact that the discourse itself may be categorized as a work of art has nothing to do with the process of producing it ... In the second place, the textual critic, as we have seen, is completely indifferent to what category of discourse he is concerned with or what category the discourse easily falls into or is more or less arbitrarily assigned to by the cultural conventions of the critic's own cultural situation. (p. 143)

If 'the activity of producing an artistic discourse is no different from producing any other kind of discourse', what is the nature of the judgement that it is complete? And what is the nature of the proposal that other people judge it to be a discourse? We cannot make these kinds of judgement without having some sort of conceptual recognition that the text fulfils our requirements of a particular text type. We judge an advertising slogan to be complete when it fulfils our expectations of what an advertising slogan should be. Our judgement about the completeness of a dictionary depends on very different expectations. We need a prior identification of text type before we can make any judgements about completeness. (Of course the fact that authors must necessarily be concerned with the category of their discourses does not imply that editors should be similarly concerned unless the intentionality of authors is taken as a guiding editorial principle.)

Imprecision about the exact nature of different kinds of judgement has led even G. Thomas Tanselle, who holds views on intentionality and editorial principle radically different from those of Peckham, to argue that an editor should be indifferent to the category to which a text belongs. In a paper delivered to the Conference on Literary and Historical Editing at the University of Kansas (1978) he argued that the fact that 'so-called "literary" works should not be accorded different editorial treatment from other kinds of writing is evident when one considers that no distinct boundary lines exist separating one type of writing from another'.[3] Tanselle's main aim in this paper is to argue for the applicability of *critical* editing to all types of text, whether literary or, as it might be, historical. His argument that all texts should be accorded the same editorial treatment is based on the 'simple reason that "literature" is not a fixed body of material and what constitutes "literature" is a matter of judgment'.[4] Tanselle does not make clear the nature of the judgement required to decide what is or is not a 'literary' work, and seems to imply that such judgements are variable between individuals. We would argue that it is possible to speak of judgement in these matters not as purely subjective and individual, but as predicated on stated criteria. E.D. Hirsch makes this argument with reference to literary evaluation very clearly:

To qualify as objective knowledge, judicial evaluation need fulfill only two criteria: (1) that it be a judgment about the work and not about a distorted version of it, and (2) that the judgment be accurate with respect to the criteria applied...accurate judicial evaluations made under explicitly chosen criteria have as much objectivity as accurate interpretations.[5]

The view that it is possible to make valid judgements relative to stated criteria appears to lie behind Peter Shillingsburg's argument that a number of basic approaches to editing (or 'orientations') are possible.[6] The four basic approaches he identifies are the historical, the sociological, the authorial, and the aesthetic, terms which are self-explanatory. Each approach involves different criteria; each is valid by its own stated criteria. Practical utility and ultimate purpose are the factors which lead to the choice of the most suitable approach. Editors may have regard not only to the character and circumstances of original production of the text, but also to the audience and market of the edition they are producing. Equally, whichever approach editors adopt, unless they produce a diplomatic reprint, the edited text will inevitably incorporate the results of their aesthetic judgements. The authorial approach is adopted by all those editors (including Tanselle) who regard authorial intention, whether 'final' or otherwise, as their central guiding principle. Given that orientation, the making of principled, objective choices between variants of demonstrably differing authority is not problematic. Further judgements, predicated on different but congruent principles, are an essential component in choices between variants of equal authority, or indeterminate origin. The resolution of these problems is what Tanselle has in mind when he speaks of 'critical editing'. Shillingsburg points out that Fredson Bowers attempts to make this exercise of critical judgement a principled one by advocating the selection of variants with 'superior' authority, but that 'his system for selecting the "superior" authority is grounded in the literary critical theory he espouses'.[7]

Tanselle considers that 'critical editing is a form of literary criticism',[8] but his discussion of the exercise of subjective judgement makes that relation unclear, and it is difficult to see how he could consistently accept Shillingsburg's conclusion:

Claims to the contrary by editors of great and small reputation notwithstanding, the principles for selection among authoritative variants in order to create a single reading text reflect values that emanate from the editor's critical preferences and acknowledged or unacknowledged aesthetic principles.[9]

In other words, as we have indicated, the objective and valid criteria for editorial choice among readings become inevitably aesthetic where that choice is between equally authoritative variants. In 'Literary Editing', Tanselle seems to suggest that aesthetic or literary critical considerations are separable from the establishment of the text:

Whether a work is 'creative' or 'nonfictional' it is made up of an arrangement of words and punctuation marks; it is a piece of verbal communication, whatever else it may be. And while one may argue that literary communication is different from other communication, the fact is that both utilize words and language; one must therefore know precisely what arrangement of words and marks is involved before one has any basis for deciding that a particular text is 'literary'. (p. 36)

This statement implies that the meaning which the marks on a page convey to any reader competent in the language has as much objectivity as it is possible to have regardless of its pre-identification as a literary type. The theoretical disputes in literary criticism of the 1960s and 1970s, however, have taught us that meaning is, at least in part, a culturally bound, systematic, encoded phenomenon, and the tension between this view and a perception of meaning as a function of authorial intention has provoked either hermeneutic richness or intolerable exegetic uncertainty depending on one's theoretical standpoint. Tanselle cannot at the same time argue for the intimate relation between editing and literary criticism and ignore developments in literary theory which would make statements such as the above at the very least problematic.

Reflections by E.D. Hirsch, in *Validity in Interpretation*, on the nature of meaning elaborate a thesis rather different from that proposed by Tanselle in 'Literary Editing':

in order to determine the meaning of a word sequence it is necessary to narrow the supposed genre of the text to such a degree that the meanings are no longer doubtful ... Now this process of narrowing the genre is a version of the principle, well known in probability theory, of narrowing the class.[10]

Hirsch, in effect, serializes meaning into a succession of judgements as to whether or not a particular object possesses the defining traits of a class. We would argue that asserting the meaning of a literary text involves a prior identification of the class to which that text belongs; and that that identification must include aesthetic judgements concerning the text's 'literary' character.

Tanselle argues in 'Literary Editing' that the main focus of editorial attention should be authors' 'intention in the act of writing, their intention to have one particular word follow another', yet he concedes that 'editors must ultimately rely on the characteristics of each piece of writing in determining what its author intended to say'. It is difficult to see what characteristics Tanselle can have in mind which do not contain some prior determination of the class of the piece of writing, including judgements of its literariness. In 'The Editorial Problem of Final Authorial Intention' he argues that 'the most reliable source of information about the author's intention in a given work is that work itself', and he asserts that an editor's 'choice among textual variants involves his understanding of the intended meaning of the text'.[11] Similarly, in an assessment of Shillingsburg's book contained in 'Historicism and Critical Editing', in which he approves Shillingsburg's distinction between an author's 'intention to do' (to write 'a specific sequence of words and punctuation') and 'intention to mean', Tanselle makes the point that 'establishing an "intention to do" involves postulating an intended meaning' and that 'the one is inextricable from the other'.[12] We agree with Tanselle's points but find them difficult to reconcile with his views on literary editing; we do not see how it is possible to postulate an intended meaning without some prior identification of the class to which the text belongs. The judgements involved in the critical editing of literary texts must be cognitive, involving first the kind of probability judgements which Hirsch identifies, narrowing the class (or genre) to which the text belongs in a continuous process with the second kind of judgement, establishing an author's 'intention to do' based on probabilities (the evidence is weighed and an editor decides what the author is likely to have written).

Nonetheless, what Tanselle has to say about the problems of identifying the nature of different kinds of work is certainly true: 'histories... [may be] read as literary works, whereas works that superficially appear to be novels may actually be historical accounts'[13] (or, as we would prefer to phrase it, may bear historical witness). But the argument that 'literary' works cannot be distinguished from other kinds of work by their intrinsic characteristics and that therefore the same editorial method is appropriate for any text appears to us to be going along a false trail. We find Hirsch's definition of literature, with its crucial codicil, to be more fruitful in an editorial context than one which aims to identify intrinsic characteristics:

Literature comprises any linguistic work, written or oral, which has significant aesthetic qualities *when described in aesthetic categories*.[14]

What are judged to be 'significant aesthetic qualities' will depend on the aesthetic (or literary critical) perspective from which the work is viewed and the category (or text type) to which it is judged to belong. A work nowadays regarded as 'literary' need not be thought of as having inherent literariness, and may not have been intended or viewed as literary when first written:

the concept of literature is not itself a privileged category for the works it embraces. Since literary works were not always conceived under a predominantly aesthetic mode, we cannot assume that a stress on aesthetic categories corresponds to the essential nature of individual literary works. Other categories, including instrumental, ethical, and religious ones, may be more correspondent to their individual emphases and intentions.[15]

Hirsch's theory helps to explain how it is possible to change the way we view works. We are able for example to regard *Pilgrim's Progress* as a literary text in spite of its religious intention. Gibbon's *Decline and Fall of the Roman Empire* would not nowadays normally be read as a factual historical account;

indeed, the most recent major study pays attention to such literary features as its structure, its style, and its rhetorical strategies.[16] Evidently, Johnson's *Dictionary* was intended primarily as instrumental, to use Hirsch's categories, and its main aim was utility rather than originality and creativity. Since Johnson's time, however, the *Dictionary* has changed its character; after the publication of the *Oxford English Dictionary* the authority of Johnson's *Dictionary* as a work of reference declined, and it was at that point, as Alvin Kernan suggests, that it came to be regarded as a *literary* classic.[17]

Hirsch's account of literature seems to us to offer more potential for flexibility in the editorial treatment of works than one which seeks only to identify intrinsic qualities. It properly shifts the focus from the intrinsic nature of the work to be edited to the way in which the work is regarded. It allows a coherent editorial method to be adopted in respect of works outside conventionally conceived literary genres. Works originally conceived within an instrumental or ethical or religious category may, according to these principles, be not only considered, but also edited, as literary works. Johnson's *Dictionary*, we argue, has features which make it possible, when it is viewed from an aesthetic perspective, to treat it as a literary work. It is necessary to identify those features in order to decide upon an appropriate editorial treatment.

We accept authorial intention as our central editorial guiding principle, our 'orientation'. It is clearly of consequence for the literary importance of Johnson's *Dictionary* that the lexicographer is also a major literary figure, and that it is the product of an intending authorial mind. The nature of authorial originality and intentionality in the *Dictionary* is very different from that in 'literary' works. Dictionaries are profoundly *traditional*, in the sense that they inherit substance and form from their predecessors. James Sledd and Gwin J. Kolb have suggested that some students of lexicography suffer from the delusion that 'in the old dictionaries they have found, or thought they found, the personalities of the dictionary makers'. This delusion springs, Sledd and Kolb argue, from 'the failure to realise that the lexicographer, like other compilers, has few opportunities for originality'.[18] The influence of Renaissance dictionaries and more immediate predecessors such as Nathan Bailey's *Universal Etymological Dictionary* (1721) and *Dictionarium Britannicum* (1730) on the *form* of Johnson's *Dictionary* is not a difficulty. What does pose a theoretical problem is how much the *content* of the *Dictionary* is verbatim quotation or paraphrase. A substantial number of Johnson's headwords are taken from the wordlists of Bailey or other lexicographers, and his definitions are often verbatim quotation from sources such as John Hill's *History of the Materia Medica* (1751) and Philip Miller's *Gardener's Dictionary* (2 vols., 1731, 1739). Johnson's etymologies are frequently copied from Junius or Skinner and even those definitions which might be thought to show the idiosyncrasy and originality of Johnson's mind – those of *oats*, *whig*, *tory*, *network*, for example – have been shown to derive from earlier writers and dictionary-makers.[19] And all this is to say nothing of the bulk of the text of the *Dictionary*, which is its illustrative material and is, of course, made up of the words of other writers. A further complication is that some of Johnson's illustrations derive, not from the original work of literature to which they are attributed, but from glossaries or 'Beauties': notably, it has been shown that the larger part of Johnson's 'quotations' from *Clarissa* come, not from Richardson's novel, but from 'An Ample Collection of Such of the Moral and Instructive Sentiments Interspersed throughout the Work, as may be presumed to be of General Use and Service', put together by a clergyman and appended to volume 7 of the fourth edition of *Clarissa* (1751).[20] These 'Sentiments' are further altered by Johnson and are sometimes so much removed from their source text as to have introduced the very word they are intended to illustrate.

The case with all these borrowings is not one of plagiarism. Johnson's *Dictionary* makes use, as it had to, of a broad spectrum of traditional lexicographical methods and material, and itself naturally became a part of that tradition. Just as he had borrowed from Bailey, so the publishers of the 'new' Bailey (1755) borrowed from Johnson. Thomas Sheridan and John Walker were among the many later eighteenth- and nineteenth-

century dictionary-makers who were guided by and took
materials from Johnson. Noah Webster was notoriously critical
of his great predecessor, but nonetheless used a remarkably
high proportion of Johnson's definitions, without acknow-
ledgement.[21] Even that great monument of late-nineteenth-
century 'scientific' lexicography, the *New English Dictionary*,
was influenced by Johnson and used his materials in its
wordlist, definitions, and illustrations. The theoretical difficulty
here is that, by the very nature of the work and its traditions,
the larger part of the verbal material in the *Dictionary* is not the
author's own. We may be fully aware that literary texts may
include, or may even to some extent be made up of, quotations
from other writers, and that the wording of any text may
be more or less substantially determined by non-authorial
agencies, but it remains the case that literary editors generally
assume that they are dealing with discourses which are more or
less integral, in some sense original, and produced by the
agency of a thinking mind whose final *verbal* intention is the
proper object of the editor's enquiry. To what extent is it
possible to identify and remain faithful to authorial intention in
a work of which the larger part of the verbal material is not the
author's own?

However 'traditional' Johnson's *Dictionary* may be, it
embodies in substantial and important ways the intentions of
an individual creating author. Evidence of Johnson's shaping
intelligence may be found in the definitions, in which he
frequently speaks in his own voice, most obviously on those
occasions when he allows liberty to his wit (he explains *irony*, for
instance, as 'A mode of speech in which the meaning is
contrary to the words: as, *Bolingbroke was a holy man*') or
introduces personal comment (the introduction of Lichfield
and the comment '*Salve magna parens*' under *lich*, for example).
Even in those parts of the work which might seem least his own,
the illustrative quotations, Johnson performs his task of
selection creatively, and his choice of authorities has an
acknowledged moral, aesthetic, and educational purpose. The
Dictionary reflects, however incompletely, Johnson's intention,
not merely to illustrate words, but to provide 'from philoso-

phers principles of science; from historians remarkable facts; from chymists complete processes; from divines striking exhortations; and from poets beautiful descriptions' (*Dictionary* (1755), b2ᵛ). Johnson provides information from chosen authors on a whole curriculum of human science, and he selects, from theological writers, philosophers, and imaginative writers a body of moral guidance. The selection of illustrative passages is an act of critical judgement and assessment, and the words of the passages chosen become part of his *Dictionary*, just as the notes he selects from earlier editors become part of his edition of Shakespeare.

The creativity underlying Johnson's authorial intention is not confined to this important exercise of selection. The illustrative quotations are brief passages removed from the original contexts which control the meaning intended by their original authors. That the determinate meaning of any sentence depends on its context was a commonplace of eighteenth-century hermeneutics. John Locke, for instance, in the preliminary essay to his *Paraphrase and Notes on the Epistles of St Paul* (1706), had insisted that any verse of Paul must be considered as part of 'a continued coherent Discourse', and that to quote verses out of their context, as 'distinct Sentences', is dishonestly to deprive them of 'any limitation or explication of their precise Meaning from the Place they stand in' (pp. vii, ix). Johnson sounds a caveat in the Preface to the *Dictionary* which demonstrates his awareness of this difficulty:

I... was forced to reduce my transcripts very often to clusters of words in which scarce any meaning is retained... The examples, thus mutilated, are no longer to be considered as conveying the sentiments or doctrine of their authors... it may sometimes happen, by hasty detruncation, that the general tendency of the sentence may be changed: the divine may desert his tenets, or the philosopher his system. (*Dictionary* (1755), b2ᵛ)

We have not, so far, found any changes so radical as to alter completely the meaning of the original passage. Much more frequent are the kinds of changes which, in effect, edit the original, condensing it or changing the parts of speech to make it fit more effectively as an illustration of meaning or simply to make it a more resonant statement. One example may serve. A passage in Bryan Duppa's *Holy Rules and Helps to Devotion* (1674) reads:

The devotion of the heart (saith St *Bernard*) is the tongue of the Soul, without this it is silent and shut up; but actuated and heated with Love, it pours itself forth in Supplications, and Prayers, and discourses with God; sometimes praising him for the infinite Blessings received from him, sometimes praying to him for those which we yet want.

In the *Dictionary* this is altered to:

The devotion of the heart is the tongue of the soul; actuated and heated with love, it *pours* itself forth in supplications and prayers.[22]

This is characteristic; an illustrative passage not only abbreviated, but made into a memorable and improving apophthegm, without being a frank misrepresentation of the original. With one class of quotations, those from his own work, he took greater liberties, providing sometimes what might be thought deliberate poetic improvement. Two lines in *Irene*, 'With mouldring Cement and with beams disjointed / And columns leaning from their central firmness', are tautened in the *Dictionary* to 'Mould'ring arches and *Disjointed* columns'.[23] It is our aim in this edition of the *Dictionary* to realize Johnson's intention, and though the illustrative quotations derive very substantially from other writers, his authorial intention is to be found precisely in how he selects, modifies, and applies them.

Ideally, a modern edition would aim to identify, as Johnson himself generally does not, the exact sources of the illustrative quotations; but we do not feel able to go a step beyond that and fulfil Lindsay Fleming's wish, that 'one day an edition of the *Dictionary* may appear restoring the quotations to their original fulness'.[24] A modern in-house editor producing a revision of, for instance, the *Oxford English Dictionary* would certainly wish to correct the errors in the illustrative quotations, and ensure that they faithfully repeat the words of the author who is quoted. For a literary editor of Johnson's *Dictionary*, however, the standard of correctness is the intention of the author quoting

(Johnson) rather than the intention of the author quoted. Donald Greene has made the same point in connection with variations within the *Rambler* mottoes: 'If the variant was not a printer's error but something Johnson intended, whether misquotation or not, it should be retained.'[25] The facts of selection, abbreviation, decontextualization, and frank alteration make the quotations in some sense Johnson's own. If an ambitious modern edition can provide fuller citations, the modern reader will be helped to trace the illustrative quotations to their original context and discover both the original tenets of the divine and (at least as much to the purpose) what Johnson has done with them.

It is our view, then, that the *Dictionary* may be legitimately regarded as a literary work and that it embodies in substantial and important ways the intentions of a creating individual author. It is our aim to recover those intentions, though we are aware that in doing so we cannot recover the *Dictionary* as a single, idealized text; we can only present a text which embodies, to some extent, our aesthetic judgements reached in accordance with our particular stated aesthetic perspective. We acknowledge that it would be possible to adopt different criteria (perhaps regarding one edition of the *Dictionary* as a document in the history of lexicography, for example) and so produce a different, but equally valid text with a different purpose and a different audience.

THE TEXTUAL PROBLEM

Having argued that it is legitimate to edit the *Dictionary* as a literary work, we must go on to specify more precisely what kind of literary work we are dealing with. It is quite clear that the *Dictionary* has a form very different from that of texts normally edited by literary editors, whether these be poems, plays, or novels, or texts not perhaps originally conceived as literary, such as journals and letters. The difference between the *Dictionary* and these texts is not simply one of genre but of discourse type, and we will go on to suggest that this has a fundamental bearing on the editorial approach we must adopt by radically affecting the way we view the textual situation.

The nature of this discourse type has been identified and described by Michael Hoey as a 'discourse colony'.[26] Hoey suggests that certain texts differ from 'mainstream' discourses in being made up of a collection of discrete elements with no cohesive ties between them. The elements 'do not derive their meaning from the sequence in which they are placed' (p. 4). He graphically compares these discourses to the colonies of a beehive or an ant-hill, in which the individual creatures serve a superior end, do not survive easily outside the colony, and enter the colony in arbitrary order. It is important to note that each individual element in a discourse colony is itself, like a bee, an independent organism. The order of the elements in a discourse colony can normally be altered with very little damage to its semantic unity, but an individual organism within the colony can be no more safely scrambled than a 'mainstream' discourse as a whole. The characteristics of a discourse colony are shared, to a greater or lesser degree, by texts as various as a hymn-book and a shopping list, an encyclopedia and a telephone directory, a dictionary and a newspaper. Some of the common features are identified by Hoey:

1. Meaning not derived from sequence; *Alphabetic*
2. Adjacent units do not form continuous prose;
3. There is a framing context; *Definitions*
4. No single author and/or anon; *Johnson*
5. One component may be used without referring to the others; *no*
6. Components can be reprinted or reused in subsequent works; *different*
7. Components can be added, removed, or altered; *from any discourse*
8. Many of the components serve the same function;
9. Alphabetic, numeric, or temporal sequencing. (p. 20)

Not all discourse colonies share all these features, but all have features 1 and 2 in common. Hoey suggests that the only discourse types which display all nine features are dictionaries and encyclopedias.

There can be no doubt that Johnson's *Dictionary*, which clearly has encyclopedic as well as lexicographic characteristics, is in Hoey's terms a discourse colony. This quality of the dictionary as a type was very well understood by an early reader of Johnson's 'Scheme', the manuscript precursor of the

Plan of the *Dictionary*. This reader, probably John Taylor, insisted that the headwords in a dictionary must be ordered, not according to any notion of their etymological class, but strictly alphabetically:

A Dictionary has no more to do w^h Connection & Dependance than a Warehouse book. They are both mere Repertoriums, & if they are not such they are of no Use at all.[27]

In its character as a discourse colony Johnson's *Dictionary* is unlike almost any other text that literary scholars edit. In some respects, of course, collections of lyric poems or essays or letters are colonies, being made up of a number of separate 'organisms'; almost always, however, such collections of literary materials have cohesive ties between the elements, of a thematic or narrative kind. Ian Jack argues against the orthodoxy of the chronological arrangement of poems in a collection for precisely this reason.[28] Collections of writings by a given author are also, crucially, linked in being made up of the words of a single intending consciousness. This is a key mark of distinction between a 'mainstream' literary text and a colony. In Hoey's words, 'a "mainstream" discourse normally has one or more named authors who take responsibility for the whole discourse; a colony on the other hand either usually has no named author or else has multiple authors who are responsible for components of the discourse but not for the whole' (p. 12). Nowadays major dictionaries and encyclopedias are presented essentially anonymously (even though an assiduous reader is given the means to discover the identity of the author of an article in the *Encyclopaedia Britannica* or *New Grove*). As Hoey points out, 'people consult dictionaries or encyclopediae as arbiters of fact and often regard them as offering a final court of appeal' (p. 12); it is precisely the impersonality of the modern dictionary which endows it with its (apparent) authority. In Johnson's time and earlier, however, dictionaries and encyclopedias generally derived their authority from a named author: Scapula, Buxtorf, Bayle, Chambers, or (as the *Dictionary*'s title page proudly announces) 'Samuel Johnson, A.M.' In ways which have already been examined, the *Dictionary* is the product of a single intending consciousness, but the words are not all those of the author and, importantly, there are very rarely any cohesive ties between the elements of the text colony. It is legitimate to speak of authorial intention governing the selection and application of illustrative passages, the framing and ordering of the definitions *within the individual organism constituted by each headword*, but to what extent is it legitimate to speak of the collection of these organisms, arbitrarily ranged alphabetically in a colony, as being the product of a single, unified, concept?

One way of answering this question may be to examine the reading strategies that we now think appropriate to the work. Hoey argues that discourse types have arisen to correspond to different reading strategies, and that the colony corresponds to the reading strategy of 'scan[ning] a discourse with a view to finding the answer to a particular question' (pp. 22–3). This is how dictionaries are normally used. To read sequentially through a dictionary would be 'an...instance of lack of correlation between reading strategy and discourse type'. (Hoey's example is Mrs Garnett in *Till Death Us Do Part* 'reading (and enjoying) a telephone directory'.) To read linearly is a strategy more appropriate to 'mainstream' texts. It seems possible to read Johnson's *Dictionary* in this way (Browning, famously, read the work through), and the writers of this essay share with many other modern readers of Johnson a pleasure not only in referring to the *Dictionary*, but in *reading* it. Nonetheless it is clear that reading the *Dictionary* is not the same as reading a 'mainstream' work because of the lack of thematic, narrative, or symbolic links between the elements.

Robert De Maria, in *Johnson's Dictionary and the Language of Learning* (Oxford, 1986), has attempted to speak of 'the whole meaning of the *Dictionary*' (p. 20), but he is able to do so only by assuming that illustrative quotations from a wide variety of sources, widely scattered under different headwords, express in a connected way an intended Johnsonian message. He asserts, for example, that illustrative quotations given under *piddle* and *gather* and *pincushion* may be taken together as in some sense an expression of an intended and coherent ironic mockery of lexicography itself; or, more improbably, that a quotation under *apophthegm* is 'a witty retort' to another under *piled* (pp. 26–7). To us it seems clear that De Maria's methodology is dubious, implying as it does the presence of large-scale cohesive ties and orderings which may be found in a novel or a play, but are not demonstrably present in that discourse colony which is Johnson's *Dictionary*.

The extent to which the choice of headwords is the product of a synthesizing, prescriptive mind, imposing order on variety, was once a matter of contention among Johnson scholars.[29] But the consensus of opinion now seems to be that Johnson was, in fact, responding to the norms of custom and usage, rather than prescriptively imposing his own system of order on infinite diversity.[30] There is much clear evidence that Johnson had given up trying to fix the language because he found it 'copious without order, and energetick without rules: wherever I turned my view, there was perplexity to be disentangled, and confusion to be regulated; choice was to be made out of boundless variety, without any established principle of selection' (*Dictionary* (1755), a2ʳ). This leads Charles Hinnant to the conclusion that 'Johnson rejects the assumption that the living language ever existed as an institution', and that 'rather than embodying a deep structure or a coherent system of differential relations, speech is composed of a *bricolage* of elements, which, though coherent in certain parts, nonetheless does not present the "uniformity" of a divinely or naturally instituted language'.[31] A reasonable conclusion from this is that it is not possible to think unproblematically of any single and unified linguistic concept underlying the *Dictionary*, and that the reading strategy appropriate to the work as a whole is the scanning technique appropriate to a discourse colony. The choice of reading strategy has a direct bearing upon the way we, as editors, approach the text, affecting how we decide, first, how appropriate it is to use the usual criteria for discriminating versions; secondly, what the implications of our argument about versions are for questions of authorial intention; and thirdly, what the consequences of the text-type are for the choice of copy-text.

It will be as well to offer a brief statement of the textual position. The first edition of Johnson's *Dictionary* appeared in

1755. Only one page of Johnson's manuscript, now in the Hyde collection, survives. The first edition was immediately followed by a second, sold in weekly numbers: this contained a few alterations, notably the abbreviation of citation details, but there is some doubt as to whether these originated from or were approved by Johnson.[32] A third edition, published in 1765, was essentially a reprint of the second, and its interest lies in the fact that it was published, as David Fleeman has remarked, 'as a kind of supplement to Johnson's edition of Shakespeare to which it served as an enlarged glossary'. The fourth edition, however, published in 1773, was very substantially revised by Johnson himself. It contains some new headwords, many new senses, and approximately 3,000 new quotations. Approximately as many quotations are omitted as are added, there are a few changes in the etymologies, and a very few words are dropped. A number of errors are corrected and, of course, a few are introduced. There are certainly many thousands of changes: one possibly overstated estimate suggests 16,000.[33] How many of these changes were caused by the exigencies of space is, at present, a matter of conjecture. On Johnson's death in 1784 a fifth edition, essentially a reprint of the fourth, appeared. The threat of competition from unauthorized reprints led the proprietors of the copy of Johnson's work to publish in 1785 the quarto sixth edition and the folio seventh edition, whose texts derive from the fifth. Editions 6 and 7 incorporate some, but by no means all, of the additions and corrections 'written by the author's own hand' in Johnson's personal copy of the fourth edition. This copy was bequeathed to Sir Joshua Reynolds, and is now in the John Rylands Library in Manchester; its autograph additions have been described in an article by Sledd and Kolb.[34] Editors taking authorial intention as their main guiding principle need not concern themselves with editions 6 and 7 since they are based on an unauthoritative text (edition 5) and the revisions they contain are copied from a text (the Reynolds copy) to which we have direct access. Fleeman argues that the corrections in editions 6 and 7 were probably transcribed on to copy from the fifth edition before being distributed to the different printers involved, a circumstance which takes us at least two removes from Johnson's own manuscript revisions. Some further manuscript materials survive. The Sneyd-Gimbel sheets at Yale are of the first edition of the *Dictionary*, not quite complete, from *A* to *Pumper*, with the exception of *Abide* to *Abolish*, *H* to *Hygroscope*, *Mactation* to *Mythology*, and *Oary* to *Pack*. They contain numerous marginal corrections, mostly by Johnson, and approximately 1,630 added slips containing illustrative quotations, mostly in the hand of Johnson's amanuenses. At the British Library there is an imperfect copy of volume 1 of the *Dictionary* (C.45.k.3.), bound as three volumes with interleaving throughout; most of this copy is made up of sheets from the third edition, but the section from the last page of the letter *A* through the letter *B* as far as *Bystander* is of sheets from the first edition, and bears many additional quotations on the interleaves in the hand of an amanuensis, and autograph revisions by Johnson on the interleaves and on the printed sheets themselves. It seems unlikely that either the Sneyd-Gimbel sheets or the British Library sheets are proof sheets.

It will be apparent, at any rate, that the two significant editions are the first and fourth. The simplest form of modern re-publication is to produce photographic facsimiles of editions 1 and 4, as has, in fact, been done.[35] Electronic publishing is also, from the editorial point of view, relatively unproblematic; the full texts of editions 1 and 4, together with the text of the surviving manuscript materials, may be recorded for example on CD-ROM, with software managing any sort of search and collation that users are likely to require. It would be possible to enable the presentation on screen, in separate windows, of parallel passages from editions 1 and 4, with corresponding manuscript materials. The editors of a 'traditional' hard-copy scholarly edition of Johnson's *Dictionary*, however, have choices to make; a hard-copy parallel-text of editions 1 and 4 would be an absurd and impossible project. Editors must decide which of the texts to base their edition on, how to make choices among substantive variants, and how to present the complexities of variants on the page. How far must the nature of these choices be determined by the special discursive nature of the *Dictionary*?

The first choice facing editors of Johnson's *Dictionary* concerns versions. Shillingsburg defines a version as 'the ideal form of a work as it was intended at a single moment or period for the author', and adds: 'A version is a coherent whole form of the work as conceived and executed by the author within a limited period of time in pursuit of a reasonably coherent or constant overall intention.'[36] The coherence of the *Dictionary* as a unified concept predicated on the author's intention is at least questionable. In 'mainstream' discourses, which are continuous and organically complete, it may make sense to speak of versions, but a discourse colony is made up of a large number of discrete elements, and components may be added, removed, or altered without having any substantial effect on adjacent components, or on the texture of the whole. That this was Johnson's attitude to his work is supported by Fleeman's observation that the disconnection of catch-words reveals that Johnson was able to make significant changes at the proof stage 'by shifting passages about, or removing or introducing others'.[37] Ordinarily, we would be looking at editions 1 and 4 as forming different versions of the work, but a discourse colony is generated by a very much more diffuse creative act than a 'mainstream' discourse, and our argument, based on a recognition of this fact, is that it is scarcely possible to speak of versions in relation to the *Dictionary*. Editions 1 and 4 are not versions, but realizations at particular moments of what was in fact a continuous process of alteration, addition, and omission; there was never a moment of which it is possible to say that Johnson's concept of the *Dictionary* was unified and complete. Even Hans Zeller's radical objections to eclectic editing allow that this sort of circumstance is an exception to his argument:

In one quite specific case contamination [i.e. eclecticism] in establishing a text is probably the correct procedure. This is when it can be proved that the author did not make alterations which bore a relationship to one another and to the whole, but simply altered things here and there in isolation. But can that be proved?[38]

Our argument is that here is a case in which it can be proved.

If it is problematic to speak of versions in relation to the

Dictionary, then, equally, it is problematic to speak of the author's 'final' intention regarding the whole work. What we have is a series of realized intentions of particular entries in the *Dictionary*, but no overall intention, whether final or otherwise, in respect of the whole work. The concept of final intention would, in any case, be difficult to reconcile with the fact that in the *Dictionary* Johnson is responding in some degree to the development of language over the years, and there is some suggestion that the composition of the *Dictionary* went on as a continuous process. We cannot know for sure why Johnson removed certain entries and inserted others; he may have reacted to criticism of his inclusion of too many 'hard words' (although he was notoriously impervious to criticism, as the retention of the definition of *Pastern* shows), he may have dropped some entries and inserted others to reflect language change between 1755 and 1773, he may have omitted some entries not because he regarded the words as obsolete, but simply to make room for new entries (trying to keep edition 4 as close as possible in size to the first edition for the convenience of the publishers). But the crucial consideration seems to be that none of these changes has any real effect on the texture or coherence of the discourse colony as a whole; even quite extensive local alterations do not bring about any fundamental change in the character of the work. The consequence of this argument is that we regard it as justified to treat the addition, deletion, and re-ordering of individual entries eclectically, without any reference to versions, and to include all authoritative entries in the final text.

What is not justified, according to this argument, is the eclectic treatment across versions of the individual organic elements of which the colony is made up. The changes which Johnson makes within individual entries include the addition, deletion, and subdivision of senses; the addition, deletion and re-ordering of illustrative quotations; the shifting of illustrative quotations from one sense to another; and changes in the editing of the illustrative quotations. *Law* may be taken as representative of Johnson's revisions within an entry. In the first edition, Johnson gives five senses; in edition 4 the word is

subdivided into no fewer than twelve senses. Senses 3, 5, 7, 9,
10, 11, and 12 are new in edition 4. Within individual senses
there are changes in the illustrative quotations; new instances
from Hooker (sense 1), and from Milton (sense 2). Quotations
originally given under one sense are shifted to another; a
quotation from *Coriolanus*, given under sense 2 in the first
edition, supports sense 4 in the fourth, and a quotation from
Thomas Baker's *Reflections upon Learning* (1699), originally given
under sense 2, now appears under sense 5. It is clear that these
changes represent a new authorial intention. They are the
result of the creative intentional processes which, despite the
apparent impersonality of a dictionary, we have insisted are
present. It is possible, therefore, to speak of versions of
individual entries. Each version in this case is the final realized
form of the complete entry for that word. Each represents a
realized form of Johnson's construction of the senses and
applications of the word. In most cases, then, we would be
aiming to reconstruct Johnson's final intention regarding
complete individual entries, and it clearly would be inconsistent
to make editorial decisions synthesizing versions within any
headword, even where the change is simple and discrete. (It
may be added that the presentation on the page of an eclectic
text of *Law* from editions 1 and 4 would be at the limits of
practicability.)

A set of proposals concerning the choice of copy-text,
following from our stated editorial orientation and our
argument about the distinctive nature of the *Dictionary* as a
discourse, might now be offered. We would suggest that in the
case of Johnson's *Dictionary* it is logical, for editors taking
authorial intention as a principal criterion, to use more than
one copy-text. Where the work is a 'mainstream' discourse
there may be an argument for keeping the copy-text single:
those factors which make the choice of copy-text important (its
privileged status in the case of accidental variants and of
substantive variants which are indifferent in authority, and its
status as the only text which can be reconstructed in its entirety
from the textual apparatus) imply coherence and unity in the
work as a whole.[39] This argument applies within the 'main-

stream' parts of the *Dictionary* which are its individual entries. But the argument for consistency over the work as a whole is far less compelling in the case of a colony than in that of a mainstream discourse. If editions 1 and 4 are not taken to represent separate versions, we need not feel constrained to adopt one or the other as the single copy-text. Copy-text may be considered separately for each individual entry, and chosen to reflect, as fully and as faithfully as possible, authorial intention for each entry. For entries which were not later substantially revised, copy-text should be the first edition of 1755. This edition must be taken to reflect most closely the author's styling (in the absence of clear evidence for later thoroughgoing authorial revision in this area). For particular entries, such as *Law*, which have been so extensively revised by Johnson as to constitute a new version, and for entries added in the fourth edition, copy-text should normally be the whole of the entry as it appears in the fourth edition. In such cases both styling and substantives must be those of the fourth edition. If we do not regard edition 4 as a new version of the *Dictionary* as a whole, there is no compelling argument for the omission from the edited text of entries which appeared in the first edition but were omitted in 1773, particularly so long as there is the possibility that such omissions might have been influenced by the publishers' rather than the author's preferences. Johnson's autograph additions and corrections, preserved in the Yale and British Library sheets and in the Reynolds copy, will be examined in detail and incorporated following the same principles. An advantage of such an editorial policy is completeness, presenting the reader with a page containing a very high proportion of the surviving printed and manuscript materials of the *Dictionary*, while the textual commentary provides individual variants and records the versions of individual entries from edition 1 superseded by the revised versions of edition 4.

All editorial tasks offer their particular problems; Johnson's *Dictionary* may be thought to offer problems of an especially distinctive kind. There are many specific questions arising out of the bibliographical and textual history of the *Dictionary* which have not yet been resolved, and to which we have not here proposed answers.[40] We have attempted in this paper to address some of the main theoretical issues raised by the special character of the work, and to derive from those issues a consistent possible practice, based on stated aims and assumptions. We are very much aware that other editorial assumptions, and other practices, are possible.

NOTES

1 Morse Peckham, 'Reflections on the Foundations of Modern Textual Editing', *Proof*, 1 (1971), 136.
2 'Ultimately an author arrives at a point in time at which he judges his production of the discourse to be complete' (p. 140).
3 'Literary Editing', printed in *Literary and Historical Editing*, ed. George L. Vogt and John Bush Jones, University of Kansas Publications Library Series, 46 (Kansas, 1981), p. 36.
4 *Ibid.*
5 E.D. Hirsch, Jr, *The Aims of Interpretation* (Chicago, 1976), p. 108.
6 Peter L. Shillingsburg, *Scholarly Editing in the Computer Age: Theory and Practice* (Athens, Georgia, 1986), pp. 19–29.
7 *Ibid.*, p. 83.
8 'Historicism and Critical Editing', *Studies in Bibliography*, 39 (1986), 40, n. 76.
9 *Ibid.*, p. 86.
10 *Validity in Interpretation* (New Haven, 1967), p. 178.
11 'The Editorial Problem of Final Authorial Intention', *Studies in Bibliography*, 29 (1976), 167–211, 179.
12 'Historicism and Critical Editing', p. 42.
13 'Literary Editing', p. 36.
14 *The Aims of Interpretation*, p. 134.
15 *Ibid.*
16 David Womersley, *The Transformation of The Decline and Fall of the Roman Empire* (Cambridge, 1988).
17 *Samuel Johnson and the Impact of Print* (Princeton, 1987), p. 197.
18 James Sledd and Gwin J. Kolb, 'Johnson's Definitions of Whig and Tory', *PMLA*, 67 (1952), 832.
19 See David McCracken, 'The Drudgery of Defining: Johnson's Debt to Bailey's *Dictionarium Britannicum*', *Modern Philology*, 66 (1969), 338–41; Donald Greene, 'Johnson's Definition of *Network*', *Notes and Queries*, 194 (1949), 538–9; Sledd and Kolb,

'Johnson's Definitions of Whig and Tory', pp. 882–5; Lane Cooper, 'Dr Johnson on Oats and Other Grains', *PMLA*, 52 (1937), 785–802.

20 See William R. Keast, 'The Two *Clarissas* in Johnson's *Dictionary*', *Studies in Philology*, 54 (1957), 429–39.

21 See Gertrude E. Noyes, 'The Critical Reception of Johnson's *Dictionary* in the Later Eighteenth Century', *Modern Philology*, 52 (1955), 175–91; Joseph W. Reed, Jr, 'Noah Webster's Debt to Samuel Johnson', *American Speech*, 37 (1962), 97–8.

22 Quoted by Lindsay Fleming, 'Dr Johnson's Use of Authorities in Compiling his Dictionary of the English Language', *Notes and Queries*, 199 (1954), 295.

23 Quoted by W.K. Wimsatt, Jr and M.H. Wimsatt, 'Self-Quotations and Anonymous Quotations in Johnson's Dictionary', *ELH*, 15 (1948), 60–8. For some other discussions of Johnson's handling of his illustrative quotations, see Fleming, pp. 254–7, 294–7, 343–7; Gordon S. Haight, 'Johnson's Copy of Bacon's *Works*', *Yale University Library Gazette*, 6 (1937), 67–73; Theodore Stenberg, 'Quotations from Pope in Johnson's Dictionary', *University of Texas Studies in English*, 23 (1944), 197–210; Katherine C. Balderston, 'Dr Johnson's Use of William Law in the Dictionary', *Philological Quarterly*, 39 (1960), 379–88.

24 Fleming, 'Dr Johnson's Use of Authorities', p. 347.

25 'No Dull Duty: The Yale Edition of the Works of Samuel Johnson', in *Editing Eighteenth-Century Texts: Papers Given at the Editorial Conference, University of Toronto, October 1967*, ed. D.I.B. Smith (Toronto, 1968), pp. 110–11 n. 14.

26 Michael Hoey, 'The Discourse Colony: A Preliminary Study of a Neglected Discourse Type', in *Talking About Text*, ed. Malcolm Coulthard (Birmingham, 1986), pp. 1–26.

27 Quoted in James H. Sledd and Gwin J. Kolb, *Dr Johnson's Dictionary: Essays in the Biography of a Book* (Chicago, 1955), pp. 53–4.

28 Ian Jack, 'A Choice of Orders: The Arrangement of "The Poetical Works"', in *Textual Criticism*, ed. Jerome J. McGann (Chicago, 1985), pp. 127–43.

29 Among those recognizing in Johnson a linguistic authoritarian in a tradition of schemes for fixing the language starting with the Académie Française are De Witt T. Starnes and Gertrude E. Noyes, *The English Dictionary from Cawdrey to Johnson, 1604–1755* (North Carolina, 1946).

30 See Murray Cohen, *Sensible Words: Linguistic Practice in England, 1640–1785* (Baltimore, 1977); W. Scott Elledge, 'The Naked Science of Language, 1747–1786', in *Studies in Criticism and*

Aesthetics, 1660–1800, ed. Howard Anderson and John S. Shea (Minnesota, 1967), pp. 266–95.

31 Charles H. Hinnant, *Samuel Johnson: An Analysis* (London, 1988), p. 79.

32 The manuscript evidence shows Johnson consistently abbreviating citations in just this way. The only evidence that Johnson disapproved of the corrections in the second edition is a letter to Johnson from Hill Boothby, dated 4 July 1755, in which she writes, 'I am sorry you have met with some disappointments in the next edition' (*An Account of the Life of Dr Samuel Johnson from his Birth to his Eleventh Year Written by Himself. To Which are Added, Original Letters to Dr Samuel Johnson, by Miss Hill Boothby*, ed. Richard Wright (London, 1805), p. 98).

33 See Arthur Sherbo, 'Dr Johnson's Revision of his *Dictionary*', *Philological Quarterly*, 31 (1952), 372–82.

34 Gwin J. Kolb and James H. Sledd, 'The Reynolds Copy of Johnson's *Dictionary*', *Bulletin of the John Rylands Library*, 37 (1954–5), 446–75.

35 Facsimile of first edition, Times Books, London, 1979; facsimile of fourth edition, Librairie du Liban, Beirut, 1978; a facsimile of the first edition is projected by Longman.

36 Shillingsburg, *Scholarly Editing*, pp. 47 and 49.

37 'Dr Johnson's *Dictionary*, 1755', in *Samuel Johnson, 1709–1784: A Bicentenary Exhibition* (London, 1984), p. 40.

38 Hans Zeller, 'A New Approach to the Critical Constitution of Literary Texts', *Studies in Bibliography*, 28 (1975), 239.

39 An argument for using two copy-texts, in the rather different case of *Vanity Fair*, has been made by Shillingsburg: see *Scholarly Editing*, p. 66.

40 An extensive study of these matters, Professor Allan Reddick's *The Making of Johnson's Dictionary, 1746–1773*, is shortly to be published by Cambridge University Press.

CHAPTER 3

'Creeping into print': editing the letters of John Clare

Mark Storey

There is considerable significance in the fact that the new Oxford text of John Clare's poetry should start, not at the beginning, but at the end.[1] As Eric Robinson and David Powell acknowledge, the textual difficulties are fewer. For the bulk of Clare's work in the asylum all that survives is the Knight Transcripts; printed texts, if they exist at all, are usually hopelessly corrupt. The main exceptions are the manuscript versions of *Child Harold* and *Don Juan*, and the lyrics of Northampton MS 19. Mention of these poems underlines the basic nature of the asylum poems: most of them were not published in Clare's lifetime, and it is doubtful whether they were ever intended to be. At best, 'publication' would consist of getting a handful of poems inserted by a friend into a local newspaper; more usually it would be a matter of passing a copy to a visitor. For the most part, these poems remained unpublished and unread. For the last twenty-three years of his life, incarcerated in Northampton General Lunatic Asylum, Clare had no audience.

The relationship between writer and audience is a crucial aspect of critical theories about the nature of works of art. It is assumed that at some point a poem, novel, or whatever leaves the artist to be received by an audience of some sort; this basic fact of literary production has led to variations on the notion of an 'implied reader' – in other words, the author creates some kind of audience, or readership, which is built into the structure of the work.[2] There is something inherently odd and unsettling about poems that lie unread in manuscript notebooks hidden in cupboards; it is even odder if those poems were written without an apparent audience in view. They have a private quality which might well keep them on the wrong side of the aesthetic boundary: for, if no audience is implied, should one in fact be supplied? A modern text places us in the role of eavesdroppers, peering into someone's private jottings. This is as true of Clare's asylum poetry as it is, say, of Emily Dickinson's work. And it seems wholly appropriate that a modern edition should at least preserve that sense of privacy, of idiosyncrasy, before these poems have, as it were, been let out of their creative crucible.

With Clare's earlier, pre-asylum work, the case is rather different and more complex. It is perfectly true that he wrote reams and reams before he thought there was any likelihood of publication; but once a publisher had been found, then he was busily going through his notebooks, copying out – or getting copied out – those poems which he thought most suitable for a volume. He would despatch the notebooks to the Stamford bookseller Edward Drury, or to Drury's cousin in London, John Taylor, and leave them to make up a book that would sell; quite clearly, he expected Taylor's amanuenses to correct his spelling and to provide punctuation. He would see the proofs, comment on them, make corrections in a way that a modern author would envy; he certainly had no intention of being presented as a country bumpkin who had no idea how to spell, and whose grammar was sometimes too quirky for polite taste; it was another matter, though, when it came to 'provincialisms', to local words and phrases that captured the precision of his thoughts and feelings, and he fought tenaciously for these to be kept. The early volumes were really collaborative efforts between Taylor and Hessey, his London publishers, and himself; that is why it can be misleading to talk simply of Clare's 'intentions'. Taylor and Hessey help him to shape what was initially 'The Peasant Boy' into 'The Village Minstrel'; they provide much of the impetus for *The Shepherd's Calendar*.[3]

The textual complexities multiply, for Clare is cavalier when it comes to preparing a long poem for the press, and Taylor is driven to distraction by the manuscripts he receives: he is appalled by their quality, but also by their illegibility. Not to mention the fact that the whole volume is getting out of hand:

Clare's prolixity, neither for the first nor the last time, works drastically against the enterprise. John Taylor's solution, in 1827, was to print a radically pruned version of *The Shepherd's Calendar*. He printed some of the Tales that had initially been intended to accompany each month's 'descriptive' sketch, but not all; in any case they came at the end of the volume, together with some other poems, rather than following on after each month. In 1964 Eric Robinson and Geoffrey Summerfield edited a version of *The Shepherd's Calendar* from the manuscripts, restoring the excised passages, and removing any attempts to punctuate or correct Clare's original version.[4] It might seem curmudgeonly, at this point, to question the assumptions of an edition that was, at the time, invaluable; but there can be little doubt that Clare would have been surprised by this editorial procedure: he might have been grateful to have his 'radical' passages restored, but it was never his intention to have all his bizarre spellings and complete lack of punctuation blazoned abroad. Furthermore, Robinson and Summerfield made no attempt to include any of the Tales in the volume, and it could well be argued that these, for Clare, were a far more integral part of the overall plan. So what we got in 1964 was by no means simply what Clare had intended, but which had been kept from the public for over a century: what we got was a compromise, a rather curious hybrid.

One concession made by the editors of *The Shepherd's Calendar* reveals the inevitably provisional nature of most editorial work, and, almost incidentally, the futility of most claims to being definitive. They printed two versions of 'July', the one submitted by Clare in the first instance, and the second version, the one actually published by Taylor and Hessey (but, again, here without the punctuation, and consigned to the back of the volume). The question behind all this is: whose intentions should we be attending to – Clare's, or Taylor's and Hessey's – and at which point? As I have said, the plan for *The Shepherd's Calendar* undergoes radical changes over several years. It is, in fact, a very unstable poem, and certainly an unstable textual object. This provisional nature of the text – which should not really surprise us nowadays, but which certainly works against notions of any one text being *the* text – is emphasized when we turn to the last volume published in Clare's lifetime, *The Rural Muse* (1835). As we now know, this was again a collaborative effort, involving a different publisher, but also Taylor, and also Mrs Emmerson: it is a long story. Initially, Clare had hoped to have published his *Midsummer Cushion* manuscript; but it was far too long, and Mrs Emmerson got to work with her pruning hooks. The 1835 volume was a rather emasculated affair. A modern editor is placed in something of a quandary. Anne Tibble and R.K.R. Thornton provided, in 1979, a text of the *Midsummer Cushion*: as a printed text of one of Clare's most remarkable and beautiful manuscripts, it is invaluable.[5] Thornton subsequently produced a version of *The Rural Muse*, based on the Pforzheimer manuscript that was used for the published volume of 1835, and therefore preserving Clare's idiosyncrasies of spelling and punctuation.[6] Once again, the vexed problem of Clare's intentions raises its querulous head. But, perhaps even more interestingly, such editions underline the curiously private, idiosyncratic quality of Clare's work; what they unwittingly demonstrate is the precarious nature of Clare's existence as a poet, the fine line he treads between private and public. It is at this point that his letters come into the argument.

Letters are usually fine and private things. We write them to particular people on particular occasions; few of us imagine that the letters we write will one day be collected and published. The same was largely true in the nineteenth century. But things had not always been that simple. There was, after all, a strong classical tradition whereby the letter was offered as, or became, a public document, and this survived into the eighteenth century. Robert Halsband has drawn a distinction between eighteenth-century letter-writers who are better known for their other works (Addison, Steele, Pope), and those 'noted mainly for their letters' (Lord Chesterfield, Lady Mary Wortley Montagu, Walpole).[7] The fact that he then introduces another category, those whose stature does not come from their letters but is 'raised by them' (for example, Gray and Johnson), suggests how readily the grey areas obtrude; but coming at things from the other angle, we can see how G. Thomas Tanselle's distinction between epistolary (private) and literary (public) texts meets a rather similar obstacle.[8] Some letters are clearly more private than others. Once we begin to edit them, even to collect them, we alter their nature and their status; it is important that, as editors, we recognize as precisely as possible what it is that we are doing.

Many have argued (and still argue) that most collections of letters should be left in the archives. The cry has gone up, 'Let them [the researchers] read *microfiches*!';[9] another version of that cry asks, 'What is wrong with facsimiles?' In other words, letters are such private and idiosyncratic documents that only a facsimile can capture that very idiosyncrasy. On an absolutist, purist level, there is something to be said for this view: simply in terms of accurate reproduction of the text as it is, a facsimile answers the purpose. It fails, though, to confront the practical problems. Anyone who has used facsimiles, let alone microfilms, knows how unsatisfactory these can be; they are also massively expensive. There is the question of legibility: it is doubtful whether many would thank a publisher who produced the best possible facsimile, certainly of Clare's letters. It is Clare's handwriting that has presented so many headaches to Clare's editors, from Taylor onwards: even those aiming at total accuracy can never be absolutely sure that they have got things right. Some words are blotted beyond recovery, others have eaten through the paper. (Clare's own recipe for the ink he used in the 1830s is a forceful reminder that some texts can alter, physically, from day to day: a manuscript seen one year might the next have begun to disintegrate, as the paper continues its inevitable process of drying and cracking.) Sometimes the handwriting is such a scrawl that it is impossible to decipher whole words and phrases. Whether the original recipient deciphered them is a question we are bound to ask, and in so doing we have to acknowledge some of the other questions that lurk beneath the surface. For in reading these letters we are, apart from anything else, trying to be that initial recipient. We become the implied reader, the sole addressee. But we are here confronted with one of the oddest aspects of reading someone else's letters (it helps, though, to answer even more conclusively the advocates of the facsimile): that sole addressee is summoned up, his ghost placated as we hold in our hands the very letter that he did, which was meant for his eyes only, in answer, most probably, to an earlier letter from him and to which he will respond later the same day, or perhaps the next week, or perhaps mislay – that addressee is summoned up only to be dismissed, because not only do we stand in his shoes, we replace him, firstly by ourselves and then by a wider audience. By gathering and editing someone's letters we not only intrude on an area of great privacy, we also alter the nature of the original document, and we alter the nature of the audience. In fact, depending on how we present these letters, we can determine the nature of that audience, and thereby the nature of the implied reader. Rather as John Taylor did, we become implicated in the whole process of literary production. Once again, the line between private and public becomes blurred, and if we do our best on one level to acknowledge the writer's intentions, on another we fastidiously put them to one side.

Even the apparently simple and innocent act of copying out a letter soon loses its simple innocence. Mixed up in the decision to copy is some kind of judgement as to a writer's worth, and hence the value of an edition of his letters. Of course there are often historical or biographical reasons for collecting someone's letters: neither Hardy nor Tennyson might pour much of themselves into their letters, but such letters supply us with a range of insights into the Victorian literary world. Quite often it is letters of relatively minor writers which tell us things we will find nowhere else: it might be that this very privacy allows them to spread their wings in ways a sense of a larger audience might not. Cowper would be an instance here, or Gray, or Southey. At the other extreme are figures like Byron, Keats, and Dickens, whose imaginative energy spills over into their letters, however carelessly these might seem to be thrown off. Whatever the biographical or historical reasons for an edition in the first place, these either merge with, or are swamped by, a belief that the letters have an intrinsic value, which might indeed raise them to the level of literature. It is here that the specifically Romantic notion of literature has a particular significance, in that in certain crucial definitions there is that very blurring of private and public that I would argue is central to much of Clare's work. I think especially of Keats, who speaks of the poet whispering his results to his neighbour;[10] and of John Stuart Mill, who talks of poetry as something we overhear.[11] It could be said that it is in a poet's letters that we truly overhear him.

Some attempts have been made to construct a theoretical account of letters, but relatively few editors have tried to see any connection between such an account and their own practice. And yet, at the most basic level, the need for accuracy and for detail is supported by various theoretical statements of recent years. As Joseph Kestner has put it, too pompously perhaps for his own good, the advantage of ordinary letters is that they are 'the essence of the genre, its *reductio*, and therefore of great value in developing a *grammaire* or a *poétique* of the epistolary form. Ordinary letters are so much what they are.'[12] In talking of Jane Austen, he argues that her letters 'are as much about themselves as about the novels or the art of the novel', but with the proviso that their survival 'does not make them art'. The letter is in a curious sense self-referential, recounting 'its own creation'. Todorov has observed that 'the materiality of the letter distinguishes it extremely from other signs or messages';[13] this is an argument for seeing it in its spatial character, and for giving some hint of that, without, I believe, necessarily resorting to an absolutely rigid quasi-facsimile approach. The letter has a specificity that sets it apart from the literary artwork: it is a specificity of surface, texture, form, but also of context. In terms of the surface, it is worth quoting Donato here, because he draws attention both to the paradoxes of structuralism, and to the connections which we cannot avoid (*pace* Barthes and Foucault) between literature and life. 'If anything', he writes, 'structuralism has taught us to apprehend the surface, and has shown us that in the past, for wanting to see too much in depth, we rejected the appearance – an appearance which structures our reality, or rather which transforms reality into the real, beyond which there is literally nothing.'[14] Jonathan Culler makes a useful distinction between a typical, everyday letter, and a poem (using Coleridge's 'conversation poems' as examples of the one becoming the other):

The [letter] is directly inscribed in a communicative circuit and depends on external contexts whose relevance we cannot deny even if we are ignorant of them. The 'I' of the letter is an empirical individual, as is the 'You' whom it addresses; it was written at a particular time and in a situation to which it refers; and to interpret the letter is to adduce those contexts so as to read it as a specific temporal and individual act. The poem is not related to time in the same way, nor has it the same interpersonal status.[15]

This is another way of saying what Kestner says, that a letter has to define itself by reacting to another letter – the writer is in fact three people, the receiver (*récepteur*), the sender (*émetteur*), and the observer of the future *récepteur*. Conveniently for those seeking support for the Hirschian notion of validity, 'the letter becomes the paradigm of shareable norms'.[16] But the other way of putting this, as Walter Ong discovers, is to touch not just on the interrelatedness of the exercise, but also on the areas of unpredictability: 'although by writing a letter you are somehow pretending the reader is present while you are writing, you cannot address him as you do in oral speech'.[17] A different kind of relationship has to be established. Ong points out that we have no way of adjusting to our friend's real mood, 'he has to assume the mood [we] have fictionalized for him'. The paradox is that, whilst apparently dealing in truths, letter-writing is also engaging in some kind of disguise: the audience is cast in a 'made-up role', and called on to 'play the role assigned'. The idea of 'shareable norms' is called into question.

The editor of letters needs to bear these theoretical, if unresolved, points in mind: we cannot rely simply on some benign notion of 'common sense', any more than we can when discussing literature. We have to acknowledge the irony that with a letter we might be able to come closest to the perfect state of a text, in terms of a relationship between writer and reader; but that text which we are making public is essentially private. And for all that what is initially most private can be most fully explained (or so it seems), there is always an element of mystery, of things not known. The privacy of the initial transaction can in the last resort assert itself, and we are left outside, barely able even to 'overhear' the 'whisperings' within.

I spoke earlier of the provisional nature of a text. This is clearly brought home to us if an edition already exists of the letters of a particular writer; any new edition has to justify itself against what is already available. In 1951 J.W. and Anne Tibble produced an edition of Clare's letters, which formed an essential part of the process of rehabilitation which had begun, really, in 1935, with J.W. Tibble's two-volume edition of the *Poems*. It gradually became apparent, however, that the Tibbles' work was not, in all respects, adequate. Their transcriptions were inaccurate to an alarming degree, their annotation meagre. Furthermore the collection was by no means complete. Since 1951 a large number of additional letters have come to light: some of these were published in scholarly journals, in each case according to rather different editorial criteria; many more were lying in the vast collections of manuscripts at Northampton and Peterborough. There were also many draft letters which, as I shall argue later, were an important part of the evidence, and merited publication. There were, it transpired, collections of unpublished letters in many different institutions, ranging from individual letters in particular libraries and museums across the country to larger collections in the States. In particular, there were letters, which had never been published, at Brown University, at Yale, at Austin, Texas, in the Berg Collection of the New York Public Library, and in the Pforzheimer Library. After appeals to practically every conceivable learned institution or library, the number of known extant letters had almost doubled, so in terms of quantity alone, the argument for a new edition had become compelling. And, as I have said, the inaccuracies of the Tibble edition were in themselves a bar to using their work as the basis of scholarship. Clare's spelling is silently corrected on innumerable occasions, often altered when it is correct, upper- and lower-case letters are interchanged almost at random, words and phrases completely mistranscribed; words, whole lines, even paragraphs, are omitted without comment; there is even no consistency towards the ampersand. Dates of letters are often either inaccurate or insufficiently precise. The Tibbles never print the texts of poems that occur in the letters – a serious omission in view of Clare's own estimation of the importance of such texts. Nor do the Tibbles make much use of the vast correspondence to Clare that survives in the British Library Egerton manuscripts. In an ideal world, these would be published in their entirety, but commercial considerations rule out such an ideal. Since it is relatively rare for both sides of a correspondence to have survived so fully, it seems especially important to catch as much as we can of that sense of ebb and flow of a true correspondence, either by printing some of the letters to Clare, or by referring extensively to them in notes. As the theorists remind us, letters are not written in a void, and one letter presupposes another. It is particularly important in Clare's case, because his epistolary relations with friends and publishers affect his verse and his view of himself, his sense of himself as a writer. His constant search for identity, on the personal and the literary levels, is traced throughout his correspondence.

My own edition has aimed at printing all the extant letters of Clare that can be found. It has to be admitted at once that the enterprise is thereby left open-ended. No edition can be complete, as there are always going to be letters that remain hidden, and others that emerge in sale-rooms from time to time. But the search has to stop at some point, and the provisional nature of the edition has to be acknowledged. As for the transcription, the aim has been to be as accurate as possible, reproducing all of Clare's oddities of spelling and punctuation; deletions and corrections are incorporated where they are interesting or important – in other words, hasty slips of the pen involving one or two letters do not have much significance, but if Clare deliberately writes a word, crosses it out, and starts again, I record the fact. In order to provide some rest for the eye, I have introduced spaces into the text where a sentence might be supposed to have ended. This is inevitably something of a compromise: some sentences clearly yearn to go on and on in an uninterrupted flow, whilst others can seem merely confusing. There is compromise, too, in the way I have treated

Clare's additions – whether between the lines, or around the
edges, or on the address panel: I have incorporated such
additions into the body of the letter, or as a postscript, as
appropriate. Nor is the complimentary close displayed. At
some point the interests of the reader have to be considered,
and I fear that behind, say, the pernickety presentation of the
text in the Oxford edition of Crabbe's letters, or the ugly and
frequent use of bold type to indicate Lamb's peculiarities in
Marrs's edition of his letters, lurks the shadow of G. Thomas
Tanselle.[18]

An important consequence of the decision to be as inclusive
and complete as possible is the printing of draft letters. In the
early and mid-1830s all that survives is often a deleted scrap;
sometimes there is corroborative evidence that a letter was sent,
sometimes not. There is a problem of definition here, as there
can be legitimate doubts as to whether such drafts are intended
as letters at all; quite often, in fact, Clare seems to be
communing with himself. But, then, that is precisely the tone of
some of the letters he actually writes and sends in those
troubled years. It is inevitable that there will be room for
debate here: I will have omitted some scraps or fragments that
others would have regarded as letters. Some of the fragments at
Peterborough would come into this category – short notes,
often deleted, attached to poems. Clare would be sending his
manuscript notebooks to Drury, or up to Taylor in London,
and asking questions, or making comments, in the margins, or
at the end of poems. It has been a matter of judging each
instance on its merits. Similarly, in the batches of manuscripts
that Clare sent to the Reverend Isaiah Knowles Holland in the
early years, there are comments that do not seem to me to
constitute 'letters', but which would seem to belong more
appropriately to a commentary on the poems. Some might
argue that some of the scraps I have included are not letters in
any conventional sense; the general rule of thumb, apart from
a desire for inclusiveness, was that if there seemed to be some
evidence that Clare had a recipient in mind, then it was
important to include the draft or fragment.

One example would be this scrap that occurs in Peterborough MS A51:

for I am going to commence cottage farmer & am on the point
of leaving the place of my birth & happ[i]ness very shortly but its no
use in indulging in feelings that we cannot live bye – & in my new
residence I hope to become independant & that will make me
comfortable – but to make a start before the flitting I shall be obliged
to make use of my money in the funds – I have little matters to make
up & a few sloughs in the road of difficulty to mend & repair & I had
hopes that a vol of ryhmes would have done that but by what I can
hear the 'days of those hopes have had their day' so I must rest
contented – yet I never got so much by my trifles as to be dissapointed
with meeting with expectations of less luck in those matters

the only thing being that I have no time left me to try such
speculations for in a few weeks I commence flitting for good – I was
very ill all last Summer & have not long been [   ] & am
[?unarmed] now for every exertion save that of

The context makes it clear enough that this was written in early
1832, just before the move from Helpstone to Northborough. It
is conceivable that Clare is jotting down his thoughts for
himself, but it seems unlikely. For a start, he was not given at
this stage in his life to the kind of autobiographical notes that
he wrote in the early 1820s; secondly, there is a clear sense of
an audience, of someone being told things. For obvious reasons,
financial considerations are uppermost in his mind: 'I shall be
obliged to make use of my money in the funds.' This is just the
kind of comment he makes in notes to Taylor, who advises
caution, at least until Woodhouse, the lawyer, comes back from
Italy and can offer sound advice. There is a *prima facie* case for
regarding this as some kind of communication, most probably
to Taylor. The note appears to be continued on the reverse side
of the scrap: the main concern seems to be the same, and once
again Clare is apparently telling someone something. Furthermore, the gap he leaves in the manuscript is itself suggestive
of an audience: it seems safe to conclude that in a private note
to himself he would not leave a gap because he could not find
the appropriate word. Another draft of a rather similar kind, in
Peterborough MS B1, seems to echo the tone of this one:

All I want is to see my own success in my own profession to stand in
my own strength to meet the storm – this will free me of hopes &
expectations that oftener end in bitterness & dissapointment then
otherwise & the longer I live there more I see the old saying justified

– if we cannot help ourselves there will be the less to help us – I have born the burthen of obligations for which a more fortunate man would not say thank ye – & suffered ta[u]nts when if I had met kindness it would have been the only profit I recieved – & under these has my spirit been so broken that I could not write a reply but suffered the ta[u]nt & the rebuke in silence – & the time was when I should have felt them as insults but I am now I hope on the threshold of better times – & if true friendships meet me they will be accidents that can never come without pleasure & I shall feel them the more from being such

There is other evidence that lends support to the idea of draft letters being scattered around unfinished in the manuscripts. For example, Peterborough MS A42 has these lines, headed 'for letter to T' (i.e. Taylor):

You held out to me the encouraging promises of a friend so warmly in the beginning that I cannot believe you will turn upon me with the extortionate exactions of a tradesman in the end tho you have the law on your side to do so which is a full liscence for knavery to do what it lists & but a poor defence for justice to expect its reward

The draft in MS Pforzheimer Misc. 198 is clearly a further and lengthier attempt at a similar kind of communication. It winds its way back and forth across three pages of the manuscript, and then apparently ends abruptly; but however muddled and unfinished it is, its biographical importance makes it an essential part of the correspondence.

I did not write sooner because you would know I recieved the dividend by other means & though I have not been over busy to plead any excuse for me I have been burthened with matters that might make apologys for longer absence but I will not trouble my letter with them – I hope you have had some intellagence from Mr Woodhouse as all my anxiety dwells upon that independance of mind that I hope to arive at by using the means which are my own & freeing myself of obligations that burthen & oppress me – I therefore eagerly hope my little money in the funds may be got at because it was not my wish or intention that it should be placed out of my power when I wanted to put it to better uses – therefore now the time is arived that it can be so applied all I wish is that you would act for me as you would act for yourself in such a matter – advice that costs nothing to the giver I have in plenty – & as it is only theory it is worth nothing to my present nessesity – some tell me that cows are excellent

profits & some tell me that pigs are excellent profits and others that
ploughed land would be far better then either – & others who have
land under the plough say that I am far better off with greensward
– & nothing disheartened I hear this confliction of opinions & strife
of tongues with the determination to trye & if God gives me health I
have a strong hope in the wind that I shall succeed – my whole
ambition is to ⟨become⟩ arive at that climax when I can say I owe
no man a shilling & feel that I can pay my way – to me this is
independance & nothing else – of money I know no other values then
of its paying its way & further then that to me it is a worthless matter
– show of wealth & pomp of luxury are shadows that never came
under the dominion of my wishes – & I often wonder that reasoning
man can keep alive that unreasonable Ape called Pride to exult
in riches & think it greatness – As soon as the house is built I leave
Helpstone & I wish to leave it out of debt – which I shall not be able
to do if I cannot get the money untill May so I hope better tidings &
shall be very anxious to hear from you – I enter upon the cottage as
a tennant – you speak as if you felt it otherwise – but I cannot look at
any right of my having any claims of extra kindness on those who
have been kind to me already all my delight is that I have an
oppertunity of having such men as the Fitzwilliams & the Miltons for
Landlords – for when a man rents anything under them it is as certain
as his own & it is as difficult to catch any cottage belonging to them
or Lord Exeter as it was formerly of catching a prize in the lottery for
in spite of political differences their fame as 'excellent Landlords' are
uniform & universal – I wrote to a friend of whom I know nothing
further then correspondence alows me to ask his advice as to
publishing a Vol of ryhmes but I have heard nothing from him yet
& as it is ⟨my⟩ the first presumption I ever took of the kind it is the
last – & yet in spite of every difficulty ryhme will come to the end of
my pen – when I am in trouble I go on & it gives me pleasure by
resting my feelings of every burthen & when I am pleased it gives me
extra gratification & so in spite of myself I ryhme on – I have got

Because this draft is so obviously directed at John Taylor, an
otherwise much more questionable scrap can be seen in a
similar light. We might at first glance think that this is a case
of Clare's venting his spleen to himself (he had cause enough
to), but the verbal similarities with the Pforzheimer draft
suggest that Clare is again trying to find the right words for his
anger:

Am I to be astonished at this matter or am I to be mad enough to think it reason – Pope says 'whatever is right' & so it seems – yet I cannot for my life make out who could give the order to get my poor little begging money into prison for life – it did no misdemeanor that I know of that deseverd imprisonment much less transportation for life – I am no leveller but I wish every mans security into his own pocket in preference to that of government security or friendly interference – where one administration cloaths her in a dress that they declare the fire proof of honesty untill another administration comes & finds out the honest cloathing to be nothing but old rags of pretention & away goes garment after garment into the Jews ragbag or somthing like it – & what would make a great coat ⟨waistcoat⟩ & full suit & to spare on [?   ] will not make out for a spencer in another – & yet the owners of property are the all that suffers – government looses nothing either in faith or security but swears herself into the friendship of the public as trustily as [   ]

It astonishes me that law can do these miracles to make deeds out of property that belongs to others without consulting the wish or satisfying the hope of the owner by showing a line or a syllable of such deeds for his approval – safety is no cannibal but to lock up saftey in such security is like putting her in a poisoned casket to eat away her existance – when it was first started I was to have twenty pound for life but years kept decreasing the salary – what with other expences it will have work enough bye & bye to amount to 10 & what with other liables it will at last I expect be liable to amount to nothing – & yet if the funds sees fit to alow me nothing I suppose I must put up with nothing on account of this deed of which I know nothing not even the sight of a [?   ] so long as my finger or word that might be coverd with the [?   ] of a pen & if this be law then tragic is a reasonable anology & nothing in the arabian Nights was ever found under the metamorphosis of stranger enchantment then this little 'fund money' that ought to call me owner – but god help it – to think that it can master the spells so far as to asume its natural shape is hopeless – therefore like the mob in a scramble I am anxious to get what I can for much of the substance has sunk to shadows – & the rest follow to the shades   I will have it if possibility be possible or reason be reason & if not – why then the Law that interferes with anothers property without his consent so far as to loose it for him that law is a rogue in the best sense of the word & I cannot help it

Anger is a significant factor in many of Clare's drafts: the more angry or the more desolate he is, the more drafts he writes. The shift from private feeling to public expression is that much harder for him to make. An early example of this occurs during the wrangle over the delays in publishing *The Shepherd's*

Calendar. Here we need, as modern readers, to get a full sense of the correspondence between Helpstone and London. What we have are the following documents: a draft letter, dated 17 April 1825, to Taylor's partner Hessey; a comment in his Journal, for the same day, 'Wrote to Hessey in a manner that I am always very loath to write but I coud keep my patience no longer';[19] a letter from Taylor, dated 18 April, and a comment in Clare's Journal for 20 April, 'Recieved a letter from Taylor in answer to mine to Hessey of last Sunday – He is very pettish respecting my anxiety & irritation';[20] a draft letter of 5 May, to Taylor; and, finally, the letter actually sent to Taylor that same day. It seemed essential to print each of the letters and drafts in sequence, with the disturbing effect that we become, in turn, Hessey, Clare, and Taylor. It is partly, too, as so often, a chronological matter, even if we are talking about one day (in the case of the draft and the letter of 5 May): just as the draft precedes the finished letter, so the letter is written with the draft by his side, and grows out of the draft. We are enabled to see the two separate stages of composition, and also get the sense of the letter received by Taylor, who of course knew nothing of the draft. In the letter that is sent Clare's hopes of seeing profits, his sense of urgency, are left vague; in the draft he is much more specific. When he gets round to the letter that is sent, he introduces, as so often, a specifically 'literary' touch: in the draft he is quite blunt about the suggestion that he find another publisher, but in the finished letter he elaborates: 'I will go no further on that head & if I did drawing comparisons from others woud not be adding praise if the complaints of authors are to be noticed & why shoud they not have cause for their lamentations as well as Jeremiah.' Once he has confronted his anger, and to some extent tamed it, he can change the tone of the finished letter, and ask about Taylor's sister, and talk engagingly about Mrs Wright of Clapham and her flowers – she is like one of those minor figures in Jane Austen, whom we never meet, but know intimately. There is no room for her in the draft, but she blooms in the letter, like one of her own roses.

A rather different kind of draft is represented by Clare's hesitations in his attempts to deceive the radical publisher, William Hone, editor of the *Every-Day Book*. But behind these, too, is the problem of self-definition, and all the more important because it bears on Clare as a poet. Practically all the surviving letters to Hone are in draft form, the first dated 23 June 1825, in which Clare tries to pass off a poem of his own, 'Death', as by Marvell. It is a double bluff, since Clare signs his letter James Gilderoy, after the famous Scottish highwayman. Five days later the poem duly appeared in the *Every-Day Book*, and Clare was rather pleased at his success; as he noted in his journal, 'I shall venture agen under another name after awhile.'[21] Sure enough, on 2 August 1825 he tried again. This time it seems to have been harder to get going: his first attempt gets stranded in the first sentence. It is worth noting that he employs an elaborate, disguised form of handwriting, as though he is consciously trying to establish a separate identity. The second draft is a complete letter, but he deletes it. Clare signs himself 'Frederic Roberts' (the name, as it happens, of a servant at Milton Hall). The next draft is also deleted and, interestingly, he has tried to erase the name of Roberts at the end of the letter, writing in Gothic lettering 'Daventry' in the margin (presumably for 'Davenant', on whom he fathered yet another poem). This draft is followed by the poem 'Farewell & Defiance to Love', which, as Clare anticipated, did not get published in the *Every-Day Book*. It eventually appeared, unsigned, in the *European Magazine*. The poem itself emerges, at this stage, as very provisional, with several deletions and alterations; it seemed important to print the poem in its equally provisional context. All these drafts form part of an unfolding narrative which reached its apogee with the recent discovery of a letter to Hone in the Berg Collection in the New York Public Library: on 29 February 1828 Clare confessed his deceptions to Hone, because he thought that Hone might be refusing to publish a recently submitted poem on the grounds that it, too, was a forgery. This is a nice example of the provisional nature of letter-writing being mirrored by the provisional nature of editing.

Another important consequence of the decision to see letters as biographical documents is the need to be as precise as possible about the dating of letters. As Jonathan Culler recognized, the temporal context is all-important. What might seem a rather dry-as-dust activity assumes critical proportions. One of the shortcomings of the Tibbles' edition was that their dates were either too vague, or just wrong. Mark Minor has demonstrated, with reference to Clare's religious conversions, how the biographical results – in terms of how we understand Clare's life – can be radically distorted if we combine an incorrect date with a misreading.[22] Initially the prospect facing an editor of Clare's letters can be daunting: there are so many fragments that are not only undated, but have no name of an addressee, no watermark, no postmark, and very little in the way of contextual clues. It is surprising how the choice of dates, in the absence of such evidence, can usually be narrowed down to within a few months. At the same time, the editor has to mistrust much of the evidence that is apparently presented to him on a plate. Postmarks, for example, are not always reliable. On the address panel of a letter to Taylor, in the Berg Collection, Clare has written 'Nov.6', without giving the year; the postmark clearly and unequivocally proclaims '9 NO 1831'. But the content and context of the letter make it abundantly clear that the year is 1821, and initial confusion is put to flight.[23] Copyists are not to be trusted, either. Several letters from the early years survive only in the form of copies: there is one, for instance, addressed to the very minor writer Chauncey Hare Townsend, the date boldly announcing 'April 10 1820'. The Tibbles took this date at its face value. However, in the course of the letter Clare mentions his next publication: 'you may have seen them advertised "The Village Minstrel" &c in 2 vols'. We know that it was not until 29 December 1820 that Taylor mooted the possibility of two volumes, and the question of the precise title and the number of volumes was still being discussed in February 1821. It is reasonable to assume that the copyist has got the month right, but has made a slip in the year (this is understandable, since Clare's 'o' and '1' can be very similar).

A rather different case is presented by the letters that survive to one of Clare's first supporters, the Reverend Isaiah Knowles Holland, Congregational Minister at Market Deeping from 1815 until his removal to St Ives Free Church in 1820. The letters form a bundle in the Norris Museum at St Ives,

Huntingdon, a mixture of poems and letters. Holland has supplied very rough dates for most of them, but the evidence suggests that these dates were added retrospectively; at least one of the dates can be shown quite clearly to be wrong, and this leads an editor to treat the others with caution. In one letter, dated by Holland '1817', Clare refers to a 'Clergyman of the Church of Engld.' who 'propos'd raising a Subsn. for me but as he spoke very coldly of pieces I sent him my proud spirit declin'd the offer'. Now, we know who this clergyman was. Drury reported to Taylor on 5 May 1819 (Northampton MS 43) that he had shown Clare's poems to the Reverend Richard Twopenny, Vicar of Little Casterton from 1783 until his death in 1843. Twopenny had replied with 'a polite & cool note of disapprobation'. Clare mentions the episode in his *Autobiographical Writings*, including the lampoon he refers to in this letter.[24] Once Holland's reliability has been questioned in this way, doubts arise over his other datings. There is, in fact, no biographical evidence that Clare knew Holland before 1819. Frederick Martin, in his *Life of John Clare* (1865), says that Clare met Holland in the spring of 1819,[25] which confirms some of the hints in the letters themselves, and also Clare's own account of his first meeting with Holland, where he declares, 'when he [Holland] first came to see me I was copying out the "Village funeral" to send to Drury'.[26] Drury's first letter to Clare is dated 24 December 1818, but it was in the following year that the two corresponded regularly, and it was not until October 1819 that Holland met Drury, and passed on to Clare what he thought of the Stamford bookseller. In spite of Holland's retrospective placing of several of these letters in 1817 or 1818, then, it does not seem unreasonable to suppose that most of them were written in 1819. Once we have acknowledged that one particular letter belongs to 1819, the others fall into place, their dates sometimes confirmed by surviving letters from Holland dated October 1819. (By a rather similar process, undated letters to Edward Drury can be placed in a sequence from April 1819 onwards, thanks to a reference in one of them to a local poet called S. Messing, and to a particular poem that appeared in the *Stamford Mercury*.)

Documents from the late 1820s and early 1830s pose their own problems. The following partially deleted draft appears in Peterborough MS A46:

You speak of publishing in the country   I dont reccolect ever saying I was going to publish anywhere – I only told you what was told me in a letter my friend Mr Sharp of the General post office who had it from Mr Hall   that is all I either know or care about the matter

do I write intelligable   I am gennerally understood tho I do not use that awkard squad of pointings called commas colons semicolons &c & for the very reason that altho they are drilled ⟨daily⟩ hourly daily & weekly by every boarding school Miss who pretends to gossip in correspondence they do not know their proper exercise for they even set gramarians at loggerheads & no one can assign them their proper places for give each a sentence to point & both shall differ – point it differently

to be sure I do not often begin a new sentence with a capital & that is a slovenly neglect which I must correct hereafter in my Essay pretentions for I fear they will be nothing else

Clare had known William Sharp, who worked in the Dead Letter Office, for some time, so that in itself provides no clue. Mention of Mr Hall is of some help, as two letters to him survive, from 1828 and 1829 respectively. S.C. Hall edited the *Amulet*, and the *Spirit and Manners of the Age*, to both of which Clare contributed. The first mention of him occurs in a letter to Taylor of 17 November 1827, and Holland had in fact first asked Clare for contributions in July 1826. So we are provided with some kind of *terminus post quem*. However, by combing through the British Library Egerton MSS we can find a clue in one of Mrs Emmerson's dreadfully long and turgid letters. On 21 December 1829 she wrote, 'I cannot advise you on the subject of your publishing your "little vol of trifles", unless I could *know more* of the *merits* of the case – certainly, I do not think you ought to publish a Volume in your *own part* of the World.' Clare's opening comments seem to be picking up on Mrs Emmerson's observations. Further, there is a draft letter to William Sharp dated 'Octr 1829', which makes mention of some publishing scheme put forward by Hall (Sharp had written on 21 September saying something of Hall's offer of paying for various possible ventures, including something in prose and Clare's next volume of poems). It is to this that Clare seems to be referring in this draft. If we need further confirmation of the date, then the second paragraph provides it. Clare became obsessed with the problems of spelling and grammar at the end of 1829 and the beginning of 1830. A letter from Mrs Emmerson to Clare, dated 10 March 1830, says, 'So you are studying the rules of "Grammar"...let me have the pleasure of a gossiping letter from you'; her letter of 22 April 1830 is clearly in reply to an undated draft of Clare's (Peterborough MS A46), in which Clare talks in a rather extraordinary fashion about grammar, and the implications of using the first person pronoun (rather typically Mrs Emmerson answers on a literal level points that for Clare have a metaphysical significance). We can, then, be fairly confident in placing Clare's draft after 21 December 1829, and most probably before the later letters just mentioned. The problems of date and addressee are solved simultaneously.

The same is true of the following, a draft in Peterborough MS A51 :

Friend D
        I have another shoot at follys as they flye in the shape of a long poem in a Familiar Epistle to a friend which you may insert if you please   I intend to follow it up from time to time by others of the kind & if my humour lives I shall pop in a stave for the coronation next may & tho it may not be much seasond with sugar plumbs it will be as truth as the best & more true no doubt then his majestys speech or the laureates Ode – In the Summons which appeard in your News some time ago I minced the matter by the omission of three verses & spoiled the Poem which I was sorry for & I here send you them for your own reading

Here we are able to address ourselves to a rather interesting textual problem in Clare's poetry whilst solving the problem of the letter's date. The 'Familiar Epistle to a Friend' appeared in John Drakard's *Stamford Champion* on 14 December 1830 (rather intriguingly signed 'H.N.'); 'The Summons' had first been published in his *Stamford News* on 25 September 1830, and was reprinted in the *Champion* on 30 November 1830 (this time signed 'N'), with three additional stanzas (*viz.* 19, 20, 21, which have clearly been inserted later in the manuscript version at Peterborough, A40, 125); however, in the process, stanzas 16, 17, and 18 were printed in reverse order after stanza 14, a point picked up in a letter to Henry Behnes Burlowe of 28 December 1830, and then again on 4 January 1831. The draft can be placed in November 1830, and Drakard is clearly the intended recipient. (The coronation Clare refers to is that of William IV, which did not take place until September 1831; Clare's poem ended 'So here's to "King Will the Fourth."')

References to particular events are often an essential way of dating otherwise apparently vaguely placed letters, especially when they are undated drafts. There is, for example, a remarkable account of fire-raising in a draft to Frank Simpson (Peterborough MS B5). It is a very hastily scribbled note, hard to decipher in many places. But it is of some historical significance, and once again the date can be fairly accurately established.

Dear Frank

    I have made a few more enquir[i]es respecting those strangers whom the 'Hue & Cry' leads me to suspect are the [?creators] of those horrid mysterys that darkness envelops & daylight discovers – The Gig was very light & apparently small for two men to occupy one was dressed in a light great coat & the other in a dark one   they came in at a end of the town no strangers ever enters as it is a bye road leading no where but to bye places – they passed my father & another & asked the way for Spalding   when near the public Hous 'Blue Bell' they met another man on horseback who either before or after stopt at the Bell & called for a glass of Gin – his appearance & manner waked the suspicions of Mrs Bradford who thought that these [?cowards] was of too much mystery to be honest – the day after this – Dr Johnsons stacks at spalding was destroyed

    Last week a strange man on horseback in a shooting jack[e]t sort of coat galloped over Mr [?Tweelys] Farm like a madman leaping a hedge & ditch & stopping at nothing   in passing a labourer making straw he hastily cried out 'Well you are getting straw   whose Farm is it' & on the mans telling him he said aye aye it will make a fine stack – & instantly galloped off & dissapeared   'Will' was the name of the labourer who declared that he had never seen the man on horseback in his life before & the ploughmen in the neighbouring grounds held their consultations on the matter of the mystery with the labourer & came to the consclusion that it must be the devil on horseback   in fact it was a 'devils drive' neck or nothing – & on

saturday night that horrid tragedy in deeping fen occured which
chills my blood almost into water to think of – Is there no trace to
track the tyger to his den whose ruinous actions are so legible & so
heartrending – the above statement is partly my own observation &
partly hearsay   if you think them worth enquirey come over your self
& do so – the people are both neighbours of mine & have the facts
fresher on their memorys then I have & will tell you more particulars
& better then I can – for I have so many other things [?   ] &
[?   ] my memory that one impression quickly wears out
another

⟨When I got home I found a commun[ication] left by Mr Clark
that need[e]d an acknowledgment so I wrote & at the same time sent
a communication viz the 'Health to the ladies' – I shall go on as a
constant contributor untill I see what payday will bring me – I am
now writing the 'Devils Drive'⟩

December 1830 was a time of general alarm and disturbance;
both the *Stamford Bee* and the *Champion* contain several reports
of similar events, and vigilante groups were formed to counter
the disturbances. (Many of Clare's letters refer to the alarming
state of the country in the early 1830s.) In the *Bee* for 17
December 1830 there was a report of an incident very similar
to the one Clare describes; the chronology, however, tells us
that it cannot be the same episode, for Clare says very clearly
that the day after the event he describes, 'Dr Johnsons stacks at
spalding was destroyed'. The *Bee* for Friday 3 December 1830
contained a report of someone setting fire the previous Monday
to the Reverend Dr Maurice Johnson's hayricks in Spalding: a
reward of £615 was offered on Friday 10 December. Already
the draft can be dated fairly precisely. The reference later on to
the 'horrid tragedy in deeping fen' helps towards greater
precision. The *Champion* for 21 December reported a fire at Mr
Clark's farm in Deeping Fen (not the Clark[e] mentioned later
in the letter, who is in fact Thomas Clarke, editor of the *Bee*),
in which many animals had been killed; it was 'the most terrific
and destructive fire...in our neighbourhood'. Finally, in the
deleted final section of the letter there is reference to a poem
Clare has sent for the *Bee* called 'Health to the ladies', and this
indeed appeared in the *Bee* on 7 January 1831. It might be
added that it was clearly no accident that Clare's poem 'The

Hue and Cry' was published in the *Champion* on 11 January
1831: quite possibly it is what he refers to here as the 'Devils
Drive'.

A rather more enigmatic document is to be found in the
small group of Clare's letters that used to belong to the late Sir
Geoffrey Keynes and is now housed, along with the rest of
Keynes's collection, in Cambridge University Library. Once
again, it transpires that a letter lurking in a private collection
not only has a peculiar and particular interest in itself, but also
sheds some light on one of Clare's most difficult poems. At first
glance, the material is not promising: a relatively brief note, in
pencil, with no date, and no immediate indication of the
intended recipient:

My dear Madam
        I have heard you sent me one of your Vols 'The Book of the
Seasons' by the Revd Mr Jones which I went for as soon as I ⟨went⟩
hear'd it & he had lent it to a young Lady a Friend of mine so I could
not think it long in coming – but Mr Wiffen who had sent me a like
present of his 'Apsley Wood' having told me that you would expect
a Letter from me to say I recieved it safe I write in the mean time to
say that when it comes in my possesion I will write agen to tell you
how I like it
        I was unlucky enough to leave Mr Wiffens Poem behind me
somewhere in Northampton or where I am which I told him &
though I had intended to have written him a Letter perhaps *my
thanks to him thro' your hands may do as well for do you know in
these sorts of places I own nothing but the cloaths on my back &
hardly them – & when I want to write to a friend I have neither Pen
ink nor paper which I do not like to explain frequently not knowing
the cause – I can assure you my home is never In such places as these
– my fancy wont even have a bed in them she fancys on & lyes
elsewhere – have you read Whartons 'Ode to fancy' I used to like it
– I have poetical sweathearts too which my fancy dwells on as it did
when I was single so in writing of these as my fancy dictates they grow
imperceptably into a Vol & then I call it Child Harold of which I
wrote much both in Essex & here which I did & do meerely to kill
time & whose more proper Title might be 'Prison Amusements'
        I am my dear Madam yours very affectionately
                                                John Clare
*Some passeges of the Poem 'Apsley wood' put me strongly in mind
of 'Child Harrold' as well worthy of Byr[o]n himself & one of the

short poems 'the last but one' as very like the strength & style of the
same writer – I should have written much sooner but I have no
communication with pen & Ink & can only write with a pencil – I
thank you kindly in giving me the hint that Mary Howitt expected a
letter to thank her for her kindness in sending me her book of The
Seasons

We can deduce that the letter is written in an asylum. The
reference to *Child Harold*, which Clare was working on in 1841,
before, during, and after his escape from the asylum in Epping
Forest, does not necessarily place the letter in 1841 or
thereabouts. In a letter of 8 July 1850 to William Knight, Clare
uses the same title, 'Prison Amusements', to describe the verses
he would write had he the inclination (he is, in fact, echoing the
title of a poem James Montgomery had written when
imprisoned in York); on 8 April 1846 Knight had written to
Joseph Stenson (Northampton MS 410): 'I think some of his
Child Harrold stanzas are very fine here is one of last week
after looking at a picture in a book'. It is as though 'Child
Harold' and 'Prison Amusements' have become catch-all titles
for anything Clare happened to be writing. This is of obvious
significance in relation to the unfinished nature of *Child Harold*
as we have it in Northampton MS 8 and even MS 6; it forces
us to reconsider the whole nature of the project, and Clare's
attitude to it.[27] The letter is made odder by the fact that it
appears to be addressed to Mary Howitt (1799–1888), whose
husband had been responsible for *The Book of the Seasons* (1831),
mentioned in Clare's opening sentence; but the final paragraph
addresses the dead poet Jeremiah Wiffen (1792–1836). It is a
remarkable instance of Clare's instability of mind, resulting in
a shift in the audience as we move through the letter. The
Howitts seem to have visited Clare twice: a copy of 'The Sleep
of Spring', addressed to Mary Howitt (now in the Berg
Collection), is dated 'Northampton, 16 July 1844'; and in
December 1846 Knight wrote to Joseph Stenson (Northampton
MS 410), 'one day this last week W. Howett called to see Clare
– but Clare talked nothing but of fiting and such like... he told
Clare how much he admired his works – and Clare only said
"Do you" then he rambled on again in his old way'. A copy of

The Book of the Seasons (6th edn, 1840) is inscribed 'John
Clare / From his Friend / Mary Howitt' (Peterborough MS
H23): a loose flyleaf is inscribed in pencil, 'John Clare /
Northborough / Northamptonshire / Octr 23d 1848'; the op-
posite page has 'Biddy Thorp / Barnoak / 1849 / Mar 19'. The
reference to Wiffen is puzzling, as he had been dead since 1836;
presumably what happened was that Clare was sent a copy of
Aonian Hours (1819) by someone else, and whilst talking about
it he became confused, and thought he was writing to Wiffen,
not to Mary Howitt, and so he ended up thanking Wiffen for
the suggestion that he write to thank Mary Howitt for the *Book
of the Seasons*. The reference to the Reverend Mr Jones could, of
course, be to anyone, but it is probably William Arthur Jones
(1818–73), the Unitarian minister, an intimate friend of
George Baker, the topographer and historian who introduced
Clare to the American writer Dean Dudley early in 1850; Jones
was resident in Northampton from 1842 to 1849. Finally, the
fact that the note is in pencil would tend to confirm a date of
about 1848–9, placing it with those other pencil drafts which
belong somewhere between 1845 and 1849. It is worth
mentioning that in a letter to his son Charles dated 7 November
1849, Clare apologizes for not writing sooner, but says that 'I
have to go down below for Ink & Paper & forgot all about it
till this Morning.'

I have dwelt on the problems of dating letters because of the
need to establish, as precisely as possible, the detailed contexts
of any one letter; annotation should serve a similar end (it
seems to me more important than, say, giving chapter and
verse for every passing literary allusion). Drafts are of
significance for the same reason: their very fragmentariness
helps us to grasp the fleeting moments which go to make up a
finished letter. We can appreciate the privacy of the letter-
writing process, and at the same time the possibility of that
privacy shading into something more public, once the letter has
been sealed and sent on its way. As I have argued, Clare uses
the letter to establish relationships between himself and people
in the world beyond, but also between different aspects of
himself; his poems explore the same relationships, and confront

the same problems, and for this reason we should take seriously those larger claims the letters make on our attention. Clare himself was aware of the paradox. As he said to Hessey on 2 April 1820, in his very first letter to him, 'I write to you & T[aylor] as I shoud do to a Country friend   I tell you my most simple opinions of things that strike me in my own rude way as I shoud have done 3 or 4 years back'; and, in the very same letter, he also writes, 'some folks tell me my letters will creep into print & that it is a serious benefit for me to try to polish I only tell them I must then make an apollagy to creep after them as a preface & all will go right – what a polishd letter this woud be if it was printed!!!' The least that an editor of Clare's letters can do is to acknowledge his awareness of the paradox pinpointed by Clare, and refrain from 'polishing'; he must then refuse Clare's 'apollagy', substitute his own, and hope that 'all will go right'.

Notes

1 *The Later Poems of John Clare*, ed. Eric Robinson, David Powell, and Margaret Grainger (Oxford, 1984).

2 See especially Wolfgang Iser, *The Implied Reader* (Baltimore, 1974), and *The Act of Reading* (London, 1978).

3 For a full account of the relationship between Clare and his publishers, see Tim Chilcott, *A Publisher and His Circle* (London, 1972).

4 *John Clare: The Shepherd's Calendar*, ed. Eric Robinson and Geoffrey Summerfield (London, 1964); but see also the same editors' account of Taylor's role in the poem's original publication, *Review of English Studies*, n.s. 56 (1963), 359–69.

5 *The Midsummer Cushion*, ed. Anne Tibble and R.K.R. Thornton (Ashington and Manchester, 1979).

6 *The Rural Muse*, ed. R.K.R. Thornton (Ashington and Manchester, 1982); the Introduction includes an excellent account of the volume's genesis.

7 Robert Halsband, 'Editing the Letters of Letter-Writers', *Studies in Bibliography*, 11 (1950), 125–37.

8 G. Thomas Tanselle, 'Literary Editing', in *Literary and Historical Editing*, ed. George L. Vogt and John Bush Jones (University of Kansas Libraries, 1981), pp. 35–56.

9 See Martin Dodsworth, 'Editorial Miscellany', *English*, 35 (1986), 108.
10 *The Letters of John Keats*, ed. Hyder Edward Rollins (2 vols., Cambridge, Mass., 1958), I, p. 232.
11 'What is Poetry?' (1833), in *Early Essays by John Stuart Mill*, ed. J.M.W. Gibbs (London, 1897), pp. 201–14.
12 Joseph Kestner, 'The *Letters* of Jane Austen: The Writer as Emetteur/Récepteur', *Papers on Language & Literature*, 14 (1978), 249–68.
13 Tzvetan Todorov, *Littérature et signification* (Paris, 1967), p. 18 (translated by Kestner, and quoted in 'The *Letters* of Jane Austen', p. 249).
14 Eugenio Donato, 'Of Structuralism and Literature', *Modern Language Notes*, 82 (1967), 549–74 (p. 558).
15 Jonathan Culler, *Structuralist Poetics* (London, 1975), p. 165.
16 Kestner, 'The *Letters* of Jane Austen', p. 266; for 'shareability', see E.D. Hirsch, *Validity in Interpretation* (New Haven, 1967), p. 66.
17 Walter J. Ong, 'The Writer's Audience is Always a Fiction', *PMLA*, 90 (1975), 9–21 (p. 19).
18 *Selected Letters and Journals of George Crabbe*, ed. Thomas C. Faulkner and Rhonda L. Blair (Oxford, 1985); *The Letters of Charles and Mary Anne Lamb*, ed. Edwin W. Marrs, Jr (Ithaca, 1975–).
19 *The Natural History Prose Writings of John Clare*, ed. Margaret Grainger (Oxford, 1983), p. 235.
20 *Ibid.*, p. 235.
21 *Ibid.*, p. 251.
22 Mark Minor, 'John Clare and the Methodists: A Reconsideration', *Studies in Romanticism*, 19 (1980), 31–50.
23 By a curious but revealing quirk, a letter I received from an American library in answer to an enquiry about dates was itself misdated by a year.
24 *John Clare's Autobiographical Writings*, ed. Eric Robinson (Oxford, 1983), pp. 101–2.
25 Frederick W. Martin, *The Life of John Clare*, 2nd edn, with Introduction and Notes by Eric Robinson and Geoffrey Summerfield (London, 1964), p. 89.
26 *Autobiographical Writings*, p. 45.
27 Robinson and Powell make no mention of this in their notes to the poem as it appears in *Later Poems*.

CHAPTER 4

Towards a mobile text

Philip Brockbank

THE HISTORY AND TRAGEDY OF *KING LEAR*

On the one hand, there is the text; on the other, the pedant, looking for fame, or scratching a living. How do we know a good pedant from a bad? It is not as bland a question as it seems, for 'we' are not indivisible but have differing dispositions and differing expectations of the texts that we encounter. It is also the case that pedantry itself becomes text. Some pedants lay the text beautifully to rest, effacing inconsistencies on an orderly sheet; others enjoy precarious text and make a feature of anomalies and inconsistencies. The text may sleep peacefully, be becalmed, may even pass away; others keep it live and kicking or, at best, live and singing. Some make it perform, like a circus horse; others play the drayman. Some see themselves as resurrecting lost life; others undertake to refine, improve, correct. This apparently skittish survey of possibilities could be soberly documented from eighteenth-century treatments of Shakespeare's text alone.[1]

The scope afforded the pedant varies according to the conventions under which he works. The conventions themselves move through historical and cultural phases, and they are exposed to differing material and ideological pressures, including those of the market-place.

Knowing that a pedant is apt to see what he is looking for, I am setting course in search of a new mode of text. In the eighteenth-century history of Shakespeare we might distinguish the poet's text, the playwright's, the essayist's, the gentleman's, and the lawyer's – all variously related to the publisher's. The nineteenth century moves from the variorum text through the age of positivist investigation into the divided or disintegrated text, distributed between different authors, or between different phases of the same author's art. From the twentieth century we are familiar with the retrieved text that we try to recover via reconstructed lines of transmission; and we remember McKerrow's disappointed confidence that exact analysis would yield a definitive text; we know that expectation continued in practice to be satisfied with an eclectic text owing more to literary judgement than to a systematic methodology. In recent years Honigmann and others have taught us to be alert to the unstable text, reminding us, for example, that in transcribing his own work an author is likely to generate a second authentic text which does not necessarily displace the first. Currently, following the publication of the Oxford Shakespeare, the divided text returns as the revised text, giving us two separate plays, *The History of King Lear* and *The Tragedy of King Lear*.

The text that I hope to present to the button-moulder at the crossroads is the mobile text. I begin within the present convention and then, in a range of senses, I move outside it. I am at present at work with the editor of *Lear* for the New Cambridge Shakespeare, Jay Halio, of the University of Delaware. In due course he will find his own solutions to the problems, but I am bound, as general editor, to offer some tentative thoughts on our editorial strategy and tactics, and in the course of doing so I must clearly take my bearings from the Oxford enterprise. I start with the *Hamlet* story before offering glimpses of the way in which we might present that of *Lear*.

I shall represent the two *Lears* (1) as an artificial abstraction from the unstable text, (2) as a version of publisher's text, and (3) as the by-product of an exhausted lineal editorial format. The editorial vehicle I wish to put on the road is not another printed format but an interactive video disc. The next variorum Shakespeare will, I am confident (but how absurd these confidences are), be compiled on a series of interactive discs – perhaps as many as one per play. I shall be satisfied therefore if for my last trick I look away from paper to pixels, and conjure with some of the possibilities.

In his lucid and persuasive paper on *Shakespeare and Revision*[2] Stanley Wells writes on the text of *Hamlet* prepared by Philip Edwards for the New Cambridge Shakespeare. In common with other editors, Edwards believes Shakespeare to have cut certain passages that are not to be found in the Folio. Since they cease to be a part of the play they should not be integrated with the edited text but confined to an appendix. This was Edwards's original intention; but in his edition (perhaps under very light editorial pressure) he compromises by retaining certain passages on the page in square brackets. This is 'cheating', says Wells ('and to his credit the New Cambridge editor thinks so too' (p. 15)). Let me assume the role of apologist for the cheat.

Like other *Hamlet* editors Edwards finds that, try as he will to establish rules for the ascendancy of one text over the other, he is compelled in practice to judge that the Folio is correct in some cases, and the Quarto is correct in others. Where the 'two early versions run parallel, the text of this edition will necessarily be an eclectic text'. Quite so. From an analysis of the textual data it is not possible to find one clear order giving place to another. Edwards by way of explanation speaks of 'degeneration' when the play was handed over to the Chamberlain's Men, and finds it 'sadly true that the nearer we get to the stage, the further we are getting from Shakespeare'.[3] But Wells is surely right to suppose that Shakespeare himself was best placed to deliver the play to the stage. There is much better reason for thinking of a changing Shakespeare-text-for-performance than of a damaging clapper-clawing by the players (of whom Shakespeare was one).

But what occasions for change, and for how many perform-ances? 'No one suggests', says Wells of the cut passages, 'that they are not by Shakespeare... only that in performance the play was preferred without them' (p. 15). But this is to assume that there was only the one text-for-performance. Are we not entitled merely to say that it was preferred without one or more of the cut passages in at least one performance? As editors we are apt to pass surprisingly easily from the recognition of a cut to the conviction that we know why and when it was made. I prefer to remain sceptical. The soliloquy cut today might have been restored on the morrow. Lines reluctantly eliminated by the actor or playwright may have retained their fascination for the poet and still invite the attention of reader or player ('Sense sure you have, / Else could you not have motion'); and passages of reflection (the 'dram of eale') that digress in performance might have been restored by the author for publication had opportunity offered.

In practice, however, I find that I differ little from Edwards in the account I would give of the nature of Shakespeare's cuts; and I am more or less content with the way in which he presents the material to the modern reader. The square brackets filleting Hamlet's admonitions to his mother (iii.iv.53–88 in Edwards's text), for example, do the job well enough. If there is cheating it is to be attributed to designing tact which makes the editorial intervention almost invisible to the unprofessional reader. But it seems that the honourable, uncompromising editor would print only the short version of 'Look here upon this picture', and, passing to a more spectacular instance, would omit iv.iv.8S.D.-66 from the play altogether, including the soliloquy 'How all occasions'.

It now surprises me that the cut scene is not only present on the New Cambridge page, it is also free from square brackets, its status simply described in collation and notes. I may myself share responsibility for this decision (I can no longer remember) but what I suspect is the intrusion of 'designer's text', for designers prefer a page free of perplexities. I have come to take the pedantic view, however, that where there is instability in the text we should expect it to make an expressive impact on the page. Working with Peter Davison on *Richard III*, I incline to believe that square brackets will not register disturbed text emphatically enough and we should go for a smaller font. I would now prefer small font for Hamlet's reflections on Fortinbras's army, but am satisfied that elsewhere square brackets do a useful job. I like to see the excised (as distinct from displaced) text held in its authentic position. In each of these cases we can be confident (1) that Shakespeare wrote the fuller text (or something close to it), and (2) that it was located close to its present position. By retaining the text in its place, therefore, we put the reader most conveniently in possession of the evidence. Is the reader therefore cheated? The more candid alternative is apparently to hide the dislodged passages (to be found, with pedantic first aid, in an appendix), and appease the reader with hermeneutic exposures of their defective art. But as such exposures cannot properly be used to make a cut, they cannot be used to justify one either; they can at best make plausible a cut made on other grounds.

I believe that Philip Edwards, disappointed by the dashed prospect of identifying two *Hamlets*, tried to find compensation in attributing to the Folio cuts a coherence and single significance they lack. I do not find the *Lear* story very different. As in *Hamlet*, the Quarto and Folio lines of transmission refuse to remain discrete. The terrain between them is not hard high ground but a kind of swamp and archipelago with many cross-currents. While it may in time prove possible to agree that the Quarto derives from Shakespeare's draft, and that the Folio derives from a transcription prepared for the playhouse, it is not likely that the hypothesis will yield a systematic editorial method. Where, to adapt Edwards's words on *Hamlet*, the texts are convergent, the editorial tactic is likely to be eclectic even when the texts are separately edited (for example, it may turn out that in any one instance the Folio may retain what was meant to be the Quarto reading).

The *Lear* editor must move adroitly between the printing-shop and the theatre, keeping in mind an array of possibilities that is simple in outline but becomes intricate and extensive when set down. They could begin with the recognition that the omission of one or more lines usually, but not necessarily, indicates a cut. Cuts may have a printing-house source and explanation (for example, bad casting-off by the compositor), or may be attributable to author, scribe, or book-keeper. A preliminary analysis would take in such topics as amplifications and additions, rewritings, substitutions and reorderings, reconstructed text, transmission errors, and authorial mistakes.

The sceptical editor would not wish any particular stance

('revisionist', 'reconstructor', 'eclectic') to determine his procedure, but rather would wish to mark the vanishing-points and discovery-points of his perspective. Revisions, for example, may be made in a first draft, but an editor is unlikely to know what they are; and they are likely to occur more freely, and sometimes more inconsequentially, in an author's transcript than in a scribe's.

But it is in the playhouse, in the preparation of the prompt-book and in rehearsal, that we are likely to find the most telling interventions. They may be spread over many years, or be concentrated on one or more occasions. They may occur in the same prompt-book used for many performances, or in a playhouse transcript made for a special occasion (for example, a provincial tour) or to replace a damaged book. They could be attributable to the author, to the book-keeper, or to another member of the company (actor or playwright), and could include: routine clarifications of performance (entrances and exits, speech-assignments, sound-effects, use of properties); responses to playhouse exigencies (change of cast, actor's indisposition, special performances for particular audiences, tours); responses to company policy, including diplomatic or legal pressures from patron of the government; local dramatic revision of isolated passages made to satisfy the author (or another company playwright); or extensive revision of a range of passages, significantly changing the impact of the play.

Wells explains the Oxford decision to print two *Lears* and only one *Hamlet* by appeal to *Lear*'s greater number of more substantial variants amounting 'to such a shift in the overall presentation of the action as to create, in effect, two different plays' (p. 15). Such a decision once made, an editor will try to vindicate it, and will be under pressure to interrelate excisions and interventions into a single act of revision. He may also find himself giving a preternatural amount of attention to divergences between the texts, and again, may be seduced into ratiocinative hermeneutics.

The sceptical editor is exempt from such pressures. The choices open to him begin as the product of the divergences and the hypothetical occasions for them. He is free to believe, for example, that for one performance the allusions to France were tempered in response to diplomatic pressure, that for another, changes in speech-assignments followed a re-casting of the roles of Edgar and Albany, and that for yet another, the therapy scene at Dover was cut because there were no musicians available on a particular occasion.

Since we may be confident that there was more than one performance, we cannot from the evidence have high hopes of preparing the performed text. The most sceptical editor, however, remains under an obligation to prepare a text for performance, and he can see to it that the reader is presented at every stage with a performable attribution, a performable speech, and a performable scene. He may not believe that episodes (Merlin's prophecy and the mock-trial) were ever part of the one performance, while retaining his confidence that each found a place somewhere in the uncharted archipelago of shows. Here, in one sense of the term, is my 'mobile text'. We are beginning to realize the theatre-text has always been mobile and must not be hypostatized (either as one text or as two).

I hope I have made my point that the Quarto and Folio *Lears* are artificial, if not arbitrary, abstractions from the debris of evidence left by the history of the unstable text. My offer to represent them as a version of 'publisher's text' is more circumspect. When Oxford and Cambridge were proposing at much the same time to bring out comprehensive new editions of Shakespeare, Stanley Wells and I aired the prospect of a collaborative project. While they received the idea politely neither Press took it seriously. Wells and I have nevertheless worked together when we have had the opportunity, and there was a moment when *Lear* seemed to offer one. In 1982 Cambridge published, inaugurating its New Cambridge Shakespeare Studies, the first volume of Peter Blayney's *The Texts of 'King Lear' and their Origins*. The second volume, after some two decades of work, has still to appear. Early in the 1980s, however, it was already clear that a revaluation of the *Lear* Quarto would generate editorial embarrassments. While Blayney was making out a strong case for a Quarto-based old-spelling edition, there seemed to be some danger of four new modernized *Lear*s emerging from the over-heated Shakespeare industry. And Why not four *Hamlet*s, *Othello*s, and *Richard III*s? As far as I know, none of us pressed for double-texts of anything other than *Lear*. Wells and I entertained the idea of each editing the play for the other's series, the one Folio and the other Quarto-based. But both Presses, it turned out, were reluctant to let go of the more familiar Folio. Cambridge already had a specialist Quarto version under way, and Oxford had (with what reluctance I am not able to say) decided to make a feature of the double-text in its one-volume edition, but deferred a decision about the single-volume annotated version. Had Oxford University Press demanded the adventurous division of the kingdom, between the *History* and the *Tragedy* of *King Lear* we should have had on our hands a publisher's text; but from my distance it looks more like acquiescence in academic enthusiasm attended by the usual (and necessary) commercial opportunism.

The Cambridge *Lear* story so far invites a different valedictory emphasis. When we issued the New Cambridge Editorial Guide in 1979 we included a few specimen pages of facsimile or old-spelling texts as they might appear in supplementary volumes. Peter Blayney allowed us to make use of a page of the Quarto edition which was then under way (see Figure 1, p. 98). Since his final version has still to appear I wish only to make the point that very few readers have skill and experience enough to read a textual score of this complexity, and the reward is hardly commensurate with the endeavour. It is of course the old spelling that creates the scale of intricacies, and it remains possible for a modernized edition to present the reader with one retrieved text while offering data enough to retrieve another. But this dual text is perhaps only an inconvenient way of presenting two edited texts, and is open to the same objections.

For the mobile text I am seeking we can make do with a synthetic text whose turbulence is marked by a busy collation, square brackets, or changed font, depending upon the convergent, divergent, or divided state of the textual traditions.

TLN 415–54]   (C2ʳ7–2ᵛ3)   [I ii 76–109

him better teftimony of ⟨his⟩ intent, you fhould run a certaine   76 (81)
courfe; where if you violently proceed againft him, miftaking his
purpofe, it would make a great gap in your owne honour, and fhake
in peeces the heart of his obedience. I dare pawn downe my life
for him, he hath wrote this to feele my affection to your honour,   80 (86)
and to no further pretence of danger.
Gloft. Thinke you fo?
Baft. If your honour iudge it meete, I will place you where you
fhall heare vs conferre of this, and by an ⟨auricular⟩ affurance
haue your fatiffaction, and that without any further delay then   85 (92)
this very euening.
Gloft. He cannot be fuch a monfter.
Baft. Nor is not fure.
Gloft. To his father, that fo tenderly and intirely loues him;
heauen and earth! *Edmund* feeke him out, wind mee into him. I   90 (97)
pray you frame ⟨the⟩ bufines after your own wifedome: I would
vnftate my felfe to be in a due refolution.
Baft. I fhall feeke him fir prefently, conuey the bufineffe as I
fhall fee meanes, and acquaint you withall.
Gloft. Thefe late eclipfes in the Sunne and Moone portend no good 95 (103)
to vs: though the wifedome of nature can reafon thus and thus, yet
nature finds it felfe fcourg'd by the fequent effects. Loue
cooles, friendfhip fals off, brothers diuide; in Citties mutinies,
in Countries difcords, Pallaces treafon; the bond crackt betweene
fonne and father. Find out this villaine *Edmund*, it fhal loofe   100 (109)
thee nothing, doe it carefully. And the noble and true harted
Kent banifht, his offence (honefty); ftrange ftrange!   [*Exit.*]
Baft. This is the excellent foppery of the world, that when we are
ficke in Fortune (often the furfeit of our owne behauiour) we make
guiltie of our difafters, the Sunne, the Moone, and the Starres,   105 (120)
as if we were Villaines by neceffitie, Fooles by heauenly compul-
fion, Knaues, Theeues, and Trecherers by ⟨fphericall⟩ predomi-
nance; Drunkards, Lyars, and Adulterers by an enforft obedience of
planitary influence; and all that wee are euill in, by a diuine

---

76 his] F; this Qq 76 intent,] Q2,F; ∼ : Q 77 courfe;] ∼, Qq; ∼ : F 79 obedience.] F; ∼, Qq
84 auricular] F; aurigular Qq 89 him;] ∼, Q; ∼ : Q2; om. F 90 him.] ∼, Q–F 91 the] F;
your Qq 91 wifedome :] ∼, Qq; ∼. F 96 vs:] F; ∼, Qq 97 effects.] F; ∼, Qq
98 diuide;] ∼, Qq; ∼. F 99 treafon;] F; ∼, Qq 100 father.] F; ∼; Qq 101 carefully.] ∼, Q;
∼ ; Q2; ∼ : F 102 honefty;] ∼. F; ho neft, Q; honeft; Q2 102 *Exit.*] ∼, F; om. Qq
104 Fortune (often ... behauiour)] ∼, ∼ ... ∼, Q–F 107 fphericall] F; fpirituall Qq
107–8 predomi- nance;] ∼, Qq; ∼. F   109 influence;] F; ∼, Qq

---

76 *fhould run*] fhal runne Q2 80 *he*] that he F 80 *wrote*] writ F 81 *further*] other F
88–90 Baft. *Nor ... earth !*] 2¼ lines om. F 92 *to*] ro Q2 93 *fhall*] will F 94 *fee*] find F
96 *reafon*] reafon it F 99 *difcords*] difcord; in F 99 *the*] and the F 99 *betweene*]
'twixt F
100+] *after* father. F *adds:*   This villaine of mine comes vnder the   100+1 (109)
                                     prediction; there's Son againft Father, the King fals from
                                     byas of Nature, there's Father againft Childe. We haue
                                     feene the beft of our time. Machinations, hollowneffe,
                                     treacherie, and all ruinous diforders follow vs difquietly   100+5 (114)
                                     to our Graues.
102 ¹*ftrange*] 'Tis F *104 furfeit*] furfets F *105* ²*the*] om. F *106* ¹*by*] on F
107 Trecherers] Treachers F

Figure 1   Page from the Quarto edition of *Lear*

But in due course, as I have indicated, we will do better to find a pixellated solution, affording much fuller and more rapid access to information, and scope for a more searching and lucid analysis of sequences and structures.

INTERACTIVE OPTICAL VIDEO *LEAR*

'*See better, Lear*'

Interactive video optical discs have been with us for several years now, but in England, in the humanities, they remain a sadly under-utilized resource. From one point of view they belong, like computers, to the world of Jonathan Swift's Laputa. Gulliver tells of his meeting with a professor in Lagado, 'in Lagod, 'in a very large room, with forty pupils about him':

> After salutation, observing me to look earnestly upon a frame, which took up the greatest part of both the length and breadth of the room; he said, perhaps I might wonder to see him employed in a project for improving speculative knowledge by practical and mechanical operations. But the world would soon be sensible of its usefulness; and he flattered himself, that a more noble exalted thought never sprang in any other man's head.

The professor has a fair understanding of the motives that prompt the design of such machines:

> Every one knew how laborious the usual method is of attaining of arts and sciences; whereas by his contrivance, the most ignorant person at a reasonable charge, and with a little bodily labour, may write books in philosophy, poetry, politicks, law, mathematicks and theology, without the least assistance from genius or study. He then led me to the frame, about the sides whereof his pupils stood in ranks. It was twenty-foot square, placed in the middle of the room. The superficies was composed of several bits of wood, about the bigness of a dye, but some larger than others. They were all linked together by slender wires...on every square...were written all the words of their language in their several moods, tenses, and declensions, but without any order...at every turn the engine was so contrived that the words shifted into new places, as the bits, moved upside down. *Gulliver's Travels*, part III, Chapter 5.

The age of Laputa is still with us, as it was some twenty years
ago when Lévi-Strauss was trying to persuade us all to set up
complex IBM card-indexing systems as a key to all mythologies.

The new technology, however, enables me to lay more
plausible claim to serve mankind with noble exalted thoughts
that never sprang in any other man's head. It is apt to recall
that when Allardyce Nicoll founded the Shakespeare Institute
he was alert some forty years ago to the prospects opened up by
the development of microfilm, which, together with the
publication of Pollard and Redgrave's *Short Title Catalogue of
English Books* (1950) made it possible for a new research
institute to undertake from the start enterprises of great pith
and moment. So it seemed also to sympathetic onlookers like
Kenneth Muir, who, writing in *Shakespeare Newsletter* (1966),
anticipated a programme of exhaustive study which would
enable us to make all the possible connections between
Shakespeare's writing and his reading. Nicoll himself, by way
of a chronological re-ordering of the STC and the initiation of
a year-by-year charting and investigation of material, hoped to
give a fuller account of the cultural ethos in which Shakespeare
worked. We are now in a good position to see why such
enterprises, depending as they do upon a positivist understanding of immutable 'fact' and a passive perception, could
only be imperfectly successful. We are better placed to recognize
the dependence of facts and their significance upon our active
perceptions, and the optical disc, used in conjunction with
ancillary computer software, promises to change the dynamics
of scholarship and indeed our radical responses to poetry and
theatre.

I shall offer some speculations about the contribution which
a combined optical disc and floppy disc project might make
towards a finer control of the text and art of Shakespeare in the
preparation of a new Variorum Edition, which the old-style
printed book is no longer able to contain. A typical single
interactive disc can hold up to 40,000 pages of text, thousands
of still photographs, and libraries of maps or fine art
reproductions. More recent technology has distinguished the
CD-ROM (Compact Disc-Read Only Memory), usually

publisher-created, the WORM (Write-Once-Read-Many), which is user-created, and the erasable optical disc, which can be both created and changed by the user. Any one of the three modes could serve the present purpose. Each has video and audio capacities, and can be divided in any proportion. If it is devoted exclusively to audiovisual performance its capacity is very limited and compares uneconomically with the cheaper video cassette (but retains over the cassette the advantage that single frames are instantly retrievable and perfectly stable). Devoted to the storage of facsimile text or image, its capacity is more evidently formidable; a typical disc can hold the equivalent of some two hundred printed books. Finally, using straight text only, one of the larger WORM discs could store a daunting total of over a billion words.

It would, of course, be possible to cover several plays on one disc, but I prefer to imagine an interactive video Shakespeare Variorum with one disc to each play. The CD-ROM or WORM once made, nothing can be added or taken away; but new material can be imposed or merged with the help of additional software. It may prove expensive in comparison with most arts projects (some years ago the estimated cost ranged from 'a few hundred pounds' using 'adapted generic course ware produced in house' to £50,000 for the preparation and processing of new material), but once made, its clones, as it were, are durable and marketable at a price close to that of the current printed volumes of the New Variorum (that is, about £50), and would provide incomparably more matter and service. At a more popular level, *King Lear* has most recently been published in two texts, as if it were two plays; even in a Variorum volume it has become increasingly difficult to manipulate the textual data to the required level of sophistication. A *Lear* disc could include 6,000 facsimile pages, covering early texts, sources, analogues and documents, and theatre history; it could take in all significant articles and books, including much in translation; and it could offer a generous service of menus and indexes.

Just what it could offer is still matter for creative speculation, for it cannot so far be said that the technological miracle has excited a wide-ranging imaginative response. Discs available when I last surveyed the scene fell into three categories: commercial sales-packages, instructional programmes, and information retrieval systems. I would hope to design a disc that not only does more efficiently what we do now through the printed page, but also encourages new modes of understanding and exploration. I do not, however, entertain any of the expectations about the heuristic technology which were recently cultivated in present-day equivalents of Lagado. All the initiatives must continue to be ours, not the machine's. But the perspectives opened up by rapid retrieval of an inexhaustible quantity of data, and by the convergences and divergences of texts and structures that can be clarified by its manipulation, are likely to make a qualitative as well as quantitative difference to our modes of thought. It could happen that in intellectual fight we will become less linear.

There has always been a distance between the ways in which the poet's mind works and the pedant's; the poet cherishes the turbulence of our common sense, the pedant its orderliness. Whenever in his plays Shakespeare alights upon poetry as a topic it is to wonder at the turmoil of the mind that makes it: 'This is a fit I have, simple, simple; a foolish extravagant spirit, full of forms, figures, shapes, objects, ideas, apprehensions, motions, revolutions: these are begot in the ventricle of memory, nourished in the womb of *pia mater*, and delivered upon the mellowing of occasion.' So says the pedantic poet Holofernes in *Love's Labour's Lost* (iv.ii.66–70). In *A Midsummer Night's Dream*, Theseus' renowned speech, 'The poet's eye in a fine frenzy rolling...', finds that 'The lunatic, the lover, and the poet / Are of imagination all compact' (v.i.2–22). And the Chorus of *Henry V* speaks of the 'quick forge and working-house of thought'. In one tradition of imaginative thought (one in which Keats, Coleridge, and Yeats were still active) poetry is less likely to depend upon consecutive argument than upon diffusions and dissipations, confluences, conjunctions and disjunctions, fusings, bondings and re-creations; and these are processes more readily imitated and traced on interactive video disc.

I say so, however, as an article of faith. What I take to be an opportunity to change and advance our imaginative thought processes a little, may turn out to be another delusion of Lagado. It may nevertheless still be possible to glimpse some precise advantages that the disc, with editorial help, could offer to the reader and player of *King Lear*.

The editorial service demanded by the disc differs in kind from that traditionally found appropriate in the book. Pressure on space compels the editor of the printed page to select, sample, exclude, and to decide (often silently) between alternatives. The disc editor can be hospitable and is not required by the format to impose boundaries upon his choice of materials or to restrict his conceptual range. Overwhelmed by opportunity, his capacity to offer creative guidance may be more severely tested, but the disc offers the compensatory advantage of allowing him to free himself and his reader from digression and distraction. He can charge the screen with apt data while keeping it clear of irrelevancies.

The editor must have an authoring system at his disposal, enabling him to order and display his material through a great variety of routes. The system would present the user with an initial choice between guided and exploratory courses. Among the guided courses would be a choice of introductory menus in a variety of languages; a voice-over-images would attend to the making of the play, and a scene or two would be presented cinematically; a lightly annotated text would be at the reader's disposal, and problems in and about the play would receive a preliminary airing. An open editorial programme could leave the user opportunity to proceed with his own editing, putting at his disposal virtually all the material (including such fine detail as close-ups of broken skeleton formes, paper-marks, and irregular font).

A screen divisible into two or more areas, with a range of magnifications, would make possible a highly sophisticated yet disarming textual display. One or two edited texts, for example, could be suspended between corresponding passages of the Folio and the Quarto; compositors' stints could be distinguished with differing ground-colours, and variants could be highlighted. Graphic analysis of text (stemmata, compositor-scans) could be pre-ordered, or, with the help of an ancillary program, prepared on-screen.

The text could be called 'mobile' merely to mark the ease with which it could be moved and manipulated. But, more significantly, the disc could simulate a hypothetical history of the prompt-book through a choice of performable states. In addition to edited versions of the Quarto and Folio it could provide perhaps as many as four texts differently 'revised' or cut for performance. The disc would also put at our disposal the prompt-books of more recent times which would remind us of the continuing instability of playhouse copy, and might or might not show, firstly, that the text of any one performance is likely to differ more from the Folio or Quarto texts than they do from each other; secondly, that the prompt-book used by a company may bear the marks of more than one occasion or production; and thirdly, that cuts frequently made in theatre tradition do not correlate closely with the differences between Quarto and Folio.

The divided screen would make it a matter of routine to compare published commentaries, while the user compiling his own commentary could have access to indexed versions of all significant articles on *Lear*, and to contemporary allusions. Passages to which the page-text can afford only references or brief citations could be generously supplied on disc. Montaigne and Harsnet, for example, would be fully available, together with all the material of the Brutan history from Geoffrey to *Locrine*.

Special topics could be covered by a choice of menus and indexes. Lear's fear that he is not in his perfect mind, for example, could invite attention to the topic 'Lear's madness'. The guided course would include an account of the king's sanity (attended by folly) in earlier Lear stories, together with a review of Shakespeare's response to *Thyestes* and the *Hercules Furens*, and of his interest in the mind's decay. The index-service offered by the disc could take in a general index to all material and any number of specialized indexes (again, within the user's ability to provide).

The true usefulness of the traditional Variorum Shakespeare has proved to be, not so much its provision of fuller and more settled interpretations, as its revelation of the changing reception of the plays through generations of reading and playing. The disc could provide menus for the study of, for example, Restoration *Lear*, Edwardian *Lear*, and *Lear* in the 1950s. This, however, is to take too parochial a view. In the twentieth century it has become increasingly clear that Shakespeare can no longer be treated as an exclusively English phenomenon. In the theatre and scholarship of other countries, often in languages other than English, the plays are finding fresh energy and significance. The *Lear* disc might be expected to include audio-visual glimpses of Chinese performances and Japanese films, with theatre stills from New York, Milan, and Georgia. The list is inexhaustible. The possibilities I have touched upon are not, of course, wholly excluded from the medium of the printed volume, but the amplitude and diversity of the material, the rapidity of its retrieval and the flexibility of its ordering, are likely to quicken and radically change the nature of our perceptions; I would expect a new vocabulary ('reflections', 'recoils', 'recoveries', 'confluences') to be needed to express relationships more oblique than those looked for in old-style analysis of sources and influences. All my expectations may be disappointed, and find their proper resting-place in a disc devoted to Lagado and the persisting or recurring vanity of mad professors. The disc, however, will carry a reflection of the truth, clarified in the opening scene of *Timon of Athens*, that the arts, depending upon patronage, are caught up in the snares of the moneyed society. For the professor from Lagado has a problem. Where is the money to come from?

Six hours a day the young students were employed in this labour; and the professor showed me several volumes in large Folio, already collected, of broken sentences, which he intended to piece together; and out of all those rich materials to give the world a complete body of all the arts and sciences; which, however, might be still improved and much expedited, if the public would raise a fund for making and employing five hundred such frames in Lagado, and oblige the managers to contribute in common their several collections. *Gulliver's Travels*, part III, Chapter 5.

If 'the managers' were ready 'to contribute in common their several collections', a team of two pedants, two 'scribes', and what Edmund in *Lear* calls a 'secretary astronomical' to do the calculating, could make a brave start on the interactive Variorum Shakespeare. Are there, I wonder, peeping round my towering microchips, any offers?

NOTES

1 For an outline history of Shakespeare editing, see J. Philip Brockbank, 'Shakespearean Scholarship from Rowe to the Present', in *William Shakespeare, his World, his Work, his Influence*, ed. John F. Andrews (New York, 1985).
2 Given as the Hilda Hulme Lecture 1987, and published by the University of London in 1988.
3 *Hamlet*, ed. Philip Edwards (Cambridge, 1985), p. 32.

CHAPTER 5

Rectifying Shakespeare's Errors: romance and farce in bardeditry

Charles Whitworth

What in the world can/should/does an editor do to the text of a Shakespeare play?[1] We are reminded by a growing host of performance critics but also, and more significantly, by textual scholars and editors, that play texts are both potential, to be realized in performance, rather than ends in themselves, and, as things in themselves, unstable. We are enjoined to privilege those early texts of Shakespeare – where there exist more than one – which appear to embody his theatrical practice or that of his colleagues, rather than those which represent his first thoughts or a scribe's transcription, and, generally, to have the *play* in mind as we edit the *text*.[2] What then is the role of the textual editor *vis à vis* a Shakespeare play? How can whatever he does make any real difference? He works perforce only with the printed signs of Quartos and Folios. The director and actors of the play may start from the text he or another editor prepares, but they can and do deviate from it, cut it, rewrite it, rearrange it, re-edit it at will, even throw it away, as the actor Richard McCabe – or was it Puck? – did with a copy of the New Penguin edition of *A Midsummer Night's Dream* in the RSC's 1989 production. Some directors go back to the original printed texts, circumventing all subsequent editions. But the vaunted indefiniteness of the dramatic text is not for the editor. He must make choices and fix them in print, however he may equivocate and canvass alternatives in his notes. He must fix that which must remain unfixed, fluid, open, ambiguous, always at the mercy, inspired or banal, of producers.[3] But if that very production, or the totality of all productions, past, present, and future, is the essence of the play, is he not in some

quixotic, perverse way engaged in denying that essence? Is not
his enterprise both subsidiary and paradoxical, at the same
time both prior to and parasitic upon the living business of the
theatre? He works for years to produce a printed text, agonizing
over accidentals, solving and resolving cruxes, emending,
guessing, inventing, admitting defeat, and delivers his text to be
printed, bound, and read. But reading is not the activity for
which that play was written. Performing is. And his text, over
which he sweated for so long, will never be performed as he
edited it. It will be reproduced, transformed, literally, in the
sweat of rehearsal and performance: Brook's *Dream*, Hall's
Hamlet, Nunn's *Macbeth*, Warner's *Titus*, not his, the editor's.
The edition used as script is rarely even mentioned in the
theatre programme.[4] 'A poem should not mean but be', said
MacLeish. An editor's text cannot mean. Can it be? Certainly
there can be no *play* on the editor's carefully constructed page.
The editor of a novel or a poem or a treatise has no such
anxiety. His text goes to its ultimate consumer, the reader, as
he has prepared it, unmediated in its essentials. The play
editor's text never goes to its ultimate consumer, the play-goer,
as he has prepared it, especially in its essentials.

The editor's quest for his text is, from one perspective, a
romantic one. He encounters obstacles, fights giants, dodges
between Scylla and Charybdis (who shall remain nameless),
comes upon ancient strongholds, smoking ruins, signs of
skirmishes, dry bones, dust, the landscape of the editorial
history of his text. When it is a Shakespeare play, that
landscape is vast, the terrain complicated, with traps for the
unwary and the challenges of predecessors, the illustrious and
the silly, the flamboyant and the hapless, with many of whom
he must pause to do battle. But the quest itself is absurd: he can
never succeed. He will think he has it, but like Sir Calidore's
Blatant Beast, it will escape again, never be finally pinned
down, penned in, tamed. What is worse, all productions of his
play will repeatedly release it, in virtually infinite mutations, all
of them the play, none of them his play. (Even if he convinces
himself that he has got the text, he may have lost, or slain, the
play.)

To what or whom is the editor of a dramatic text responsible? To the author? He, in Shakespeare's case, is long dead, and besides, we do not, cannot, know what exactly he wrote or wanted. He is, in a crucial sense, irrelevant. To the reader? To the director, to the actor, all of whom are also readers, but who read to different ends than do the student, the teacher, the literary critic, the 'mere' reader? And those to whom the ultimate, infinite re-creations of the play belong, theatre practitioners, amateur and professional, great and small, have no responsibility to any *editor's* text. They may rely upon a single edition, which they will still cut and rearrange as it suits them, or they may work from several, picking and choosing, referring to earlier printed texts, even preferring less reliable texts to more reliable ones.[5] Their responsibilities are various: to that chimera, 'the play', in the objectivity of which they sometimes display a touching faith, to the audience, society, the box office, sponsors.

The two activities, reading a printed text and seeing/hearing a performance, are, obviously, radically different.[6] The one thing you cannot do as you read the book is really see and hear a performance (imagination is something else); at a performance, you see, hear, even smell sometimes (as in the 1980 RSC production of *As You Like It* when the most delicious aroma of roast chicken wafted over the stalls as the banished duke and his men sat down to their feast in Act II, scene vii), but you cannot read the printed text of the play, the book, simultaneously. To the reader, the medium is print; to the spectator–auditor, the media are many, but print is not normally one of them. The editor provides for the one activity, the director, actors, designer, composer, and others for the other. The editor may hope fervently that his edition is adopted by some director and that his cherished readings will be spoken and thus achieve a fleeting immortality. But he knows that even if that happens, his *text*, what he edited, will be only part of the *play*. He cannot provide for those other essential parts, including the way each phrase and line of his text is delivered. The actor *gives* meaning to words, can indeed give different meanings to the same words, meanings which the editor cannot entertain or even imagine.[7] His text is thus at an even further remove from final or definitive meaning. Whether blueprint or skeleton (or some other, always inadequate, metaphor), his text will be the merest starting-point for the performance, that text which was the goal of his long arduous quest. Not only is it destined to be rehandled in the very act of being realized, it is doomed, even as allegedly fixed, permanent, printed, preserved artifact, to be superseded. The beast breaks out as it is being apprehended.[8]

On the other hand, is it really as hopeless as all that? The writing of a play is an act of literary composition. The editor deals with a literary artifact, written, printed, as any literary work is. Written words are the medium, as they are for a novel or a poem. We cannot edit what is not there, that third dimension: the performance. (Nor should the editor, however much he may yearn to do so, stage the play on the page; to do so is to limit the text's potentiality.) We can only edit that text which is different in its structure and layout – speech prefixes, stage directions, act and scene divisions, and so on, rather than authorial voices, paragraphs, quotation marks, chapters, and so on – but similar in its medium: words. The editor of a dramatic text will always have divided, irreconcilable loyalties: to the written text he works from, the material cause (in Aristotelian terms) of what he aims to make, and to the performed play, the final cause.

These and other related questions have occurred to me, a moderately experienced editor of Renaissance dramatic texts but a relative novice as a Shakespeare editor, as I have worked on an edition of *The Comedy of Errors* for the Oxford Shakespeare. They are, some of them, simple matters, but they are also, I am convinced, fundamental matters. They are theoretical, or rather philosophical, questions about the nature of the editing enterprise where dramatic texts are concerned, and about the nature of those texts themselves. I do not wish to belabour the obvious, nor to over-dramatize harmless drudgery, but I do wish to pose such questions, even the more naive-sounding ones, and to worry, and encourage my fellow-editors to worry, about what we do. This concern has not sprung *ex nihilo*, but neither is there yet any articulated theory of dramatic textual editing that addresses these and related questions. Greg's famous theory of copy-text and the guidelines for editors that were derived from it went unchallenged for a surprisingly long time, such were Greg's stature and authority.[9] But even as editors, the great majority of whom have not considered themselves textual theorists *per se*, have worked, they have recognized the limitations and contradictions in Greg's impressive rationale. Its shortcomings are more clearly seen as the peculiar extra-literary nature of early play-texts, the differences between playwriting and authoring, and the primacy of performance over mere reading emerge and are articulated. I am one of that majority, just an editor, not a bibliographer or textual critic *tout court*, and the questions and sceptical reflections which have arisen in the course of the workaday business of editing a Shakespeare play-text (scepticism has not yet induced paralysis) have led, not to a new theory, but to a preoccupation with the peculiarity of that business.

With these queries pending, or looming, I propose to engage in a sort of quizzical intermittent trialogue with recent Shakespearean textual theory, specifically as enunciated by the editors of the Oxford *Complete Works* and related publications, and by other textual critics, all on one side, and 'my' play/text, *The Comedy of Errors*, on the other.[10] On this side too is some limited experience of testing editorial solutions in the arena of performance when I had the opportunity to advise the director Phyllida Lloyd on textual matters as she prepared and rehearsed a production of *The Comedy of Errors* for the Bristol Old Vic.[11] Like Antipholus of Syracuse, I am 'smothered in *Errors*'. I can only hope that my efforts do not prove me, as he claims to be in the second half of that line, 'feeble, shallow, weak' (III.ii.35).

The Comedy of Errors is not a particularly difficult text, compared with others in the Shakespeare canon. It does not raise the 'two-text' issue since the Folio of 1623 contains the only early version of the play, and it is not radically corrupt, incomplete, or otherwise maimed. It has its own peculiarities, to some of which I shall return later: a small handful of cruxes, some confusion over characters' names, an occasional vagueness in stage directions, as well as the usual misprints, verse–prose transpositions, unmetrical lines, lacunae, and the like. It is a uniquely Shakespearean amalgam of disparate genres, romance and farce, an early comedy that has more in common with *Twelfth Night* and *Pericles* than with the other plays more nearly contemporary to it, and little of the comedy of young love so prominent in most of Shakespeare's first ten comedies.

I want to discuss here some of the problems and puzzles, critical and editorial, it poses, within the framework of the theoretical and procedural issues adumbrated above. The romance and the farce of editing Shakespeare's plays will, I hope, be both evoked and illustrated in this context, the particular surprises and misprisings, double-takes and double thinking involved in doing the mundane job of editing this text framed, as it were, by the larger questions, as the immediate, hectic business of the farcical comedy is framed and overarched by the mythical, romance motifs of erring, losing, seeking, and finding. The harmless, hopeful drudge sets forth, in the giant shadows of his predecessors, equipped with the tools of the trade, instinct, and some notion of what the achieved thing should be like. He should not deceive himself that he has a perfect idea of the thing-in-itself. Romance versus farce; editing texts for readers versus performing plays for theatre audiences; the editor's need to choose, to set something and not something else down in print, but with space for glosses, collations, explanations versus the performer's need to say one thing and not another, despite the 'openness' of the text, with no place for verbal glosses or commentary, but virtually unlimited scope for glossing by gesture, expression, inflection; telling, in narrative and in introductions and commentaries on the page versus showing, in performance, with sets, costumes, and music on the stage; diegesis versus mimesis – these complementary, often contradictory sets of conventions, requirements, and procedures seem to me to be reflected in the play, *The Comedy of Errors*.

Romance is essentially a narrative genre, not a dramatic one. I take it that there are fundamental differences between those two modes, which are more or less identical to Plato's diegesis and mimesis.[12] Drama, as theatre, occurs in the present, is immediate, visual as well as aural; narrative is usually in the past tense, is mediated by a narrator who may or may not be the 'author', and nowadays is experienced silently and privately, by reading, though it used more commonly to be experienced aurally and with others. Romance depends upon discursive passages of description, scene-setting, and mood-making, and upon the omniscient narrator's mediation, guidance, information, suspense-building, reassurance, and so on. The time scale is, or can be, vast: 'Once upon a time, long ago' is not the dramatist's opening gambit, but it is the essence of the romancer's. Consider Shakespeare's various ploys to overcome that initial obstacle. He uses prologues and epilogues, choruses, frames (themselves either narrative or dramatic), lumps of narrative within the plays (for example, Prospero, Orlando, the Third Gentleman in *The Winter's Tale*, or Egeon at the beginning of *Errors*), even a real historical poet, Gower, who appears in *Pericles* to tell the story that we are unlikely to credit without his assurances as to its authenticity. Only after forty lines, with references to his book, does Gower hand us over to 'the judgement of [our] eye'; not content, he presents dumbshows, refers often to his sources, and in all, appears seven times throughout the play, speaking some 300 lines, including an epilogue, all in order to mediate the romance narrative to a theatre audience, to turn telling into showing. Shakespeare's practice in many of his plays amounts to an inversion, or turning inside out, of Plato's and Aristotle's 'mixed mode' (a narrative with some direct dialogue): he writes drama, with a lot of narrative, external and internal, to account for that which is beyond the dramatist's and his audience's reach. An Elizabethan paradigm of this kind of mode-switching is George Peele's marvellous little fantasy, *The Old Wife's Tale*, which announces itself as 'tale' but is a play, but a play in which a tale being told turns into a play being performed for an audience which includes the tale-teller herself and her auditors, a play in which several characters tell romance-like tales of travel, hardship, and enchantment.[13] In the vogue of performance studies, we must acknowledge that there are limits to the dramatist's art, even as we claim that his written text is not fully realized until it is performed. Shakespeare's and others' metadrama is a recognition of those limits; it is also a challenge to them, pushing out the circumscribing walls of the wooden O's and concrete caverns in which the performance is confined. There are things the dramatist cannot do, *qua* dramatist, when it comes to story-telling, that the romance narrator can do. But in the theatre the theatrical naturally prevails.

To come to cases: in the theatre, will comedy and its vigorous stepchild, farce, where they are present, inevitably overwhelm, if not subvert, romance? Does romance have a chance where farce pops in its zany face (or arse)? Is *The Comedy of Errors*, romance in its form and in much of its matter, doomed to live *on stage* in a single dimension, that of farce? Is the romance to be left to readers only, while theatre audiences get farce(d): two works living under one title? Farce is a viewerly, spectator-friendly genre; romance is a readerly, imagination-friendly one. Romance requires imagination, farce leaves nothing to it. As readers of romance, we have to create our own Arcadias and Faerylands, Illyrias, Bohemias, and Ardens (or Ardennes if we are reading the Oxford Shakespeare). Romance is not visual; it is, 'to speak metaphorically, a *speaking* picture'. Farce has to be seen to be (dis)believed.[14] Is it wrong for directors, designers, and actors to take the farce and let the romance go (or worse, send it up)? Or do the improbabilities of romance pushed further, treated comically on stage, necessarily *become* farcical? That is, is the difference I am talking about one of degree and not of kind? But if so, why isn't *Cymbeline*, of all the outrageously improbable plays, called a farce, or *Twelfth Night*? What is the point of Shakespeare's having encased his 'farce' – if that is what it is – in a romance, a story which, on its own, has all the sentiment, pathos, and wonder of *Pericles*? Will we even agree that *The Comedy of Errors*, in its larger dimension, *is* romance? For we are told and have been told for a long time that the play is a *farce*, and theatre practitioners have, it seems, always treated it so.

In 1819, Frederick Reynolds turned the play into an operatic farce. He added songs from other Shakespeare plays, with musical settings by various composers, including Mozart. A reviewer for the *European Magazine* found Reynolds's enormities just the remedy for a silly, incredible play:

It was attended by the most crowded house since the beginning of the season, and the audience were throughout in a unanimous temper to applaud…No illusion of the stage can give probability to the perpetual mutations of four persons, paired in such perfect similitude, that the servant mistakes his master, and the master his servant: the wife her husband, and the husband his wife. All this so strongly contradicts common experience, that it repels us even in description; but on the stage, with the necessary dissimilarity of countenance, voice, manner, and movement, that occurs between the actors, however disguised by dress, the improbability becomes almost offensive.[15]

The anonymous reviewer is carried away by his own rhetoric: no husband mistakes his wife, because there are no twin women.[16] Even the farce, let alone what was left of the romance, failed to work for this dyspeptic critic, but whether audiences liked the play or not, farce it was and farce it remained. C.E. Flower, in his preface to the play in the Memorial Theatre acting edition, makes much of the text of the 'Comedy, or as we should now call it Farce' being fully restored in the 1881 Stratford production.

Many of us would concur in Dr Johnson's opinion that 'Shakespeare's plays are not in the rigorous and critical sense either tragedies or comedies, but compositions of a distinct kind', accurately reflecting 'the real state of sublunary nature' with its 'chaos of mingled purposes and casualties'.[17] It is well known that Shakespeare drew upon Plautus' comedy, *The Menaechmi*, about twin brothers from Syracuse, accidentally separated in childhood, one of whom journeys in search of the other. It is also clear that in Act III, scene i, he had in mind the first scene of Plautus' *Amphitruo*, in which Jupiter and Mercury impersonate Amphitruo and Sosia, master and servant.[18] But the ingredient that Plautus did not provide was the plot which frames, overarches, and ultimately subsumes the comedy of twins mistook, servants beaten, masters maddened, and merchants thwarted. That plot, which sets *The Comedy of Errors* in another mode altogether, belongs to a different tradition, one which also went back to antiquity, which Shakespeare knew well and turned to again and again, in which he seems to have been more at home than ever he was in the strictly-structured, rule-governed school of classical comedy. Dr Johnson, keeping to the Folio's tripartite division of the plays into comedies, histories, and tragedies, opined of Shakespeare that 'in comedy he seems to repose, or to luxuriate, as in a mode of thinking congenial to his nature... His tragedy seems to be skill, his comedy to be instinct.'[19] I would refine Johnson's distinction and suggest that it was particularly *romance* and the dramatic genre that approximates it that were most congenial, even instinctive, to Shakespeare throughout his career. He manifests a peculiar fondness for romance, for old, hoary, much-told tales of wonder and wandering, of storms, shipwrecks, pirates, mistaken identity, oracles and mysteries, treachery and betrayal, bravery and devotion, of parents and children, husbands and wives, brothers and sisters torn asunder and tossed by Fate, but brought together at last against all odds. All of his comedies and tragicomedies contain such elements, some are essentially of that kind.

Just such a tale, of course, is that of old Egeon of Syracuse, his wife, and twin sons and twin servants, shipwrecked, separated, rescued, lost, finally reunited after years of despair and searching, but not before further trials, danger, and anguish. *The Comedy of Errors* begins with it and ends with it, and its dominant moods and motives run right through the farcical comedy, tempering it and transforming it into a new kind of whole which cannot, without distortion, even denaturing, be described or performed simply as 'farce'. That long discursive opening scene, in which the actors, especially the one who plays Egeon, must grip the audience's attention and imagination with pure tale-telling, holds the cruel promise of execution for the sad, worn-out old man.[20] The comedy which follows must be coloured by it. Johnson may have had in mind that scene, among others, when he complained of the tediousness of Shakespeare's passages of narration:

He affects a wearisome train of circumlocution and tells the incident imperfectly in many words which might have been more plainly delivered in few. Narration in dramatic poetry is naturally tedious, as it is unanimated and inactive and obstructs the progress of the action;

it should therefore always be rapid and enlivened by frequent interruption. Shakespeare found it an encumbrance...'[21]

Well, maybe, but he repeatedly brought it upon himself by his choice of romance material. The language of Egeon's narrative is stylized, formulaic, the language of romance: 'Once upon a time, long ago...' is the mode; and Egeon's story begins a long time ago, at the beginning of his life, in fact: 'In Syracusa was I born...'

Within a few lines of the start of the next scene, we see that the two plots, Plautine comedy and Hellenistic romance, are related, that the promise of doom will not be kept because the elements necessary to avert disaster and to bring about the happy dénouement begin immediately to assemble. Scene ii begins, in sharp contrast to the deliberate narrative tempo of Scene i, dramatically in mid-conversation, in mid-sentence, with a friendly local merchant warning the newly-arrived Syracusans of their danger as proscribed foreigners in Ephesus, and pointing the warning with news of another Syracusan who is to be executed that very afternoon. The 'wearisome train of circumlocution', the narrative, ends, and the brisk, immediate action of drama begins: 'in medias res' takes over from 'Once upon a time...' The frequent reminders of the time of day in the play – in eight of its eleven scenes – keep Egeon and his impending fate constantly in mind while he is absent from the stage, in tension with the expectation raised by the romance conventions of the first scene that it will be averted. Shakespeare's observation of the unity of time, here as nowhere else before *The Tempest*, heightens that effect. The theme was rendered visually by the clock in Theodor Komisarjevsky's 1938 Stratford production: its hands moved as the hours ticked away, and sometimes ran to catch up. Reference to Egeon (not by name, of course) in the second scene links his plot to that of Antipholus and Dromio of Syracuse: father, son, and servant, unknown to each other, are in the same place at the same time, aliens all three, despairing seekers for each other and the rest of their family.

Furthermore, the two stories are linked immediately and explicitly by references in both to money. Egeon desperately needs money to save his life; barely half-a-dozen lines after he goes off, 'hopeless and helpless', to seek it, Antipholus receives back from the merchant the money he had held in safe-keeping, the very sum, we are soon told (I.ii.81), that Egeon requires. And the place where all of them are, the alien town of Ephesus, is established as one where money counts, and where the making of profit has priority over the taking of pleasure: the merchant excuses himself from accompanying Antipholus on a sight-seeing tour because he has an appointment with 'certain merchants/Of whom [he] hope[s] to make much benefit' (I.ii.24–5).[22] Shakespeare's changing of Plautus' Epidamnus to Ephesus was no doubt suggested by the primary source for his Egeon plot, the famous story of Apollonius of Tyre in Gower's *Confessio Amantis*. It was in Ephesus, where his long-lost wife had been restored to life after shipwreck and become a priestess in the temple of Diana, that Apollonius was reunited with her at last. Egeon finds his long-lost Emilia in Ephesus. Thus, years before he dramatized the story in its entirety in *Pericles*, he seized upon it as the unlikely frame-plot for his most classical comedy. The alteration of Diana's temple to a Christian priory and Diana's priestess to a Christian Abbess are probably due to the prominence of Ephesus and its affairs in St Paul's New Testament writings, in Acts and the Epistle to the Ephesians, although Gower supplied a hint by referring to Apollonius' wife as an 'Abbess'. From Paul, Shakespeare would certainly have known about the reputation of Ephesus for strange goings-on, with evil spirits, sorcerers, exorcists, and others who practised 'curious arts', as well as its artisans and merchants. Perhaps Demetrius the silversmith in Act XIX who makes idols for the devotees of Diana suggested Angelo the goldsmith who purveys trinkets for the servants of Venus. Plautus' Epidamnus survives, however, in no fewer than seven references in the play.[23] In his choice of Ephesus, whatever the origin of that choice may have been, Shakespeare gave himself both the strangeness, the menace, and the surreal atmosphere of the typical romance setting, and the urban, mercantile, domestic scene of Roman comedy. The very setting embodies the two primary modes that he fused in this play.

Egeon's story of separation at sea introduces *that* central motif, and sea imagery recurs frequently. Metamorphosis and loss of identity are introduced in the second scene, expressed in the sea image in Antipholus' first soliloquy:

> I to the world am like a drop of water
> That in the ocean seeks another drop,
> Who, failing there to find his fellow forth,
> Unseen, inquisitive, confounds himself,
> So I, to find a mother and a brother,
> In quest of them unhappy, lose myself.
>
>   (i.ii.35–40)[24]

Adriana uses the same image later when, ironically, she is pleading with this Antipholus, the wrong one, not to tear himself away from her (ii.ii.128–32). Transformation, dissolution, loss of oneself – this related group of states and their various images form a major theme, or super-motif. In Act ii, Adriana wonders if age is diminishing her beauty, causing her husband to seek his pleasure in the company of other women; in Act v, when his own son does not recognize him, Egeon exclaims that grief and time must have altered him beyond recognition (both characters use the rare word *defeatures*, its only two occurrences in Shakespeare). Time's ravages, added reminders of the immediate, real time that is passing in the play's day, and related to the transformation and dissolution motif, become the subject of two comic exchanges (ii.ii.; iv.ii.). Metamorphosis is mentioned repeatedly, sometimes humorously, sometimes fearfully. The workaday city of Ephesus itself is curiously animate: its very buildings are called 'Centaur', 'Phoenix', 'Tiger', and 'Porcupine'.

Enchantment continues to work upon Antipholus: someone hands him a gold chain, Dromio brings him a bag of gold. Convinced they are bewitched, he calls upon divine aid – 'Some blessed power deliver us from hence' – whereupon a courtesan appears (iv.iii.44) (in Adrian Noble's 1983 RSC production, she rose spectacularly from beneath the floor, scantily clad in red and black). Antipholus and Dromio behold not a heavenly rescuer, but Satan herself. Divine aid will come, and in female form, when the Abbess appears and gives them sanctuary, but not just yet. (Parenthetically, we may notice that Antipholus of Syracuse falls under the spells, as he believes,

of a series of enchantresses: Adriana in ii.ii., Luciana in iii.ii.,
the courtesan in iv.iii., finally the Abbess in v.i. – one en-
chantress per act, a neat distribution – with, as prelude, the
soliloquy in i.ii. in which he voices his fears of sorcerers,
witches, and the like. This underlines his vulnerability and
impressionability, and is reminiscent of the case of a famous
hero of chivalric romance, Sir Percival, one of the Grail knights
of Arthurian legend, whose experiences with women during his
quest, including his mother, his sister, and the fiend in female
guise several times, similarly underline his susceptibility to
error and his innocence. In contrast, Antipholus of Ephesus
is always accompanied by men only – his servant, friends,
business acquaintances, creditors, the officer who arrests him –
until iv.iv., the conjuring scene, when at last he is surrounded
by women, who insist that he is mad; his brother thinks *himself*
mad, the victim of witches. Another way in which Shakespeare
differentiates the brothers, making the Syracusan the romance
protagonist while the Ephesian retains the role of the thwarted
and irate husband of domestic comedy, is by giving the former
no fewer than six soliloquies and asides, totalling fifty lines,
while his brother has none.)

A new order, that of genuine divine authority, not Dr Pinch's
sham, intervenes in the person of the Abbess. Her claim to be
able to heal the supposedly mad Antipholus and Dromio is the
claim of a power superior to those of mere magic, sorcery, even
the devil. Now the Duke returns, leading old Egeon to
execution. At its height of frenzy, the comical–farcical action,
which, as we have seen, is far from being only that, is
interrupted by the resumption of the tragicomic one. But its
progress is halted too, literally, physically, by the prostrate
Adriana, imploring the Duke to intercede with the Abbess and
get her husband restored to her. Farce impedes romance
temporarily. At this moment, the two plots merge, under the
auspices, as it were, of both spiritual and temporal authority,
both benign, the Abbess and the Duke. Romance resumes, and
subsumes farce. To be sure, the unravelling will take some 300
more lines and there will be further supposes and surprises,
even pathos, along the way.

Time, which Dromio claimed had gone back an hour, has

now gone back years, to when the family was whole, before the events narrated by Egeon a few hours earlier took place. The boys were infants then, new-born. It is, fittingly, the Abbess, the holy mother, who gives explicit utterance to the metaphor of rebirth, describing this moment as one of nativity, repeating the word (if the Folio is right) for emphasis:

> Thirty-three years have I but gone in travail
> Of you, my sons, and till this present hour
> My heavy burden ne'er deliverèd.
> The Duke, my husband, and my children both,
> And you the calendars of their nativity,
> Go to a gossip's feast, and joy with me.
> After so long grief, such [nativity].
>
> (v.i.403–9)

Both Pericles and Cymbeline use similar language when they are reunited with children whom they had believed long dead.[25] The imminent death with which the play began is transfigured into birth: then we met with things dying, now with things, as it were, new-born. That same death-dealing Duke becomes the life-giving lord: 'It shall not need. Thy father hath his life.' Patron already to one Antipholus, the Duke becomes godfather to both at their re-christening. Even the little coda, with its comic business between the pairs of twins, not yet entirely free from error though beyond its more baleful effects, ends on that note. The Dromios resolve that since they do not know which is elder, but came into the world 'like brother and brother', they will now go hand in hand, not one before another, a visual image of recognition and reunion, the joining, not the confounding, of water drops, and a verbal reminder of birth and rebirth. Komisarjevsky's clock should by now have been running furiously backward, whirling away the years, for in the biggest and best of the comedy's errors. Time has indeed gone back, all the way from death to birth, from the intense dramatic final moment to the expansive narrative 'Once upon a time', from the end of the play to the beginning of the story. But that, essentially, is what happens in romance.

The editor in his quest may face anything from minor, uncontentious emendations to hopeless cruxes, from mere commas and full stops to be distributed judiciously, to gaping blanks where text should be, and to heaps of text where less, or none, should be. He will be grateful, in the present case, for the relative brevity and relative cleanness of the Folio text of *The Comedy of Errors*, and that there is only the Folio text to contend with, no two- or three-headed monsters. *Errors* is the fifth play in the Folio, following *The Tempest*, *The Two Gentlemen of Verona*, *The Merry Wives of Windsor*, and *Measure for Measure*, all of which were set by the compositors from transcripts made by Ralph Crane. The four plays which follow *Errors* – *Much Ado About Nothing*, *Love's Labour's Lost*, *A Midsummer Night's Dream*, *The Merchant of Venice* – are all reprints of Quartos.[26] *Errors* stands alone among the first nine plays in the Folio in having apparently been set from Shakespeare's foul papers, a genesis it shares with only seven others in the volume. This orthodox view, held by Chambers, McKerrow, Greg, and nearly everyone since, of the nature of the printer's copy for *Errors* has recently been challenged by Paul Werstine.[27] His argument that authorial foul papers might have been used in the theatre, and thus that the standard 'foul papers versus prompt copy' dichotomy may not be so rigid after all, is rebutted by Wells and Taylor.[28] Some of the confusions in the text are of the sort usually attributed to unperfected authorial copy: descriptive or narrative stage directions, imprecise distinctions between characters, uncertain or alternate names for characters, missing or imprecise entrances and exits, and so on. All of these require editorial emendation but not all are necessarily problematic for performers.

Take the names, for example. No editor is likely to hesitate before emending '*Iuliana*' and '*Iulia*' in the stage direction and first speech prefix at iii.ii. The character in question is clearly Luciana, Adriana's sister, who has already appeared and been named at ii.i.3. But the misnamings occur in column a of gathering H4, probably the first column of this play set by Compositor C; meanwhile, C's partner, Compositor D, was getting it right seven times – *Luc.* – in column b of the same page (this is not to suggest that they were necessarily setting the page simultaneously, side by side). Surely Shakespeare, writing his play seriatim and not by formes, did not forget his character's name between the end of ii.ii., where she has the last line, and the beginning of iii.ii. Did he on the spur of the moment decide to change her name to 'Juliana' to avoid confusion with Luce, who had just made her one and only appearance barely eighty lines before, then revert to 'Luciana', the aberration preserved in the foul papers? Compositor D was in no doubt, nor was B, the third *Errors* compositor, and C himself conformed subsequently, though he vacillated between *Luc.* and *Luci.* on three other pages. Such speculation need not trouble even an editor intent on establishing a consistent text; he emends ⌐whether it was Shakespeare the composer or C the compositor who erred.⌐A director may never know if he has not seen the Folio text or an apparatus that records such things.

But Luce is a different, more substantial matter. This character, later identified as the kitchen-maid, appears in iii.i. and engages in a slanging match with Dromio and Antipholus of Ephesus, who vainly seek entry to their own house, while their twins are inside, enjoying their usurped places. In the Folio, Luce is named once in a stage direction, seven times in speech prefixes, and three times in the dialogue. This is her only scene, though in many productions she returns in the general mêlées in iv.iv. and v.i. (usually taking the small part of the messenger in v.i., which justifies her presence on stage), and to be reunited with the right Dromio as her master and mistress are reunited. John Dover Wilson, in his first Cambridge Shakespeare edition of the play (1922), listed the character as 'Luce, or Nell' and he has been followed by many editors since. A few imply that there are two characters, one of whom does not appear. Only the new Oxford edition goes so far as to change the character's name to 'Nell', and to give only that in Dramatis Personae, stage directions, speech prefixes, and dialogue. Luce is expunged.

The basis for this emendation is Dromio of Syracuse's reference to the woman in question as 'Nell' in his comic set-piece duologue with Antipholus of Syracuse in iii.ii. There is no reason to identify Luce, who appears in iii.i., with Nell the kitchen-maid described as globular in shape by Dromio in iii.ii.

But the person who stood behind the door and 'reviled' Antipholus of Ephesus, that is, Luce, is identified as the kitchen-maid at iv.iv.75–6. So did Shakespeare begin with a maid called 'Luce', then change her name to 'Nell', perhaps to avoid confusion with Luciana, or did he originally plan a second maidservant for the second Dromio? If the latter, then he changed his mind before the end where Dromio of Syracuse gratefully relinquishes any claim in the kitchen-maid to his brother (v.i.417–19). In any case, as the text stands in the Folio, the name 'Nell' occurs only once, in a set-piece, where Dromio is desperately inventing witty replies to straight-man Antipholus' questions. The scene, with Dromio's (geo)graphic anatomizing of spherical Nell, is the comical counterpart in prose to Antipholus' lyrical wooing of Luciana in rhyming verse in the immediately preceding seventy lines of the same scene; we witness the first wooing, Dromio reports the other, with grotesque embellishment. 'Nell' is an *ad hoc* invention by Dromio; it allows him (and Shakespeare) their harmless necessary pun on 'ell': 'What's her name?' 'Nell, sir. But her name and three-quarters – that's an ell and three-quarters – will not measure her from hip to hip' (iii.ii.110–13). He even spells it out to be sure we get it, as bad punsters usually do. The actor might pause momentarily before replying 'Nell, sir', as if inventing the name and lining up his gross pun on the spot. This single occurrence of the name in this highly artificial context hardly warrants changing 'Luce' to 'Nell' eleven times.[29] No editor, to my knowledge, has bothered to mention the name 'Dowsabell', let alone proposed that Luce be called that. Yet this same Dromio calls this same woman 'Dowsabell' at iv.i.110.

Nevertheless, a director may choose to call the character 'Nell', as Phyllida Lloyd did in her 1989 Bristol Old Vic production. She read and was persuaded by the Oxford editors' argument, liked the jingle of 'If thy name be called Nell, Nell thou hast answered him well' (iii.i.53), and thought the name suited the actress playing the role. My arguments for retaining 'Luce' did not prevail; the director simply chose to do otherwise as she was free to do, citing a recent major edition of the play, and no one could protest that the text was grievously violated or directorial whim irresponsibly indulged. The Oxford editors print 'Nell', I would print 'Luce', and both of us will have done as we did for good reasons. Who will be right? What are the criteria for deciding that question? Shakespeare's intentions? Whatever they were, we cannot recover them, and they may anyway have been one thing at one time, another at another. The beast has not been slain or caught, greasy Nell is forever loose.

Other names and other creatures are less troublesome. The place-name 'Epidamium' occurs seven times in the Folio, three on pages set by Compositor C, four on pages set by B. Though minim error is a distinct possibility, the agreement of two compositors makes it more likely that they set what they were reading in their copy. But there was no such place.[30] May an editor rectify Shakespeare's errors? Some would not: the Riverside Shakespeare and David Bevington, in both his last revision of Hardin Craig's edition (1980) and his new Bantam (1988), read 'Epidamium'. Most editors, however, including the Oxford, follow Pope in emending to 'Epidamnum'. But the place in question is Epidamnus, the setting of Plautus' *Menaechmi*. Why the classicist Pope should have chosen the accusative form of the noun (which occurs in various declined forms in *Menaechmi*) is mildly puzzling. Feeling slightly giddy at venturing where no fool editor has ever rushed before, I would propose 'Epidamnus', the correct Latin name for the city Shakespeare apparently had in mind. But does it matter? In performance, not a whit. A fictitious place, a mere name on two romance characters' Mediterranean itineraries, that is all it is. But for the editor, it must matter, however insignificant it is: something must be printed and justified against the contending alternatives. In performance, almost anything can be said and no one will blink.

The Courtesan's house is called the Porpentine. This is an archaic spelling of 'porcupine', so a modernizing editor should prefer the modern form. Shakespeare used only 'porpentine' though 'porcupine' was already current; it occurs eight times in his works, five times in *Errors*. But it is a proper name here.

Is that then an argument for retaining its archaic form? No.
That is to opt for quaintness, a practice that mars the otherwise
splendid Riverside edition. A quaintness quotient has no place
in a scholarly modernizing editor's set of guidelines. We
modernize other spellings, so why not this? Curiously, it has
been relatively modern editors, starting with Aldis Wright in
the famous nineteenth-century Cambridge Shakespeare, who
have reverted to 'Porpentine', while Rowe modernized the
spelling and was followed by editors until Wright. The Oxford,
like eighteenth-century editions, has 'Porcupine' (and thus
obviates the need for a gloss). No editor, I believe, has retained
the Folio spelling 'Tyger', another house-name, at III.i.96, nor
'Centaure' for the inn where Antipholus of Syracuse lodges at
I.ii.9. And in the context of those other recognizable beast-
names which abound in the play, 'Porpentine' sounds odd in
performance as well as looking odd on the page.

Another problem facing editors, but which causes little or no
difficulty in the theatre, is the unmetrical line, whether short or
long. The New Cambridge editor of *Errors* rhetorically asks *à
propos* of one such, 'Need we be worried by a line which is
metrically short?'[31] Editors, *pace* Dorsch, usually are, assuming
that Shakespeare always wrote regular iambic pentameter and
that verse lines which contain fewer or more than the standard
number of syllables (excluding feminine endings) must be
faulty. But perhaps Dorsch is right and the assumption needs
re-examining; Shakespeare, like Homer, must have nodded
now and then. Metrifying Shakespeare is harder when a
syllable or a word is missing than when there are too many;
adding something requires that we invent or reconstruct
Shakespeare. The line 'A meane woman was deliuered' (I.i.54)
has been regularized by most editors, usually by adding F2's
'poor' before 'mean', though some recent editors, from Peter
Alexander (1951) to Bevington, leave the line as it stands in F.
In performance it is easy and natural for an actor to pause a
beat before saying 'mean' or to emphasize it to mark the
difference between this woman and Egeon's own wife, about
whom he has just been speaking, and thus fill out the line. The
same holds for many other such lines, short by a mere syllable.

A good actor will not chant verse or mark the metre obtrusively anyway (nor will he reduce it to prose), and a missing syllable here and there, provided the sense is clear and the surrounding flow of the verse is maintained, is hardly going to be disastrous. But again, an editor, producing a printed text, may feel the lack more keenly and will probably at least consider whether or not to supply it, even if he finally decides not to, or writes a note asking whether we need be worried by it.

Gary Taylor's eloquent advocacy of invention by editors must be endorsed with caution and caveat (note 10 above). It will seem to many chillingly like an unrestricted licence. The naturally conservative editor and the naturally, or supernaturally, inventive poet seldom cohabit in one mind, and Taylor is right when he observes: 'It is because those who have the facility seldom possess the judgement to restrain their inclination that those with a gift for emendation...invariably indulge in it too often' ('Inventing', p. 43). Though no harm may be done by adding a word to fill out a line of verse, will enough be gained to warrant the in(ter)vention? Taylor's own 'mean-born' in the line under discussion seems to me to be a scant improvement over F2's redundant 'poor mean'. The condition of *her* birth is not relevant, and to refer to it here points away from the birth that is relevant, that of her 'burden, male twins' (1.i.55). The point is that she is now 'mean', that is poor, of low estate, and so is willing to sell her twin sons to Egeon to be servants to his. If the compulsion to metrify proves too strong, I would favour 'A mean young woman was deliverèd', but, like many editors, most actors, and any audience, I can live with the Folio's mere nine syllables. In general, editors seem less troubled by F's long 'Vnwilling I agreed, alas, too soone wee came aboord' (1.i.60), which some retain, or the very short one resulting from breaking it up into two: 'Unwilling I agreed. Alas, too soon / We came aboard' (following Pope).[32] Sometimes when the latter choice is made, a note solemnly remarks on the rhetorical effect of such a short line at this decisive moment in Egeon's narrative. Such 'effect' has been imported by the editor, of course, in breaking up the long line, and an actor can impart rhetorical effect in his delivery by pausing, sighing, whatever, if such an effect seems appropriate at this point, whether or not the line is printed as one or as two in his script.

The inventing editor will find somewhat more fertile ground in Dromio of Syracuse's frantic outburst at II.ii.192–3: 'This is the Fairie land, oh spight of spights,/We talke with Goblins, Owles and Sprights.' Here is another short line, lacking two syllables this time. The Second Folio, that anonymous first edited text of the First Folio, recognizes the problem, but does not get it right somehow, reading 'and Elves Sprights'. Pope changed 'Elves' to the unmistakably bisyllabic 'elvish'. Theobald transformed 'owls' to 'ouphs'. Most modern editors, however, have stuck with F's three unmetrical monsters. Even the Oxford retains an octosyllabic line, but modernizes Theobald's 'ouphs' to 'oafs', a lexically legitimate move all right, but one that creates a misleading and therefore undesirable secondary meaning for modern readers and audiences (as any modernization may run the risk of doing). The short line invites expansion. Is it not plausible that, by haplography, Compositor D conflated 'oules and elues and' in his copy to 'Owles and'? 'We talk with goblins, owls, and elves, and sprites' seems appropriate to Dromio's terrified state, his fevered brain coining monsters pell-mell.[33] But, of course, the actor has even more reason here to pause, engage in business, break the line up, and hence stretch it that extra foot, than was the case with Egeon's line in the first scene discussed earlier. If in performance, where and only where his text can become a play, it does not matter if a word is missing, is the editor justified in indulging the inventing itch? Of course, we edit for *readers*, who can interrupt their reading of the text, who indeed are invited to do so, to jump to the fine print at the bottom of the page where we discuss the options and defend our decisions, as theatre-goers at a performance cannot. For the play editor's peace of mind, the ideal reader of his edition will be a literary reader and not a theatrically-minded one, and will read it as he or she reads a novel, a poem, Johnson's *Dictionary*, or Lawrence's letters. When Shakespeare was but the prince of poets, happy drudges lost less sleep.

Lacunae of a whole line or more, even in a rhyming verse passage where it seems clear that something is missing, are dealt with in performance, while the editor sweats and strains and, maybe, invents iambic pentameter. A case in point occurs in *Errors* iii.i., at the height of the furious row between those inside the Phoenix and the rightful occupants and guests outside. In a long rhymed passage, immediately following the line in which Luce's name appears twice, the Folio reads as follows:

ANTI[PHOLUS OF EPHESUS]. Doe you heare you minion, you'll let
   vs in I hope?
LUCE. I thought to haue askt you.
S. DRO.   And you said no.
E. DRO. So come helpe, well strooke, there was blow for blow.

Theobald emended 'hope' to 'trow' in the first line, producing a triple rhyme, of which there are four others in the passage: lines 19–21, 64–6, 67–9, 76–8. But he produced no more sense. Some modern editors have followed him, including Cuningham, Foakes (new Arden), Wells (New Penguin), Levin (Signet), and Dorsch; the last is peremptory in dismissing Malone's conjecture that a line rhyming with 'hope', perhaps ending with 'rope', had dropped out (p. 68 n.). Just as many, however, have preferred to retain F's 'hope', usually citing Malone's conjecture: Wilson (1922 and 1961), Alexander, Jorgensen (Pelican), Riverside, Bevington, Tetzeli. Only the Oxford, though, both retains 'hope' and leaves a space in brackets to indicate that a line is missing before 'Do you hear…I hope?' Gary Taylor admits ('Inventing', p. 43) to not having the temerity to insert his own line into Shakespeare's text in another play, but says further that he would feel no compunction about marking a lacuna and mentioning the conjecture in a note. This he did in the present case, recording: '*E. Dro.* Thou wouldst answer well to hanging, if I had a rope.' This supplies the rhyme, but leaves Luce's (in the Oxford text, Nell's) 'I thought to have asked you' still unattached. What did she think to have asked whom? Bevington thinks the missing line should follow rather than precede the 'hope' line, but does not conjecture.[34]

As textual adviser to the Bristol Old Vic production of *Errors*
in 1989, I discussed the lacuna with the director, who, while
using the Arden edition as her script, studied the text very
carefully, consulting several other editions. Prior to one
rehearsal, I composed several alternative lines, one of which she
might choose to insert in the gap. Alas for my inventions, I
arrived to find that she had decided to ignore the lacuna, keep
the Arden's 'trow', and try to make sense of what was there.
The actors had invented business to that end. Nell's and
Dromio of Syracuse's half-lines were a resumption of a
hypothetical previous conversation, a further sally in the
former's attempt to seduce the latter. A little personal drama
was simmering away indoors even as the larger, more public
drama boiled over outdoors. The large Nell spread-eagled the
small Dromio against the door. In the fever of the moment, it
worked. Dromio's 'And you said – no?' became a plea for
mercy. No one gave a further thought to the dread lacuna,
which in any case was filled from outside when the other
Dromio, in mime, thrust a privy member through the letter
slot, and the outraged, frustrated Nell inside applied a vacuum
cleaner to it. The audience roared its amusement at the
mayhem which ensued, and the rejected inventing editor had,
willy-nilly, to join in. An emboldened editor may invent, but if
he cannot insert his invention in his text, and performers who
know about it do not want or need it, it can only survive as a
conjecture, buried in a note. What then is its status or point?
Inventing Shakespeare only to lose him in the apparatus seems
an unprofitable expense of spirit. Yet Taylor's plea is a
powerful one, and it enhances that task of helpful drudgery to
which editors earnestly commit themselves. It urges the editor
to re-create as well as to recover, to become Shakespeare in
some sort, momentarily. That his invention, which may not
become text, will *be* only if it is spoken in performance and if it
is, will *be* only for an instant, are the absurd odds against which
he plays. Taylor's description of such inventive emendation as
game is reminiscent of the late Philip Brockbank's advocacy of
'festive scholarship'.[35] Ludic editing serves Shakespeare, the
play, and the reader, not just the black signs on the white pages

of F1. *Ludus* – the medieval Latin word meant *game* and *play*, as students of medieval drama well know. But games have rules and boundaries, as Taylor reminds us. Because he cannot cheat and write his invention into Shakespeare, the gaming editor offers it and hides it wistfully, playfully, at the same time. It may be in print all right, but it is out of bounds, off stage, below the line. A director like John Barton may write hundreds of lines of 'Shakespeare' in his adaptation and they get spoken at every performance. The inspired editor invents, and directs furiously in his head. ⌉*CAP.*

May an editor adopt a reading recorded only in acting *ORAL* editions? If we mean what we say about the primacy of *TRAD.* performance, why not? A crux or a confusion may be clarified by an actor or director who *has* to get or make sense out of it, and that reading may be passed down in playhouse tradition, unknown to scholarly editors who collate those dozens of other scholarly editions. In *Errors* i.ii., Antipholus of Syracuse speaks his first soliloquy, quoted earlier (p. 119). In the Hull adaptation of the late eighteenth century, revised by John Philip Kemble in 1811, the Folio's 'falling' in line 37 is emended to 'failing'. Thus the parallel drawn by Antipholus between the water drop and himself is exact: it seeks its fellow in the vast ocean, and failing to find it, loses (confounds) itself; he, seeking his family in the wide world, unhappy (unsuccessful) in his quest, loses himself. When this emendation was suggested to Owen Teale who played Antipholus in the Bristol production, he grasped it immediately, perceiving the logic and clarity it achieved. An eighteenth-century theatrical emendation lived again in performance 200 years later. It is a tiny change, to be sure, an *i* for an *l*, and the improvement in sense is slight if real. But should we continue to resist or ignore it in modern editions because an actor not an editor first invented it, and when a simple explanation, compositorial misreading of *i* for *l*, is available anyway? Which reading would Shakespeare have opted for, the actor's, the compositor's, or the editor's? His own – but that begs a few questions.

We have, it would seem, come almost full circle, from making a text by remaking another text which never was, and never will be, what it is meant to be, unless it is performed, and then will be something else quite, to realizing that performance not only makes the play, but can, and often does, make the text itself. Of course, the example just given is a very small one, one word, one letter, in an entire play. We do not edit performance, or base our scholarly editions solely or mainly on texts derived from performance – at least, we do not *say* that we are doing so. But what of those Shakespeare revisions preserved in the Folio? A modern edition of *Hamlet* based on the Folio text may, it would seem, be said to be derived from a performance text. But we as editors unmake and remake that particular early text upon which we base our editions, wherever it emanated from, by modernizing its spelling and punctuation, correcting its obvious misprints, spelling out speech prefixes, adding and expanding stage directions, even reconstructing, as the Oxford editors reconstructed the *Pericles* Quarto, and by emending cruxes, mending lacunae, inventing Shakespeare. In each repeated effort to fix *our* text, pin it down, get it right, we make *the* text more, not less, unstable. For each edition is another text, different from all others, be it by no more than a few commas (it is of course always more than that), as each production is a new text, in that larger sense of the word, as well as enunciating a new text in the narrower sense. Every edition is, and is not, definitive. And each performance of a single production has its peculiarities of rhythm, mood, tempo, 'feel', as performers are always telling us.

Actors and directors talk readily about remaking Shakespeare when they do a new production. Indeed, most believe that is what the theatre is about.[36] Editors are more reluctant to acknowledge that they too remake Shakespeare, even when they are engaged in producing diplomatic texts or facsimiles. This implies – and this is no earth-shaking discovery of mine – that that TEXT of Shakespeare which we believed, avowedly or tacitly, it was a duty to attempt to recover *in toto* and exactly, not only is not there to be recovered, that that concept itself is faulty, but that if it were it could never be 'restored' in our editions, old- or modern-spelling, diplomatic or inventive. Editors of multi-text plays such as *Hamlet* and *King Lear* have come to realize that, if they have the courage of their convictions, they cannot have all the *Hamlet* or *Lear* that Shakespeare may have written in their edited texts. They cannot print the complete words of *Hamlet* and call it Shakespeare's play. To print all the *Hamlet* that Shakespeare wrote at different times, on first, second and subsequent thoughts, even if one is convinced that he did write all of it, is to produce something under Shakespeare's name that he never invented.[37] We can only edit texts, finally, not plays, not authors. Once we accept that our control-text, be it Folio *Hamlet* or *Errors*, Quarto *Lear* or *Pericles*, is itself only a version, and perhaps a partial one, of Shakespeare's own total *Hamlet*, *Errors*, *Lear*, or *Pericles*, and that the very existence of that entity is doubtful and unprovable, we may find ourselves freed from the old idolatry. And if we further accept that all our texts are remakes of versions of uncertain provenance, well, we shall be in no worse company than that of the poets banished by Plato from the commonwealth for making counterfeit copies of imitations of the Forms.

This freedom should in turn help us to overcome the *Still.* 'inhibition of seriousness', as Taylor calls it, the po'-facedness of scientistic textual scholarship which has prevented editors from realizing the playful truth that the object of the quest is given much of its substance and shape by the quester himself. The editor does not return with the captured TEXT in hand, but emerges at the other end of the labyrinthine way with the text that he has found, *trouvé*.[38] Such a concept of the editor's art, partway between setting out to find and retrieve a determinate object that is known to exist *a priori* out there, and the free, frivolous invention, the parlour-game that Taylor, as he predicts, will be accused of encouraging, seems to me a fruitful one. What I find will, of course, be partly determined by what I look for, and it is no game of blind man's buff that I play, or random hunt I set out upon. Not just any treasure trove will do; ghastly roadside warnings like *The Other Shakespeare* and the deformed corpses of A.L. Rowse's brood litter the way. But what I cannot come back with, however I may 'struggle for the vision fair', is the one and only *Comedy of Errors* by Shakespeare.

I might have multiplied the examples of textual puzzles and problems in *The Comedy of Errors*, and proposed or speculated about them at length. I have avoided the most notorious crux in the play, Adriana's speech beginning 'I see the jewel best enamellèd' (II.i.108–12). Whatever an editor decides to print in these lines is bound not to be right. The actress Rosie Rowell managed to make the passage sound quite meaningful as it stands in most modern editions when she played Adriana in Bristol in 1989. Editing inevitably complicates such cruxes, while performance, also inevitably, simplifies them: it must. As Stanley Wells suggests, 'For some reason – perhaps because an edition can be annotated – one is more willing to confront a reader than a playgoer with nonsense' (*Re-editing*, p. 49). But often, what is nonsense on the page is given sense on the stage, or at least an audience is easily persuaded that it makes sense. The moment comes and goes in seconds, and an audience which is not going to worry whether it is 'Epidamium' or 'Epidamnum' or 'Epidamnus', or fret over Luce or Nell, will be swayed by the gist of what Adriana says as she grieves at her husband's supposed desertion. They will not see the collations and commentaries, or the whole articles devoted to emending and explaining the five lines spoken in fifteen seconds in performance.[39] To return to one of the issues raised at the beginning, it is because he must print this or that but not both that the editor has to resolve cruxes, but he sets about it knowing that he can canvass, collate, comment, and explain also, while the actor has to say it, play it, and be done. Shakespeare, of all people, knew that reading a speech and playing it were worlds apart, that obscurity can evaporate in the action of the stage. May it be that some of the famous cruxes are our own inventions, as readers, critics, and editors? Shakespeare did not count on us getting in the way.

I am not yet sure whether to stick to the Folio's double 'nativity' in the Abbess's final speech (v.i.403–9, quoted above, p. 121). Double nativity at the end of a play about two pairs of twins lost at sea, separated, then reborn, in the words of their new-found mother, is fitting. Besides the play was performed, probably for the first time, at Christmas 1594.

Nativity was seasonal. Johnson proposed 'festivity' in the final line, Dyce adopted it and was followed by the Oxford edition, but Hanmer's 'felicity' fits the line and sums up the tragicomic action best: 'After so long grief, such felicity.' Whichever word is spoken in performance, the joy, the felicity, the festivity of comic dénouement and romance rebirth are ambient. Editors will make various decisions; performance will variously fix that particular word at that moment, but will unfix and remake the very text it speaks, playing and showing nativity, festivity, felicity, and more, where the edition can read one of them, collate others, comment on all, but convey none. Text and performance merge, and the printed word, apparently always the same but, as a famous son of ancient Ephesus, Heraclitus, would have known, always in flux, is confounded by the act that gives it being but is itself evanescent, rushing headlong to its own closure, the final curtain.

Romance and farce merge at the end of *The Comedy of Errors*, I have argued. The local absurdities, cruxes, and confusions of the latter are confounded in the eternal improbabilities and incredibilities of the former. Both genres flaunt unlikelihood, the one calling us to witness with our own eyes that it is true, the other telling us even as it shows us that it cannot possibly be true. To attempt to create a coherent whole out of such unlikely components seems doubly unlikely, ludicrous. But Shakespeare brazenly pulled it off. Setting out yet again to edit a Shakespeare play-text may appear an unlikely, quixotic venture, but we do it all the time, put our names to it, package it and sell it – Wilson's, Foakes's, Wells's, Bevington's, Dorsch's, Whitworth's *Errors* – claiming, or at least acquiescing in publishers' claims, that we've got it, the play, right here. Performance too is risky, volatile, ephemeral, over as soon as it is done, and just as brazen, each new show – the Lord Chamberlain's Men's, Kemble's, Komisarjevsky's, Nunn's, Noble's, Lloyd's *Errors* – implying each time that for that time, this one is it, the play, Shakespeare's *Comedy of Errors*.[40] Rectify Shakespeare's *Errors*? Perform Shakespeare's, the whole of Shakespeare's, and nothing but Shakespeare's *Errors*? Not very likely. Yet on and off we and they go, doing it because it must be done, repeatedly. None of the products of these efforts, the myriad performances, the endless editions, though they stretch out to the crack of doom, can be Shakespeare's *Errors*. All of them, hypothetical and actual, future, present, and past, not one before another, may be so called.

NOTES

1 A prior question, in the poststructuralist era, might be to do with how 'text' in such a context should be construed. I shall use the term in a conventional sense, to denote the written or printed pages which collectively make up a single work of dramatic literature, a play as it is read in book form. The differences between a play text as edited and read, and a play as performed and seen/heard are crucial to this discussion.

2 Among the fuller arguments for this general case is Stanley Wells's *Re-editing Shakespeare for the Modern Reader* (Oxford, 1984); one of the most recent and vigorous is T.H. Howard-Hill's 'Modern Textual Theories and the Editing of Plays', *Library*, Sixth Series, 11 (1989), 89–115. Especially pertinent to the concerns of this essay is Howard-Hill's 'Playwrights' Intentions and the Editing of Plays', *TEXT*, 4 (1988), 269–78, in which testimony is adduced from an unexpected quarter: C.S. Lewis, half a century ago, anticipated central issues in the current text–performance debate.

3 I do not mean that an editor should interpret in the text itself. An example of editorial overfixing is the Oxford Shakespeare's 'under-stand' in the speech of Dromio of Ephesus at *Comedy of Errors*, II.i.51–3 (all references will be to the Oxford *Complete Works*, in modern spelling, ed. Stanley Wells and Gary Taylor (Oxford, 1986), unless otherwise indicated). In modern as in Elizabethan English, *understand* is not hyphenated. To hyphenate it is to interpret reductively, to accord priority, with a nudge and a wink, to the secondary meaning, 'stand up under his blows'. An editor as annotator may of course do that in his commentary, if he judges it necessary; it is an actor's job to do so in delivering the line, if he judges it necessary.

4 The New Penguin Shakespeare is the RSC's 'house' edition and is frequently mentioned in programme credits. Directors there often use others as well or instead; the Arden is a favourite because of its copious annotation, which, however, actors often admit, can be either an encumbrance or irrelevant to their work. Antony Sher writes that the company used both New Penguin and Arden editions when rehearsing *Richard III* in 1984: 'and when there are

discrepancies we'll choose whichever is more useful for our purposes' (*Year of the King* (London, 1985), p. 156).

5 In his 1988/9 production of *Hamlet* for the RSC, director Ron Daniels transposed a scene in accordance with the 'bad' Quarto of 1603. He also cut 900 lines from the New Penguin text, itself based on the 'good' Quarto of 1604/5, with liberal helpings from the Folio.

6 On hearing versus seeing a play in Shakespeare's time, see Andrew Gurr, *Playgoing in Shakespeare's London* (Cambridge, 1987), pp. 85–97.

7 A good example of this occurred in Deborah Warner's 1988 production of *King John*, when Salisbury (Edward Harbour), as he spoke the lines 'My arm shall give thee help to bear thee hence, / For I do see the cruel pangs of death / Right in thine eye' (v.iv.58–60), to the mortally wounded Count of Melun, reached behind his back to receive a misericord from his companion Pembroke, with which he put Melun out of his agony. The stage business not only conferred a novel meaning upon 'My arm shall give thee help to bear thee hence', but was appropriate in the context, a soldierly act of mercy to a dying, noble enemy who had done the English lords a good turn by warning them of treachery.

8 At least three noteworthy editions of *The Comedy of Errors* have appeared since I undertook my own in 1985: that in the Oxford *Complete Works*, T.S. Dorsch's New Cambridge (1988), and David Bevington's Bantam (1988). There was a bilingual German–English edition by Kurt Tetzeli von Rosador in 1982, and the script used in the BBC television production was published in 1984. Meanwhile, a variorum edition is in progress in the United States, and the Arden is being revised.

9 The classic essay 'The Rationale of Copy-Text' is reprinted in Greg's *Collected Papers*, ed. J.C. Maxwell (Oxford, 1966), pp. 374–91. Howard-Hill challenges the rationale and the editorial tradition since Greg in the first article cited in n. 2 above.

10 Besides works already referred to, I would include in this body of recent work in the immediate light of which my (and others') current editing of Shakespeare is being conducted: Stanley Wells and Gary Taylor, *Modernizing Shakespeare's Spelling, with Three Studies in the Text of 'Henry V'* (Oxford, 1979); the same authors' (with John Jowett and William Montgomery) *William Shakespeare: A Textual Companion* (Oxford, 1987); Wells, *Shakespeare and Revision*, Hilda Hulme Memorial Lecture, University of London, 3 December 1987 (London, 1988); Gary Taylor and Michael Warren (eds.), *The Division of the Kingdoms: Shakespeare's Two Versions of 'King Lear'* (Oxford, 1983), and several articles written

in response to this volume; Gary Taylor, 'Inventing Shakespeare', *Jahrbuch 1986* (Bochum, 1986), 26–44; Taylor, 'Revising Shakespeare', *TEXT*, 3 (1987), 285–304; Taylor, 'Metrifying Shakespeare', *Shakespeare Studies*, (forthcoming), other articles by Taylor and the other members of the Oxford team, and reviews of their books and edition. To these could be added a host of articles, both theoretical and on specific matters relating to the Shakespeare text, such as Folio and Quarto printers and compositors, published in the last decade by such scholars as Fredson Bowers, G. Thomas Tanselle, D.F. McKenzie, Paul Werstine, Howard-Hill, and many others. Among all of these, the Oxford *Textual Companion* is the one for a desert island, or for the editor-errant travelling (moderately) lightly. It is a monumental work of scholarship, and while editions continue to bloom and fade, it will fertilize them and fodder their editors and critics for generations to come.

11 Preliminary consultations on the text were held in November and December 1988, when Miss Lloyd was Sir Barry Jackson Fellow in the School of Performing Arts, University of Birmingham, with practical work on text and performance with drama students. Several such sessions also took place with the Bristol Old Vic company during rehearsals of the production, which ran from 16 February to 11 March 1989 at the Theatre Royal, Bristol.

12 Aristotle, typically, complicated this straightforward distinction: for him, in drama, the poet's agents, the actors, imitate for him by taking on the characters of the persons; thus drama is in one sense a mediated form (*Poetics*, 1450a–b). But since for Aristotle action is more important than character, the immediacy of the representation or imitation gives the dramatic genre, tragedy, its superiority over the narrative one, epic (1462a–b). Conversely, Homer is a good narrative poet to the extent that he speaks little in his own person and a great deal in the (assumed) persons of his characters. Another Aristotelian tangent worth pursuing would be the consequences for the subsequent study of drama as *poetry* of Aristotle's relegation of the elements of *performance* – spectacle, music, etc. – to positions of minor importance.

13 This dimension of Peele's play is discussed more fully in the introduction to my *Three Sixteenth-Century Comedies* (London, 1984), pp. xlvi–xlviii.

14 I realize that I have oversimplified both romance and farce for the sake of my argument. There can be more to farce than buffets and pratfalls. But critics who label *The Comedy of Errors* 'farce' also oversimplify the genre in focussing on those elements, and thus fail to do justice to the play.

15 Reprinted in Gāmini Salgādo, *Eyewitnesses of Shakespeare* (New York, 1975), pp. 68–9.

16 But this is as nothing compared with the hash made of the play by one reviewer of the 1989 Bristol Old Vic production. Among other things, he names the wrong actor in the part of Angelo, refers to Adriana's entrance in a swimming pool when it was Luciana who appeared thus, says that the Abbess comes out leading the Ephesian Antipholus, and that Shakespeare unforgivably marries off the Abbess and Egeus (a double howler); that Egeus (again) is 'bailed' at the end when, of course, he is pardoned and released unconditionally. Finally, he says, we shall never know which Dromio ends up with Nell (as that production called Luce), when it is perfectly clear a few lines from the end that the Syracusan resigns her with relief to his Ephesian twin (*Financial Times*, 21 February 1989).

17 Preface to Johnson's edition of *The Plays of William Shakespeare* (1765), reprinted in W.K. Wimsatt (ed.), *Dr Johnson on Shakespeare*, (Harmondsworth, 1969), p. 62.

18 The fullest, often irksomely exhaustive treatment of sources for the play is T.W. Baldwin's *On the Compositional Genetics of ' The Comedy of Errors'* (Urbana, Illinois, 1965).

19 *Johnson on Shakespeare*, p. 64.

20 Phyllida Lloyd, in her 1989 Bristol Old Vic production, had the courage, as most modern directors have not, to put Egeon alone on stage with the Duke for the first scene. Egeon was lit by a single white spot. Some of the Duke's questions were given to recorded voices off, as of a crowd or press corps, but the theatre audience were not distracted, as so often, by a stage audience busily listening and reacting.

21 *Johnson on Shakespeare*, p. 67.

22 The word 'money' occurs twenty-six times in *Errors*, more than in any other play in the canon. *Marks* and *mart* also occur more times than in any other play. *Gold/golden* are found more times only in *Timon of Athens*; *ducats* and *merchant(s)* more times only in *The Merchant of Venice*.

23 Plautus, incidentally, set one of his plays, *Miles Gloriosus*, in Ephesus, and another, *Curculio*, in Epidaurus, mentioned in Egeon's narrative; most are set in Athens. Epidamnus was in Illyria.

24 On the reading 'failing' for F's 'falling', see below, pp. 131–2. Antipholus' lines about seeking and failing to find his mother and brother are an abbreviated romance narrative on the same theme as Egeon's: another link between the plots. The inner plot, the

farcical comedy itself, sounds a romance chord. In *Menaechmi*, the romance story is told briefly in the Prologue, outside the play.

25 *Pericles*, xxi.183–5; *Cymbeline*, v.vi.369–71.

26 Wells, Taylor, *et al.*, *William Shakespeare: A Textual Companion*, p. 39.

27 '"Foul Papers" and "Prompt Books": Printer's Copy for Shakespeare's *Comedy of Errors*', *Studies in Bibliography*, 41 (1988), 232–46.

28 *Textual Companion*, p. 266.

29 But see the note in its defence (*Textual Companion*, p. 267).

30 Compositor C also set 'Epidarus' at another place on the same page where 'Epidamium' appears twice. F2 corrected the former to 'Epidaurus'. But Shakespeare might have gone back and changed it if he had revised his foul papers, because Emilia later says that she and the children with her had been picked up by men of 'Epidamium', not Epidaurus (v.i.357).

31 T.S. Dorsch (ed.), *The Comedy of Errors* (Cambridge, 1988), p. 64 (n. to II.ii.181).

32 Henry Cuningham (old Arden) thought 'We came aboard...' an incomplete line and proposed to complete it thus: '...and put to sea, but scarce', an intelligent conjecture, if one accepts the short-line hypothesis.

33 Gareth Roberts has strengthened the case for 'owls' and against replacing it with 'elves', arguing that it is quite plausible for Dromio to fear being sucked black and blue by a *strix*, a screech-owl's body housing a witch or other malign spirit ('*The Comedy of Errors* II.ii.190: "Owls" or "Elves"?', *Notes & Queries*, N.S. 34 (1987), 202–4).

34 *The Comedy of Errors* (New York, 1988), p. 29n.

35 His presence in this celebratory volume is a reminder of the loss of a friend, colleague, and festive, creative spirit.

36 Though the kind of informed, sensitive inventiveness that Gary Taylor urges editors to exercise is sometimes in the theatre, unfortunately, usurped by directorial arrogance, duncicality, or perversity.

37 *Ergo*, we cannot edit *Hamlet*, but either the bad Quarto or the good Quarto or the Folio of *Hamlet*. If *Hamlet* is an eclectic edition, Shakespeare did not write it. If Shakespeare wrote different versions at different times, which survive as Quartos and Folio, eclectic editions are amalgamations and adaptations, misleadingly labelled. A comparable case-history from Elizabethan non-dramatic literature is that of Sidney's *Arcadia*(s). He may have written all of the 'old' *Arcadia* and all of the incomplete 'new' *Arcadia* which breaks off in mid-sentence in Book III, but he did not

write the composite *Arcadia* published in 1593. That was constructed after Sidney's death by his literary executors, who also rewrote some of the 'old' *Arcadia* used to piece out the 'new', and, with a link passage by yet another author, Alexander, was the version read for more than 300 years: the Countess of Pembroke's *Arcadia* more than her brother's, in a significant sense. Yet even after the discovery and publication of the complete 'old' *Arcadia* early this century, some editors (e.g. Maurice Evans) and critics (e.g. C.S. Lewis, Walter R. Davis) have edited and written about the composite version, insisting, in some cases, on its primacy (see Lewis, *English Literature in the Sixteenth Century* (Oxford, 1954), pp. 331–3).

38 As in Provençal *trobar* – find, make, invent, compose, as the *troubadours* did.

39 The latest and most detailed discussion, of many, is Gary Taylor's 'Textual and Sexual Criticism: A Crux in *The Comedy of Errors*', *Renaissance Drama*, N.S. 19 (1988), 195–225. My use of masculine pronouns throughout this essay when referring to Shakespeare editors reflects the fact observed by Taylor at the beginning of his, namely, the virtual absence of women from the field.

40 I have deliberately excluded film and television from this discussion. They are quite different media from the stage, and Shakespeare's plays were not written for them. Film is a cool medium, its message frozen.

CHAPTER 6

Victorian editors of As You Like It *and the purposes of editing*

Russell Jackson

Some recent writing has discussed the ways in which Shakespearean texts are mediated by editors, and the work the texts are made to do in the society within which they are reproduced. Gary Taylor's provocative *Reinventing Shakespeare* (1989) and Michael D. Bristol's *America's Shakespeare. Shakespeare's America* (1989) insist on the material contingencies that have governed the seemingly (or would-be) 'pure' pursuits of editing the plays.[1] Who is speaking to whom in an edition of a Shakespearean play? Decisions as to how the play speaks are clearly visible in the work of Victorian editors of the Shakespeare plays, and their place at the beginning of a 'popular' tradition of editing practices for these works makes them especially interesting. This essay takes *As You Like It* as the basis for a discussion of two groups of Victorian Shakespeare editions, the popular and the scholastic, which illustrate the range of Victorian Shakespeare publishing.

Modern editors of a Shakespearean text have to take account of the work of their predecessors, even if the goal is not a revised Variorum and the readership envisaged is primarily that of 'general readers'. Some scholarly Victorian editions are bound to appear in this shopping-list: notably those of Collier (1842–4), Dyce (1857), Halliwell (1853–65), and the 'Globe' edition of 1864. These more austere works, mostly addressing themselves to a scholarly audience, were highly priced or limited initially to private and institutional subscribers, and represent only a small portion of the range of Victorian editions of the plays. The principal explicit aim of most of the participants in this activity was furthering a more or less idealized pursuit of knowledge. Dewey Ganzel has given a vivid

142

picture of the internecine strife among mid-Victorian editors in his account of the career of John Payne Collier, *Fortune and Men's Eyes* (Oxford, 1982).

These Victorian editors frequently figure in new editor's notes. The editors discussed here for the most part lack their quasi-canonical status in the hermeneutic tradition, but it was entirely possible for a Victorian editor to combine social zeal with recondite scholarship – F.J. Furnivall, founder of the New Shakspere Society, was a case in point. In similar fashion Charles and Mary Cowden-Clarke (in an edition first issued in parts in 1859–60), Charles Knight, and Henry Morley directed their labours towards a wider readership, with the genial social ambition of bringing Shakespeare into the family home by making his work available in well-printed, scrupulously prepared presentations at prices and in forms that would attract readers other than wealthy scholars. The Cowden-Clarke *Concordance*, first published in monthly parts in 1844–5, was a move towards increasing the accessibility of the texts, enabling common readers to move about them with ease. In these works bringing Shakespeare to the people was combined with scrupulous explication of meanings and the provision of 'background' information.

The introduction to *As You Like It* in Charles Knight's *Illustrated Shakespeare*, published initially as a part-work (London, 1844–8), identifies and locates the meaning of the play in terms appropriate to a wide popular readership, comparing Shakespeare's work with his principal source, Thomas Lodge's *Rosalynde*:

> Perhaps there is no play more full of real moral lessons than *As You Like It*. What in Lodge was a pastoral replete with quaintness, and antithesis, and pedantry, and striving after effect, becomes in Shakespeare an imaginative drama, in which the real is blended with the poetical in such intimate union, that the highest poetry appears to be as essentially natural as the most familiar gossip; and the loftiest philosophy is interwoven with the occurrences of everyday life, so as to teach us that there is a philosophical aspect of the commonest things. (II, 208)

Lodge is clearly guilty of the self-conscious cleverness that gets in the way of clear and humane thought. The lessons of the play, in Knight's account, amount to this: the realization that 'the feelings of social life alone' can give us 'Sermons in stones'; a demonstration by gently characteristic satire of the 'the vanity of the things which bind us to the world'; and the understanding that '*life* has its happiness in the cultivation of the affections – in content and independence of spirit' (II, 208). A similar emphasis on social virtues informs Henry Morley's presentation of the play in Cassell's National Library (1886). As a tireless proponent of popular education, Morley shared many of Knight's assumptions.[2] 'All who read Shakespeare', he begins, 'are content to hear his works described as a Lay Bible, but many pause when it is added that they are not so by chance' (p. 5), and Morley goes on to show that *As You Like It* resembles Shakespeare's other plays in expressing a practical Christianity, splendidly free of dogma and always subservient to the imperatives 'Love God; Love Your Neighbour; Do Your Work' (p. 6). Shakespeare may be miraculously gifted, but it is his kinship with common readers that Morley cherishes, reassuring us that 'the best truths are the simplest – never difficult, abstruse or dark' (p. 8). Using a musical analogy, Morley proceeds to demonstrate how each discord in the play is resolved by a concord of good feeling and true thinking. So, to take an important example, the 'false moralising' of Jaques is 'immediately followed by entrance of Orlando, and again there rises the full music of the brotherhood of man' (p. 16).

Morley and Knight were anxious to provide such guidance as would lead inexpert readers most directly to the poetic and moral strengths of the work rather than to an appreciation of the editor's qualifications (although when he wishes, Knight can deal authoritatively with the follies of his predecessors). Knight's edition has copious engravings, illustrating not only incidents in the play but also objects, persons, or incidents referred to, and it has useful explanatory notes on the page and at the end of each act. The effect is accessible and attractive, a popularization of scholarship. Henry Morley's edition in Cassell's National Library is a plain text with an introduction and, as a supplement, the *Tale of Gamelyn*, but lacks explanatory notes. It is compact, clearly and pleasantly printed, and cheap.

In such popular Shakespeares for the general reader, commentary on the moral meanings of the text is provided not out of blindness to the need for some other kind of critical activity, but as part of a project to make the plays intelligible and pleasing. The elucidation of moral significance not only in individual works but in the author's *œuvre*, construed as documents of a spiritual life, was central to the audience's habitual way of enjoying the works. There is plenty of evidence to show that the enjoyment of Victorian popular culture usually began from the elucidation of more or less conventional moral lessons from plays, paintings, stories, and poems.[3] The fostering of this attitude in relation to the products of higher culture was, admittedly, a dominant element in programmes for popular education. In the view of Morley and Knight, if the arts were democratically available and rightly understood, people of all classes would be more likely to live better together, because the masters of literature offered finer and more forcefully expressed morality than that available in the cruder, cheaper work of melodramatists and hack novelists. This was a means not of levelling social strata, but of using culture to facilitate harmony in diversity. The difference between popularized Shakespeare and popular melodramas lay in the quality of the plays rather than the process by which the cultural exchange between audience and work took place. Consequently the moralizing bent of the editions of Knight and Morley, which would be out of place in a modern commentary, was designed to recommend the plays to the tastes and inclinations of a wide audience. Another group of editions was constituted in response to the increasing use of Shakespeare's plays in the classroom, and as material for examinations in the later decades of the century. These exemplify the sterner tasks that could be devised with Shakespeare as a pretext.

Neither Morley nor Knight expurgate, although they refrain from giving explanatory notes for passages (such as the jokes about horns) which might be thought offensive. Theatre texts, and editions prepared for reading aloud, usually offer a cut version: C.E. Flower's 'Memorial Theatre' editions (of which *As You Like It*, the last, appeared posthumously in 1894) are expurgated, not to make them fit for children, 'but rather to present such an edition as can be read aloud in general society' (p. vii). In the remaining text, Flower cuts some passages altogether, but he includes others in a smaller typeface to indicate that they will not be needed in performance but may well be read – a practice derived, via Bell's acting texts, from Pope's edition of the *Works.* Other texts for reading aloud include one published in 1910 by the British Empire Reading Society, giving no commentary but following a similar plan of using smaller type for passages that may be cut. Such editions are a reminder that Shakespearean production had many locations in Victorian social life: reading aloud in the home and in clubs occupied a position midway between performance and solitary reading, and publishers responded to its requirements. Bowdler's *Family Shakespeare*, in its various editions, although a by-word for the sanitizing of the plays, is as significant for bringing Shakespeare into the middle-class home.[4]

Something of the same ground is occupied by editions designed to woo the youngest readers into an appreciation of the plays. The *Tales from Shakespeare* of Charles and Mary Lamb, conceived as an interim measure for those (especially girls) not yet mature enough to read the plays, found their way into the classroom. *The Children's Shakespeare. Scenes from the Plays with Introductory Readings from Charles and Mary Lamb's 'Tales from Shakespeare'* included an *As You Like It* (London, 1910) in which continuous narratives and stretches of dialogue are grouped as episodes with 'composition exercises' after them. The questions are less formidable than those encountered in full-fledged school editions of the play, but they firmly direct the young reader to a conventional Victorian view of it. For example: '"Sweet are the uses of adversity" – Write a short essay on this', or 'Write a short life of Orlando.' Another essay title begins with a quotation from Horace Howard Furness's *New Variorum*:

Although the scene is laid in France, *As You Like It* 'is through and through an English comedy, on English soil, in English air, beneath English oaks; and it will be loved and admired, cherished and appreciated, by English men as long as an English word is uttered by one English tongue'.

'Write any comment you can on this extract', the reader is instructed. It is interesting that an appreciation of 'Englishness' could be expected in readers so inexpert that they could be invited indulgently on the same page to 'Quote either from memory or from the book, some lines that you admire very much. Say, if you can, what it is in them that attracts your fancy.' Before they grew to man's estate, they would have to face up to sterner tests, and texts, than these.

As Shakespeare was established as a subject in the examinations that accompanied the professionalization of administrative careers, publishers began to commission editions for use in schools, modelled on the editions of Greek and Roman authors then in use. The most thorough-going of these show clearly that the texts could be used as a quarry for information, as a repository of brain-teasing points of grammar and philology, and as the basis of exercises in deduction. The notes sometimes make absurdly heavy weather of the text's meaning in order to secure a thorough understanding of its grammar. A representative example is the note provided by Lionel W. Lyde's edition (Blackie's Junior School Shakespeare, 1894) on 'I will go buy my fortunes' in Act I, scene i:

> The preposition *to* is neither a necessary sign nor an essential part of the simple infinitive, but it ought to be used before the gerundial infinitive or infinitive of purpose. Contrast 'I *want* (to) buy' with 'I *went* to buy.' See note on ii.5.56.

It must be allowed that the language of this note would be more familiar to schoolchildren of the 1890s (or indeed the 1950s) than to most adults in the 1990s, but it still leads the reader towards rather than away from difficulty. This is an edition prepared by teachers (according to the general editors' preface) to meet 'the needs of the youngest students of the dramatist' and of 'junior candidates in the University local and similar examinations'. *As You Like It* in *Chambers' Edition of Shakespeare's Plays for Schools* (1892), like many similar works, includes specimen examination papers on the model of those used for 'the Civil Service, the University local and similar examinations'. In these the emphasis is on the recall of philological and historical information and comprehension of the play's events and characters, which become a cognate exercise. Thus, pupils are invited to 'Give the history of the possessive pronoun *its*', and to 'Discuss the gerundial infinitive, and give instances from the present play.' They may comment on the etymology of 'carlot, character, conned, curtle-ax', and many other words. There is a list of passages in which the student should 'Explain the allusions...and in each case give the name of the speaker and some brief account of the context.' These include such knotty points of explication as 'It is the right butter-women's rank to market' (II.ii.). Each play in Chambers's edition includes a 'Plan of Study for Perfect Possession' which sets out systematically the points on which a student should be word-perfect. The principal headings are 'The plot and story...the characters...the influence and interplay of the characters upon each other...complete possession of the language...power to reproduce or quote... power to locate'. Another edition, by Thomas Page, in the series *Moffat's Plays of Shakespeare* (1893), includes a helpful list of 'notable passages (suitable for committing to memory)' and 'proverbial expressions and familiar quotations'. Its specimen examination questions are rather more ambitious: 'Write a short essay on the Dramatic Genius of Shakespeare as exemplified in *As You Like It*' or, as a task more likely to show the ability to manage data, 'Illustrate from this play the use of the Imperative mood in English.'

The use of the text to exercise skills of comprehension and memory often produces what seems like a parody of the worst excesses of character-centred criticism, in which the information bearing on a given personage is to be sifted and collated. Stanley Wood and the Reverend F. Marshall, in their *Oxford and Cambridge Edition* (London, 1904) offer fifty pages of introductory material in which the 'Characteristics of the Play' are classified. They provide a revealing one-page guide to 'Character Interpretation', and then set out the evidence in due order, so that an attentive reading of their introduction would get one through the specimen questions offered at the end of the volume. Thus Rosalind is summed up under the following headings: 'Her personal appearance...her love for Celia...Her changed life in the forest...the love of Rosalind...her sympathy...her vivacity and sparkling wit...she is spirited...her womanliness...her common sense'. On all these there is little room for discussion: the process is one of illustrating a given description. As one might expect, the account given of Rosalind has little to surprise anyone who had read the then-current standard works on Shakespeare's plays (by Mrs Jameson, Mary Cowden-Clarke, and others), but the writing of Wood and Marshall is worth quoting at length for its illustration of the assumptions behind their practice of reading:

> Rosalind is one of the most delightful of Shakespeare's characters and the brightest of his heroines. But the depths of her character are not revealed in the play and she evades analysis. We may surmise, but we cannot know how she would play her part amid the daily trials and troubles of our workaday world. We feel that she is perfectly charming, and that we could wish for no more exhilarating companion with whom to fleet the time carelessly, as they did in the forest of Arden. But her actions spring more from caprice than from character, and she is as difficult to analyse as a perfume. We can but follow her through her butterfly existence, and draw attention to the qualities which have impressed upon us a feeling of pure delight. (p. xxiv)

The celebration of the unfathomable is to be achieved by as much collation of the available evidence as possible; the character (as a woman, it seems) defies analysis partly because she behaves from caprice rather than 'character' – that is, implicitly, some deep-seated principle of action and thought; her behaviour in the play does not tell the whole story. At least the intellectual confusion of this is made patent by the openness with which the authors declare themselves. They hardly follow their own advice on character analysis. Thus, on Rosalind's behaviour during and after the wrestling, they comment:

> She has all a woman's admiration for physical courage. She endeavoured to dissuade Orlando from wrestling with Charles, but thinks more highly of him for refusing to be persuaded than she would have thought of him had he followed her advice. (p. xxix)

The sentiments are not original – they had long been part of the received opinions on the character and the play – but it is the failure in reasoning that is most striking. It may be that in the absence of any suitable language for the analysis of the effect of dramatic fictions, editors were simply unable to say anything useful. Shakespeare's own personality was just as accessible and as examinable, given the prevailing conventions, and the 'questions' accept this, inviting pupils to show by quotations ' 1. Shakespeare's love for and exact description of natural objects. 2. His high appreciation of the virtues of (a) temperance (b) courage (c) forgiveness'.

When we do find 'moral' commentary, drawing conclusions from the effect of the play on its readers (never its spectators) in the late Victorian 'educational' editions, it is usually at its strongest in the introductory accounts of the play's characters and action, although it sometimes seeps into the notes and questions, where it seems to offer a relief from the incessant parsing and etymology-tracing.

An edition 'for the use of Rugby School' (Rugby, 1868) lacks the systematic orientation towards examinable 'fact' found in editions for general scholastic use, but shares their interest in the history of the language. Its literary observations are conventional enough, with an emphasis, appropriate enough for Rugby, on the play's place in Shakespeare's life-struggle. *As You Like It* dates from a period when the dramatist's 'powers of thought were maturing, and his language was pure, manly and simple in the highest degree' (p.v). It was a time when 'he was preparing for the highest flights of his genius'. This is clearly a Shakespeare endowed with the mid-Victorian sense of a man's spiritual and material career, his path through the world. Shakespeare's adaptation of 'a hoary and com-monplace tale' is notable for 'the shade of real and thoughtful sorrow which mingles in the general brightness of the piece', and Jaques reflects the likelihood that Shakespeare 'was battling with a disposition to despondency in himself' (pp. vi–vii). It is not surprising that when Orlando rejects Jaques's overtures – 'I will chide no breather in the world except myself, against whom I know most faults' – the Rugby editor observes 'again the tone of true healthy reflection puts Jaques to the rout' (p. 47).

This reading of Jaques is put forcefully by other school editions, as if to forestall any relishing of the character's cynicism at the Duke's expense. The *Canadian School Shakespeare* (Toronto, 1919) states simply that 'It is quite evident that the attitude of Duke Senior rather than that of Jaques is Shakespeare's own ideal' (p. xiii). In *Blackie's Junior School Shakespeare*, Lionel W. Lyde describes Jaques as a 'sensitive, sullen, self-centred [and] utterly useless man, whose sole aim in life is "to think"'. Against his example we may set Rosalind, who is 'above all things womanly, thorough and healthy, both in mind and body' (pp. 12–13). The briskest version of this camp-fire aesthetic is to be found in the *Australasian Edition* (1917, by Frank Tate, Director of Education in Victoria): 'part of the charm of the play is the healthy robustness and cheery optimism of all the forest dwellers except Jaques. They are hearty wholesome folk who fill out their day pleasantly and go to bed thoroughly tired' (p. xiv). When the exiled courtiers leave the forest they show good sense, and the editor advises us:

By all means visit Arden when in holiday mood, refresh and recreate your spirit there, and then
> Go out into the dust and heat
> And justify the food you eat.

Henry Morley had insisted that 'the poet had no faith in an ideal of Arcadian idleness' (p. 17), and one sometimes senses that the educational editors feel it necessary to police the bounds of Arden, keeping Jaques's cynicism and the play's over-indulgent pastoralism equally under control. A comment in *Arnold's School Shakespeare* (London, ?1895) suggests the need to avoid subversively romantic applications of the Arden lifestyle. After describing its attractions and suggesting some modern parallels, the editor (S.E. Winbolt) observes, 'Touchstone [is] always at hand as a check to any extravagant nature-worship which might tend to lead to the extreme conclusions of a Jean-Jaques Rousseau' (p. xxiv).

Some of the school editions tried not to break the plays down into examinable, quantifiable chunks of information. William Aldis Wright's Oxford edition (1876) does this austerely by simply presenting the best available scholarly annotation and omitting any apparatus adapted to the specific requirements of examination boards. All the material is there, but the user is left to seek for it without further aid. In many respects this edition reads like a 'grown-up' text, making no concessions to popular readership or scholastic use. A.W. Verity's edition for The Pitt Press Shakespeare (Cambridge, 1899) is less austere – it includes introductory comment on the play's characters and literary quality – but has similar standing, and like Wright's, it tends to figure in the footnotes of modern editors. Other editions made a positive move towards a more humane presentation of the plays. *Arnold's School Shakespeare*, cited already as warning readers against cynicism, was under the general editorship of John Churton Collins, who claimed in his general preface that it had been 'designed for the use of those students who are encouraged to study Shakespeare liberally, rather, that is to say, from a literary and historical, than from a philological point of view – a class of students which, owing to the salutary reaction against philological cramming now setting in on all sides, is rapidly increasing'. Unfortunately the questions proposed for essay-writing in the *As You Like It* (1895) betray a spirit not so far removed from that of the philological crammers: 'What do you mean by *paraprosdokian*? Quote instances...Give instances of: archaic plural, confusion of genders...[etc.].' And the 'literary' questions are hardly an advertisement for departure from this mode: 'What portion of this scene [II.vii] is purely Shakespearean?' is merely an invitation to ponder the barely fathomable.

The Warwick Shakespeare was far more successful in this aim (according to its general preface) of presenting 'the greater plays of the dramatist in their literary aspect, and not merely as material for the study of philology or grammar'. J.C. Smith's *As You Like It* in this series, first published in 1894, includes notes that show the dramatic purpose of each scene. Smith's attempts at literary comment are surer than those of most of his rivals. He seems to have acquired a Paterian penchant for impressionistic description of aesthetic effect. In Act II, scene i, for example, he notes that 'coming where they do, these forest scenes supply a broad bar of neutral colour between the somewhat gloomy hues of Act I and the radiant mirth and tenderness of Act III' (p. 129). He also pays some attention to technical effects, inviting students to 'Note, the abundant alliteration throughout this scene, especially the labials *p*, *f*, *b*, and the liquids *l* and *m*, which English verse loves. There is little of this in the plain narrative of Act I: its use now marks a more elaborate and brooding style' (*ibid.*). The success of this edition was reflected by its continuing in use well into the middle decades of the present century.

In these 'anti-crammer' editions, as in the 'popular' editions of the plays, the alternative to philological rote-learning is usually conceived of as a training in the apprehension of moral significance and the understanding of 'characters' – both of them central in the popular Victorian conception of the craft of reading fictions. The influential American scholar Henry N. Hudson put the case eloquently in the essay on 'How to Use Shakespeare in School' which prefaced his *Shakespeare's 'As You Like It'...for Use in Schools and Families* (Boston, Mass., 1880). Hudson argues against the usual abuses of rote-learning, recitation from memory, and so on. He thinks pupils should not approach Shakespeare 'until they have got strength and ripeness of mind enough to enter...into the transpirations of character in his persons. For this indeed is the Shakespeare of Shakespeare.' This is 'nothing less than to hear and see the hearts and souls of the persons in what they say and do; to feel, as it were, the very pulse-throbs of their inner life. Herein it is that Shakespeare's unapproached and unapproachable mastery of human nature lies.' It is in this, with its close relationship to the experience of life, that Hudson centres the students' work, rather than in 'a mere formal or mechanical or routine handling of words and phrases and figures of speech' (p. xiv).

Sometimes the questions raised by editors, although scarcely those a modern teacher might choose, show a willingness to think outside the strict preserve of what might be examinable. Perhaps it was the freer atmosphere of the New World that encouraged O.J. Stevenson, in the *Canadian School Shakespeare* (Toronto, 1919), to ask 'How is it that the spectacle of two young men (Ganymede and Orlando) carrying on a pretence of wooing does not appear ridiculous to the audience?' or 'Orlando admits that his education and training have been neglected. How is it that the audience are so ready to admire him?' This is also the only Victorian schools' edition that I have so far encountered which offers any elucidation of the 'horn' references – inescapable in Act IV, scene ii but ignored by most commentators: 'There is a coarse reference here to the old fancy that a man whose wife was unfaithful to him wore horns on his forehead' (p. 124).

Schools' editions from this period are especially useful to a historian because they are forthright in their recommendation of conventional Victorian methods of reading, and their sometimes crude predications of the results to be anticipated from an exercise ('With reference to the text, show that...') often make clear the orthodox Victorian interpretations of 'Shakespeare' (the man and the plays). They orient students towards participation in a hermeneutics of the canonical texts, and make use of that exercise as a test of skill in sifting and collating information. Similar structures are found in biblical and classical literary texts prepared for the same users. But some educators were beginning to argue for a more 'liberal' use of the plays, if only in the sense of freeing them from this particular kind of pedagogy.

A reminder that there was yet another life for dramatic texts in the school, but one still further removed from the rigours of the examination syllabus, is provided by the Swan, Sonnenschein company's series of *Standard Plays for Amateur Performance in Girls' Schools*, in which *As You Like It* was published in 1900, in an adaptation prepared by Elsie Fogerty, who was later the founder of the Central School of Speech and Drama and a formative influence in the development of verse-speaking technique in theatrical training. Fogerty's edition has no introductory matter except for advice on staging and performance (evidently influenced by the work of William Poel, she advocates a draped stage with no representational scenery).

The margins of her adapted text are filled with suggestions for motivation and stage-business, some of them clearly derived from contemporary custom. It is pleasing to think that in some schools at least, young women were learning the pleasure afforded by such rituals of the Victorian and Edwardian stage as Audrey's turnip:

Audrey giggles sheepishly [on 'features'] and begins to hunt awkwardly in her pocket for her turnip. She cuts junks [*sic*] out of it with a big knife, and eats them in the pauses of her remarks. This business must not be overdone.[5]

However, Fogerty's work is a rare sign of an engagement between pedagogy and the theatrical origins of the plays.

A common feature of the majority of the schools' editions considered in this essay is that they use the play to construct 'Shakespeare' as natural phenomenon, whose creations can be analysed with the confidence appropriate to positivist science – Sherlock Holmes, the arch-deducer, would be best equipped for the task. The philological knowledge and circumstantial information to be gleaned from the play testify to the work's richness even as they test the user's management of data and powers of memory. It is rare in these editions to find any approach to criticism, as constituted in late Victorian literary discourses and modified in the work of twentieth-century writers. At the same time the forays into moralizing and 'character' inference do reflect popular ways of reading. It should be added in their defence that popular Victorian culture accommodated a zest for scientific knowledge that may have been catered for in the parts of these works that seem most abstruse or unappetizing. Many features of these editions – and in some cases the editions themselves – survived into the middle of this century, tumbling out of classroom cupboards when a play was to be read round the class. Moreover, their unspoken assumption that the theatrical occasion of the work has no significance fed similar attitudes in subsequent decades and on higher planes of learning. It is a paradox of the work of the popular educators that their labours bring Shakespeare to the people rather than assert his works as being of the people. The

ambitions and methods of Victorian Shakespeare, in this as in
other manifestations, give an insight into the practices that
superseded them, and the directness with which they are
sometimes stated provides a means of questioning what editors
do when they 'produce' the texts they edit.

NOTES

1 In addition to the books by Taylor and Bristol, see Aaron Y.
Stavisky, *Shakespeare and the Victorians: Roots of Modern Criticism*
(Norman, Oklahoma, 1969); Derek Longhurst, '"Not for All
Time, but for an Age": An Approach to Shakespeare Studies', in
Peter Widdowson (ed.), *Re-Reading English* (London, 1982); Alan
Sinfield, 'Give Some Account of Shakespeare and Education...',
in Jonathan Dollimore and Alan Sinfield (eds.), *Political Shake-
speare: New Essays in Cultural Materialism* (Manchester, 1985);
Terence Hawkes, 'Swisser-Swatter. Making a Man of English
Letters', in *That Shakespeherian Rag* (London, 1986), and Graham
Holderness (ed.), *The Shakespeare Myth* (Manchester, 1988).
Chapter 10 of Louis Marder's *His Exits and his Entrances: The Story
of Shakespeare's Reputation* (Philadelphia, 1963) describes Shakespeare in Victorian education, drawing mainly on American
sources. A brief survey of Victorian attitudes to Rosalind will be
found in my article '"Perfect Types of Womanhood": Rosalind,
Beatrice and Viola in Victorian Criticism and Performance', in
Shakespeare Survey, 32 (1979), 15–26.
2 On Morley's career, *cf*. Russell Jackson, 'Shakespeare in the
Theatrical Criticism of Henry Morley', *Shakespeare Survey*, 38
(1985), 187–200.
3 On the practices of reading in Victorian popular art, theatre, and
fiction, see Martin Meisel, *Realizations: Pictorial, Narrative and
Theatrical Arts in Nineteenth Century England* (Princeton, 1983).
4 On the Bowdler phenomenon, see Gary Taylor, *Reinventing
Shakespeare*, pp. 206–7.
5 The stage-custom of Audrey's turnip is described by A.C.
Sprague, *Shakespeare and the Actors: The Stage-business in his Plays,
1660–1905* (Cambridge, Mass., 1944), pp. 37–8.

CHAPTER 7

Bentley our contemporary; or, editors, ancient and modern

Marcus Walsh

Notoriously, literary theory over the last half-century has moved steadily away from the author. The New Critics thought of the poem as detached from its writer, making its way beyond the author's control or intention; structuralism found in the literary text an expression of common *langue* rather than of individual *parole*; Roland Barthes proclaimed in 1968 'la mort de l'auteur'; Derrida has called into question the whole 'metaphysics of presence', of which the ideas of 'author' and 'authorial meaning' are part. The author and authorial intention have not been without their defenders. Their most sophisticated and persuasive apologist has been E.D. Hirsch, who has argued, in the teeth of the prevailing gale of scepticism, that genuine knowledge is attainable in the humanities; that such knowledge must be based on the valid interpretation of texts; and that the validity of an interpretation of any text can be judged only in relation to a determination of the intention of its author.[1] On this last point Hirsch and, for example, Barthes are not in disagreement. Hirsch believes that the object of valid interpretation is the author's intended meaning: 'to banish the original author as the determiner of meaning was to reject the only compelling normative principle that could lend validity to an interpretation'.[2] Barthes similarly acknowledges that the death of the author makes interpretation impossible: 'Once the Author is removed, the claim to decipher a text becomes quite futile.'[3] The question is, what are we doing when we read? Are we interested in author's meaning or reader's meaning? Do we deal reverently with a Book, a Scripture (to use Barthes's term a 'work'), seeking in it the truth enunciated

by its author, 'reading for closure', seeking the final signified?
Or do we prefer to deal with a 'text', from which the author
has been banished, a 'galaxy of signifiers' rather than a
'structure of signifieds',[4] which we consent to re-write, whose
unlimited plural we appreciate?

This fundamental question, or something very like it, has
raised its head even in the world of scholarly editing. For long
a powerful assumption has been that the aim of the literary
editor was to recover the text 'intended' by the author; in her
Clarendon Press edition of Milton's *Poetical Works* (1952) Helen
Darbishire felt able to write, without irritable self-doubt: 'My
aim has been to offer a text as near as possible to that which
Milton himself would have given us, if he had had his sight'
(Preface, p. vi). 'The ideal of textual criticism', writes James
Thorpe, 'is to present the text which the author intended';
Fredson Bowers insists that 'the main scholarly demand is for
an established critical text embodying an author's full
intentions'.[5] In recent years the intentionalist or re-cognitive
position has been occupied particularly tenaciously by G.
Thomas Tanselle. In Tanselle's view, the scholarly editor has a
definable goal, 'the historical reconstruction of the text which
reflects the intention... of its creator(s) at a particular time'.[6]
The reconstruction of the author's text is inevitably and
intimately connected with an act of objective interpretation of
the author's intended meaning; and that interpretation must
be validated against the cultural and linguistic contexts of the
text's original moment of production:

> The scholarly editor is in the same position as the critic who is
> concerned with the author's intended meaning. Regardless of how
> many meanings he finds in the text, the scholarly editor makes
> corrections or emendations on the basis of the one he judges most
> likely to have been the author's intended meaning...the editor...is
> concerned only with that intention which his knowledge of the author
> and the period allows him to attribute to the author.[7]

Here Tanselle works within a Hirschian understanding of
objective 'meaning' and its interpretation. In Hirsch's theoretical writings intention and context, far from being her-

metically distinct interpretative criteria, are inevitably inter-
linked. The word sequence which is the text 'cannot',
according to Hirsch, 'under the general norms of language,
delimit a determinate meaning'; determinate meaning must
therefore be construed by as exact as possible a knowledge of
the norms that hold for a particular utterance.[8] The determination of authorial intention, and hence of meaning,
depends on 'knowledge of the author and the period'. Hence,
the interpreter, in Hirsch's words, must 'posit the most
probable horizon for the text', must 'reproduce in himself the
author's "logic", his attitudes, his cultural givens, in short, his
world'.[9] Re-cognitive interpreters base their interpretations on
a sense of the context beginning with 'the words that surround
the crux' and ending only with 'the entire physical, psycho-
logical, social, and historical milieu in which the utterance
occurs'.[10] It is knowledge of the context that allows editors to
choose between readings, as it allows interpreters to choose
between possible and impossible connotations of a word. For
neither Tanselle nor Hirsch can the task of the editor be
reduced to mechanically bibliographical terms, the finding and
collation of texts, the derivation of stemmata, the choosing
between alternative readings. The Tansellian editor 'soon
realizes that his...choice among textual variants involves his
understanding of the intended meaning of the text'.[11] Hirsch
insists that 'the aim of the textual editor is to determine what
the author wrote or intended to write, and no purely
mechanical system which ignores interpretation could ever
reliably reach such a determination'.[12]

Tanselle's position is evidently underwritten by the Hirschian insistence on the distinctness of 'meaning' from 'significance'. Meaning is historically constituted, objective, determinate, unchanging, sharable; *Paradise Lost* means now
what it meant when Milton wrote it. 'Significance', which is
the object of criticism rather than of interpretation, 'names a
relationship between...meaning and a person, or a conception,
or a situation, or indeed anything imaginable.'[13] Significance,
by definition, is therefore subjective or intersubjective; the
significance of *Paradise Lost* is inevitably different to every

reader, and always has been. Tanselle is prepared to concede
that certain kinds of non-scholarly editing might concern
themselves not with determinate, objective 'meaning', but
with variable, subjective 'significance'. Writing of eclectic,
belletristic editing, Tanselle remarks: 'editing which does not
have as its goal the recovery of the author's words is not
necessarily illegitimate – it is creative, rather than scholarly,
but not therefore unthinkable'.[14] It is possible to edit
subjectively and aesthetically, rather than objectively and
scientifically. Some critics or editors may conscientiously prefer
a 'good' to a 'correct' (that is, authorially intended) reading;[15]
'every interpreter' (writes Hirsch, in resonant words quoted by
Tanselle[16]) 'has a touch of the medieval commentator looking
for the best meaning, and every editor has a drop of Bentley's
blood'.

Indeed, text theories much more sceptical, much more
subjective and creative, than Tanselle's have been adumbrated
in recent years. Tom Davis and Susan Hamlyn, for example, in
an essay considering the treatment of textual variants in *She
Stoops to Conquer*, argue that the literary work is not an objective
reality, but a 'subjective construct, any physical manifestation
being an approximation'. Davis and Hamlyn's position derives
its theoretical justification partly from the Saussurean distinction between *langue* and *parole*. *Langue* they understand as
analogous to the play or poem itself, *parole* to its particular
texts. 'The play...does not exist in any of its performances or
published forms, but none the less only by them is it known.'
The editor consults, and is bound by, evidence, including
evidence of authorial intention, but authorial intention is
'ultimately unknowable'. The textual critic's statements are
'potentially objective', but derive from 'his own intuitions'. In
the end the editor can only construct a text 'that represents his
subjective perception of the work itself'.[17] Tanselle, who is a
good deal more convinced of the knowability of authorial
intentions, concludes that Davis and Hamlyn conceive of
editorial judgement as seeking 'readings that appeal to the
editor's own literary sensibility' rather than 'authorially
intended readings'.[18]

One of the most thoughtful and original text theorists of our time, Jerome McGann, has insisted, against the Hirschian and Tansellian position, that editing in itself has nothing to do with interpretation.[19] McGann complains that 'establishing texts for editions too often begins and ends in the pursuit of the so-called author's intentions'. He argues that textual editing, at present too much 'author-centered', should be based on a much more fully socialized model of literary production, and should pay more attention to 'nonauthorial textual determinants'.[20] McGann offers what he calls a 'finished program of historicist textual criticism', divided into three categories; 'the Originary Textual Moment' (including not only the author but also 'other persons or groups involved in the initial process of production'); 'Secondary Moments of Textual Production and Reproduction' (including reception history); and 'the Immediate Moment of Textual Criticism' (which 'calls for an analysis of the critic's own programmatic goals and purposes').[21] McGann argues for a comprehensive theory of textual criticism whose functions would include not only 'an editorial operation that will result in the production of an edition' but also 'a critical operation for studying the character of that edition', and 'an interpretive operation for incorporating the meaning of the (past) work into a present context'.[22] Neither in his own editorial work nor in his theoretical statements can McGann be accused of neglecting any part of a text's history, including its immediate authorial context. Nonetheless, as compared with Tanselle, McGann has shifted the emphasis from the meaning intended by an author in a past originary moment, validated against the author's own context, to the significance of the text for the present. Not surprisingly, McGann calls to his support Coleridge's preference for the generative power of the imagination over the empirical perception of fixed objects, and Barthes's preference for the producible, the *scriptible* 'text' over the consumed, the *lisible* 'work':

The great strength of this tradition lies in the freedom it can give to the critic-as-reader. Authority for literary creativity emerges from a dead past to a living present.[23]

McGann is aware that a criticism based on such assumptions must know its own limits, and be aware of its own nature; aiming not 'to study the text of the critic but to generate the text of the reader', it 'can generate literary experience only, not literary knowledge. Such criticism should not mean but be, and as it yearns to embrace its own aesthesis, it also tends to abandon knowledge and science.'[24] The polarities are clear, then, not only in critical but also in editorial theory. On the one hand we have the advocates of an objective, scholarly, contextual re-construction and re-cognition of the author's meaning; on the other the advocates of a subjective, poetic experience of the text and creation of the reader's meaning.

Such a debate amongst literary critics and scholars is by no means without precedent. In this paper I will be concerned to show that Richard Bentley's notorious edition of *Paradise Lost* represents an early case of non-objective editing, and that the controversy which it immediately provoked parallels sur-prisingly exactly the modern polarizing of opinions I have described.

From the moment Bentley's edition of *Paradise Lost* was published in 1732 it has been an obvious, and in some respects an easy, Aunt Sally. It needs to be said that Bentley was the most significant early eighteenth-century commentator on Milton, with the exception of the brilliant Zachary Pearce. It is true that Bentley's critical judgements were often idio-syncratic, and that he was poorly served by conjectural methods which had been conspicuously successful in his classical editing. It is also true that he brought to the examination of Milton's sense, expression, and argument a precision and intensity of critical attention which has continued to make him, explicitly or implicitly, a central and necessary antagonist in such major twentieth-century commentaries on *Paradise Lost* as Denis Burden's *The Logical Epic*, Christopher Ricks's *Milton's Grand Style*, or Alastair Fowler's Longman's Annotated English Poets edition.

By the time Bentley's edition appeared, *Paradise Lost* was an accepted classic. Dryden's famous epigram, which found in Milton the culminating combination of Homer's loftiness of thought and Virgil's majesty of style, was first printed in the splendid subscription-printed folio fourth edition of 1688. A number of smaller format editions followed, of which the most notable were the quarto sixth edition of 1695, with Patrick Hume's notes, and the handsome quarto edition of 1720, with a subscription list including an imposing galaxy of men of arts and affairs.[25] Bentley, however, had higher, and more specific, editorial ambitions than merely to attach his name to the latest in a sequence of editions of England's greatest modern poem. In his Preface, he presented his edition of *Paradise Lost* as an attempted 'Restoration of the Genuine *Milton*'. Bentley argued that the text of *Paradise Lost* had been subject to corruption in four ways:

(1) the amanuensis, taking down the dictation of the blind poet, was responsible for 'Errors in Spelling, Pointing, nay even in whole Words of a like or near Sound in Pronunciation';

(2) the bookseller and 'that Acquaintance who seems to have been the sole Corrector of the Press' were so negligent as to allow the first edition to appear 'polluted' with numerous typographical faults;

(3) Bentley argues that Milton's 'Acquaintance' or 'suppos'd Friend' in fact behaved as an 'Editor', and, taking advantage of Milton's blindness, 'thought he had a fit Opportunity to foist into the Book several of his own Verses';

(4) finally, to be laid 'to the Author's Charge' are a number of 'Inconsistencies' in the poem which Milton would no doubt have corrected had he not lost his sight.

It is clear that Bentley is fully, and rightly, aware that the textual problems of *Paradise Lost* are at least in part constituted by the circumstances of its original transmission. To the usual questions regarding the accuracy of the press have to be added special questions about the effect of the poet's blindness and his use of an amanuensis. Bentley's concern for what McGann calls 'nonauthorial textual determinants' is clearly a necessary part of establishing Milton's texts, by McGann's, or Tanselle's, or Darbishire's criteria. However, Bentley raises these principles, not as an objective textual editor, but as a re-interpreter seeking a larger freedom. By insisting that he was dealing with an extensively corrupt and adulterate text, Bentley seized for himself a wide liberty for emendation. The 'Printer's Faults' may be corrected, he argued, 'not from a Manuscript, (for none exists) but by Sagacity, and happy Conjecture'; the 'Editor's Interpolations are... easily cured by printing them in the *Italic* Letter, and inclosing them between two Hooks' (that is, in square brackets), though '*Milton*'s own Slips and In-advertencies cannot be redress'd without a Change both of the Words and Sense'. It has been easy enough to detect stratagem and disingenuousness here. Bentley knew of the existence of the manuscript of Book I of *Paradise Lost*, and indeed used it extensively himself.[26] Above all, the device that gives Bentley his greatest latitude, the '*Persona* of an Editor', has caused suspicion. Bentley insisted that this was not 'a mere Fantom, a Fiction, an Artifice', but not all readers have been convinced. David Mallet accused Bentley of 'Calling *Milton* himself, in the person of this phantom, fool, ignorant, ideot, and the like critical compellations'; and Samuel Johnson described Bentley's hypothesis as 'a supposition rash and groundless, if he thought it true; and vile and pernicious, if, as is said, he in private allowed it to be false'.[27]

The question of Bentley's honesty in securing his licence to amend seems less interesting than the effect his extensive suggested alterations produce. Bentley makes more than 800 substantial emendations to the text.[28] All the words and passages for which he proposes a change are italicized in the body of the text, and the alternative is given in the margin (or, in the case of longer passages, at the foot of the page). The 'spurious' verses allegedly inserted by the editor are dis-tinguished by their 'hooks' as well as by their italic type. It is hard for the reader's eye to escape Bentley's re-writing, nor did Bentley intend it should. From the start Bentley enlists the reader into his re-creation of the text. 'Every Reader has his free Choice', promises Bentley in the Preface, 'whether he will accept or reject what is here offer'd him.' Changes made to Milton's 'Slips and Inadvertencies' are 'suggested, but not obtruded, to the Reader: they are generally in this Stile; *It MAY be adjusted thus: Among several ways of Change this MAY be one.* And if any Person will substitute better, he will deserve every Reader's Thanks.' So when Milton has Satan surmise that 'A chance but chance may lead' him to further information about new-created man (IV, 530),[29] Bentley remarks: 'If any are offended with this Jingle; as unbecoming *Satan* in this serious Juncture to catch at little Puns; they may easily alter it thus, or several other ways; SOME LUCKY *chance may lead.*' So variants of the text are offered in the footnotes for the reader to take or leave or choose between. Pope describes, in the *Epistle to Dr. Arbuthnot*, the pestering hack cheerfully surrendering his own authorial responsibility and status:

> 'The Piece you think is incorrect: why take it,
> I'm all submission, what you'd have it, make it.'
>
> (lines 45–6)

Like the hack, and as modestly, Bentley surrenders Milton's authorial status to his own conjectures and his reader's response. Modesty and submission are not however Bentley's most common style. Some notes, indeed, are tentative: 'Perhaps it was given thus' (I, 746; *cf.* I, 107). The great majority of Bentley's textual decisions are more confidently stated: 'without question the Poet's Words were', 'no doubt the Author spoke it'. Very frequently the notes make no pretence merely to establish the text, but express a critical judgement on Milton's writing: 'he had better have said', 'he had better have given it thus'. Often what Milton wrote is decided on the basis of what Bentley feels he ought to have written: 'here it should, or might have been, or was' (II, 1001). And, in a highly significant change of tense, the author is kidnapped from his past context to be admonished in Bentley's present: 'he must give it thus' (IV, 472), 'he must give it here' (IV, 264). Speculation, with an increasing degree of confidence, becomes the exercise of retrospective authority. There is a prevalent preference for what Tanselle would call the 'good' as opposed to the 'correct' reading; so Bentley changes 'the secret top / Of Horeb' (I, 6–7) to 'SACRED top', arguing 'I have such an Esteem for our Poet; that which of the two Words is the better, That, I say, was dictated by *Milton*.' 'Better thus' is a repeatedly used phrase. In extreme cases Bentley not only amends the text, but adds new verses of his own. At the end of Milton's *Paradise Lost* Adam and Eve 'hand in hand with wand'ring steps and slow, / Through *Eden* took their solitary way'; this, it seems to Bentley, 'contradicts the Poet's own Scheme', so Bentley's poem ends on a rather more upbeat note:

> THEN hand in hand with SOCIAL steps their way
> Through *Eden* took, WITH HEAV'NLY COMFORT CHEER'D.

Addison, similarly unhappy with Milton's last two lines, had merely wished them away (*Spectator*, 369, 3 May 1712); Bentley, more confident of his abilities, has given the poem his own, quite different ending.

'Conjecture has all the joy, and all the pride, of invention', as Johnson puts it in his Preface to Shakespeare. Bentley's contemporaries knew very well that his conjectural procedure was not simply a matter of textual mechanics, but a new creation, a replacement of author's sense by editor's or reader's sense. The anonymous author of *Milton Restor'd, and Bentley Depos'd* (1732) pointed out that

The same Liberty may be assumed by every Reader, as by you, Doctor; and so the whole of Milton's, or any other Poem, extinguished by degrees, and a new one set forth by Editors, challenge the Title not of Notes, but of a Text variorum. (p. vii)

In the course of a lengthy attack on Bentley, Jonathan Richardson *père* urged the reader not to presume 'on his Own Sense of a Passage' but rather 'to come Honestly to receive *Milton*'s Sense'.[30] Benjamin Stillingfleet, in the letter preceding his manuscript notes on *Paradise Lost*, complained that Bentley's alterations 'often totally destroy the Author's meaning'.[31] And David Mallet famously wrote, with a proper irony, of Bentley 'to *Milton* lending sense', making the English poet, as he had made Horace, 'write what never Poet writ' (*Of Verbal Criticism* (1733), lines 135–6).

In his re-writing of *Paradise Lost* Bentley was concerned, then, with his own sense rather than with Milton's, with significance (to refer again to Hirsch's distinction) rather than with meaning, with re-interpretation rather than with interpretation. The cultural context within which he worked was his, sometimes personally his, rather than Milton's. In re-making Milton's epic he was subjecting it to an evaluative and interpretative process using standards of taste, and a horizon of knowledge, different from Milton's own. Bentley's impulse to re-create is analogous to that which led Dryden to write a 'dramatic transversion' of *Paradise Lost* (*The State of Innocence and the Fall of Man* (1677)); or to that which led Nahum Tate to revise *King Lear* (1681) and give it the 'Regularity and Probability' which Shakespeare's play lacked (Epistle Dedicatory, A2ᵛ); or with that which led Isaac Watts to produce a Christianized version of David's Psalms, 'Imitated in the Language of the New Testament, and apply'd to the Christian State and Worship' (1719). Swift's 'Bookseller', in his address to the reader in *A Tale of a Tub*, gives comparable examples of the tendency of modern writers to produce new versions of old works, 'fitted to the Humor of the Age'; a new Quixote, a new Boccalini, a new La Bruyère.[32]

Bentley's tastes were essentially classical, as well as distinctively personal. He consistently prefers the genuinely heroic to the romance element in *Paradise Lost*, the logical to the apparently inconsistent, the literal to the metaphoric. He expects that the poem should conform to his own criteria of stylistic decorum, and to his own understanding of the world, its philosophy, its natural philosophy, and its history.

Bentley imputes to the 'Editor', and so banishes from the poem, elements of romance, of pagan fable, and of popular mythology. The list of romance heroes to which the devils in hell are compared (I, 579–87) is described as 'Romantic Trash', the invention of Milton's 'Acquaintance and Editor'. It is the 'pragmatical Editor' who brings into the description of the bower in Eden allusions to the 'salvage and beastly

Deities' of pagan myth, Pan, Sylvanus, and Faunus (IV, 705–8). And the 'fabulous *Night-Hag*', '*Dance of Lapland Witches*', and '*Smell of Infant Blood*', which are found to be 'less abhorr'd' than the figures of Sin and Death (II, 659–66), are 'idle' and 'dangerous' stories with which the 'Editor' has contaminated the poem.

Bentley everywhere finds offences against logic and consistency in the poem. 'Darkness visible', for example, 'will not serve to *discover Sights of Woe*' (I, 63). The devils cannot have 'dig'd out ribs of Gold' (I, 690) if we find them, a dozen lines later, melting the ore and scumming off the dross. Can Eve be said to have 'marriageable arms' (V, 217)? 'Why she was *wed, spous'd* already in the Verse before.' (Here, 'among several ways of Alteration', '*Arms* LASCIVIOUS' is offered.) Occasionally Milton's logic is so defective as to impel Bentley to write new explanatory material for insertion in the poem. Bentley wonders that Ithuriel, knowing Eve's bower was 'sacred and sequester'd to *Adam* and *Eve* only', should not at once identify as Satan the toad at Eve's ear (IV, 810), and so rectifies the poem with a new line:

> *Him thus intent* Ithuriel *with his Spear*
> KNOWING NO REAL TOAD DURST THERE INTRUDE,
> Touch'd lightly.

This indeed is re-writing English.

The stylistic decorum of Milton's writing was as inconsistent, as far as Bentley was concerned, as his logic. Bentley's ideal of fit heroic style was of 'Grandeur' combined with 'Simplicity' (X, 1092n.), of 'Propriety' controlling 'magniloquence of Stile, and Sublimity of Thought' (VI, 212n.). Against these classicist principles Milton often offends; to have 'th'Apostat Angel' speak 'though in pain' is 'low and vulgar' (I, 125). It is indecorous to allow God the Father to speak of 'Furies' (X, 620). Christ's enemies will find out, in the phrase given him by Milton, 'whether I be dextrous to subdue' the rebels to God (V, 741); Bentley would prefer Christ to 'prove able', rather than 'be dextrous', for 'the simplest and nearest Word is the best'. A regular and strict application of the Horatian test of the *usus loquendi* results in the purging of idiosyncratic usages: so Eve's question to the serpent, 'How cam'st thou Speakable of Mute' (IX, 563), is re-phrased 'How Thou cam'st VOCAL THUS', since '*Speakable*, in common Use, is not *What can speak*, but *What can be spoken.*'

A revolution in attitudes to the proper wit of poetry lies between Milton and Bentley. Consistently Bentley reveals his distaste for what Addison would have called 'false wit' in Milton; verbal play, puns, equivocations. The 'affected jingle' of 'At one slight bound high over-leap'd all bound' (IV, 181), for instance, is remedied by the change 'high overleap'd all FENCE'. More fundamentally, Bentley everywhere rejects, or is blind to, metaphoric levels of discourse and metaphoric logic in *Paradise Lost*. To call Proserpine a 'Flour' (IV, 270) is in Bentley's view 'but fit for a Madrigal'; there is no allowance for, and probably no apprehension of, the recurrent resonance of the flower image as applied to Eve, 'fairest unsupported Flour' (IX, 432). Milton tells us, of the fallen Satan, that 'Princely counsel in his face yet shone, / Majestick though in Ruin' (II, 304); Bentley confesses 'How *Counsel* could *shine*, or be *Majestic*, or be in *Ruin*, is beyond my Understanding', and defuses the metaphor by suggesting 'Feature' for 'Counsel'.[33]

The philosophy and natural philosophy of Milton's poem, in questions large and small, are similarly tested by Bentley against his own standards. Milton's reference to 'the Female Bee' (VII, 490), for example, puzzles Bentley, who wonders whether the phrase refers to 'an *Amazonian* Race without Males, or...one Female, common Mother of all the Hive'. Neither explanation consists with Bentley's knowledge, and both are dismissed as 'idle and idiotical Notions, against the Course and stated Rule of Nature'. On the larger scale, Bentley the Modern is especially disturbed by Milton's lament over his poetic disadvantages: 'unless an age too late, or cold / Climate, or Years damp my intended wing' (IX, 44–5). 'What's the Meaning of an *Age too late*?' expostulates Bentley; 'surely he could not think the World is superannuated, and Mens natural Powers diminish'd.' Milton, of course, could think precisely that; as Alastair Fowler's note points out, such a 'cosmic pessimism' was 'common in Milton's time'.

The central characteristic, then, of Bentley's reading of

Paradise Lost is his consistent refusal to work within appropriate horizons of knowledge. In discussing matters of lexis, of style, of biblical reference, of natural science, of the history of ideas, Bentley makes little allowance for the relation of Milton's poem to its own moment of production. There are few attempts to draw on the literary affiliations of *Paradise Lost*, to engage with the state of scientific, or theological, or even biblical knowledge in Milton's time, or to determine, still less to allow for, differences in linguistic usage.

That Bentley should seem to provide, beside Johnson's notes to Shakespeare, or certainly beside Alastair Fowler's notes on *Paradise Lost*, a startlingly impoverished context, is no surprise. More significantly, several of Bentley's contemporaries, and even one predecessor, offer a far more fully contextualized concern for Milton's sense.

Certainly the most striking feature of the earliest substantial commentary on *Paradise Lost*, Patrick Hume's *Annotations* (1695), is the volume of knowledge that Hume thinks it necessary and proper to bring to bear on the poem. Classical and modern poets, historians, and natural scientists; philosophers from Plato onwards; biblical commentary of all ages and kinds; Latin, Greek, Hebrew, Anglo-Saxon, and Dutch etymologies; all these, and much else, are laid under subscription. Milton's allusion to the Garden of Adonis (*Paradise Lost* IX, 440) is partly accounted for on etymological grounds: 'Adonis, seems to be derived of Ἡδονὴ, Gr. Pleasure; and it is very probable, that the *Gardens* of *Adonis* were an ignorant imitation of that of *Eden*.' The discovery by the 'Tuscan artist' of 'new Lands' in the moon (I, 290) is explained by a reference to Galileo's *Siderius Nuncius*. The appearance of the pagan gods Pan, Silvanus, and Faunus (IV, 707–8) is compared with passages in Virgil's *Eclogues*, *Georgics*, and *Aeneid*. Above all, and most usefully, Hume identified a very large number of Milton's biblical allusions. The 'secret top / Of Horeb' (I, 6–7), which would be changed by Bentley with so little ceremony to 'SACRED top', is given a scriptural explanation: 'Its Top or Summity is said to be secret…from that thick Darkness which cover'd the Mount, when God spake there with his Servant

Moses, as in private, *Exod.* 19.16.' That Adam was made 'for God only', Eve 'for God in Him' (IV, 299) is 'maintainable from St. *Paul*'s Doctrine', as stated in 1 Corinthians 11: 3.

The most impressive reply to Bentley was Zachary Pearce's long and scholarly *Review of the Text of Milton's Paradise Lost* (1732–3).[34] Pearce offers amendments of his own to *Paradise Lost*, but only either 'to propose words of like sound, which a blind Poet's Ear may be presum'd to have been sometimes mistaken in, when the Proof-Sheets were read to him', or to correct errors at points where 'it is not improbable that *Milton* trusted much to the Care of the Printer and Reviser' (p.v). That is, Pearce confines himself to genuinely likely 'non-authorial textual determinants'. Bentley's notion that 'there was any such *Person of an Editor*, as made Alterations and added Verses at his Pleasure' is rejected.

Typical of Pearce's response to Bentley's complaints about the lexis of *Paradise Lost* is his comment on Bentley's note on this line describing Abdiel's assault on Satan: 'So saying, a noble stroke he lifted high' (VI, 189). 'Vulgar Use (says the Doctor) has long since made *Noble Stroke* base and unfit for Heroic. But how long since? was it base before *M*'s writing of this? unless it was, the Objection is frivolous.' Pearce's insistence is that the linguistic standards of 1667, not those of 1732, are the true basis for evaluation. There is a telling disagreement with Bentley's classicism at *Paradise Lost*, v, 741, where Pearce prefers Milton's poetic and peculiar 'be dextrous' to Bentley's prosaic and clear 'prove able' since, in poetry, 'a Metaphorical and more Remote word is often preferable to the Simplest and Nearest, because it throws the Diction still more out of Prose'. Pearce is generally prepared to work harder to account for the idiosyncratic in Milton, offering interpretation rather than conjecture. Bentley rejects Satan's 'memory / Of what he was, what is, and what must be' (IV, 24–5), complaining that one cannot have 'Memory of Future'; 'but no doubt, in stead of *Memory*, the Author gave it ... THEORY'. Pearce justifies Milton's word by comparing it with the phrase 'remember that you must die', and with the Latin *recordatio*: 'the thinking and reflecting upon any thing, as well present and future as past'.

Pearce is almost always more sympathetic to Milton's figurative methods. Where Bentley objects to 'fierce Ensigns' (VI, 356) Pearce explains, with a weary irony, '"tis a Figure call'd Metonymy of the Part for the Whole, well known among Poets and Orators'. Even where he finds Milton's expression unsatisfactory, Pearce does not reject the 'correct' for the 'good' reading; the quibbling 'high over-leap'd all bound' (IV, 181) is accepted as Milton's intention (against Bentley's 'fence' and Pearce's preferred 'mound') because of the confirmation offered by the Argument for Book IV ('overleaps the bounds').

Pearce is especially aware how far the language of the Authorized Version influences, and warrants, Milton's usage. When Bentley comes across Eve's 'Virtue and the Conscience of her Worth' (VIII, 502) he objects, as usual applying the Horatian principle of the *usus loquendi* rather narrowly, that '*Conscience* is here taken in a Signification unwarranted by Use', and changes the word to 'Consciousness'; Pearce restores 'Conscience', on the grounds that 'in our English Version of the Bible the word is often us'd in this sense', citing 1 Corinthians 8:7 and Hebrews 10:2. Similarly, where Bentley had objected to the 'Rites / Mysterious of connubial Love' at IV, 742–3, changing the 'threadbare' epithet 'mysterious' to 'solennious', Pearce restores the original reading, 'for [Milton] plainly alludes to St. *Paul*'s calling Matrimony *a mystery*, Eph. v.32.'

The natural science of *Paradise Lost* is often biblical, as Pearce knew. Bentley objects to Leviathan's 'skaly rind' at I, 206, pointing out that 'the Whale has no Skales'. Pearce's contextual refutation is exact, and simple:

[Milton] does not mean a Whale. He meant what *Job* did by Leviathan in ch. 41. where by his Description he makes it as much a *Beast* as a Fish, and in *v.* 15 speaks of its *Skales*.

Pearce appreciates too that Milton's natural science depended on the state of knowledge in his own day. When Raphael tells Adam '[the Moon's] spots thou seest / As Clouds' (VIII, 145–6), Bentley objects that '[the Spots] of the Moon are permanent, and have appear'd the same since the first Memorial of them; and therefore cannot be Clouds'. Pearce answers by referring to Auzout's observations of change in the moon-spots reported in the *Philosophical Transactions* of 1666; 'and *M.* who wrote this Poem about that time, might approve of *Auzout*'s observation, tho' the Doctor and I do not'. Similarly, Pearce defends Milton's description of bees as female and drones as male (VII, 490), on the grounds that 'both those Opinions had been strenuously maintain'd by Mr. *Charles Butler* in the 4th Ch. of his curious Treatise upon Bees, entitled the *Feminine Monarchie*, printed in 1634: and it seems to have been the prevailing doctrine in *M*'s days'.

Very much less well-known than Pearce's *Review*, but in their way as representative of contemporary responses, are Benjamin Stillingfleet's manuscript notes on *Paradise Lost*, composed before April 1746.[35] Stillingfleet's comments on *Paradise Lost* are especially characterized by his conviction that the explication of Milton's sense is dependent on a knowledge of Milton's contexts, and more especially his literary contexts. Many difficult passages can be understood only by 'recurring to [the] very same sources, from whence they were originally taken'. To Stillingfleet a major failing of Bentley's was his 'never once making use of the Advantage his Knowledge of the Greek & Latin tongues gave him'.[36] Stillingfleet's own notes make especially extensive reference to classical analogues and sources to explain and justify Milton's usages. Where Bentley had objected to Milton's phrase 'the deep Tract of Hell' (*Paradise Lost*, I, 28), because 'tract' signifies 'a plane expanded Surface', Stillingfleet points out that the word is used 'by the best Authors without the least regard to the Nature of the Surface', citing, amongst others, Pliny's application of the word to the Alps.[37] Like Pearce, Stillingfleet is aware too of the importance of the Bible as a key to Milton's meaning. Milton's use of the epithet 'secret' in connection with Horeb (*Paradise Lost*, I, 6), for example, is justified by reference to the account given in Exodus 24:18 of Moses' receipt of the Law in 'the midst of the cloud'. And, like many other answerers of Bentley, Stillingfleet considers that evidence for interpretation may especially reliably be sought amongst materials that have the closest relation to the text in hand; that is, in other works by Milton himself, or in other parts of *Paradise Lost*. In this stress on the hermeneutic value of exactly appropriate contexts, as in much else, Stillingfleet is a Hirschian.[38] That Milton intended 'night-founder'd' (altered by Bentley to 'nigh founder'd') at *Paradise Lost*, I, 204 is evidenced by a similar figurative usage in *Comus* (line 482).[39] The passage on 'Fable or Romance' at *Paradise Lost*, I, 580 ff. might seem 'Romantic Trash' to Bentley; it need not have done so to Milton, who had written appreciatively of the topics and tales of romance in both *Il Penseroso* (lines 116–17) and *Paradise Regained* (III, 339). Like Pearce, Stillingfleet is insisting, against Bentley, on the authenticity and coherence of passages in *Paradise Lost* by reference to the mediate and immediate contexts required in interpretation.

William Empson, in his well-known discussion of Bentley and Milton, lamented that 'Bentley has been used as a bogey; he scared later English critics into an anxiety to show that they were sympathetic and did not mind about the sense'.[40] The sense that Bentley cared about, however, was very often his own. It is evident that Bentley's contemporaries were sympathetic precisely because they did care, contextually and often exactly, about Milton's sense. The general tendency of the opposition to Bentley was re-cognitive. A major effort was to reconstruct Milton's past imaginative world, rather than to reconstrue his poem in a modern light. Where Bentley boldly amended, other editors and commentators attempted to find the validating contexts for Milton's language and ideas. Where Bentley sought the poem's significance for himself in 1732, others looked for the poem's meaning as determined by knowledge of its own historical moment.

The debate between Bentley and his answerers was a battle in the (continuing) war of Ancients and Moderns. To his opponents, Bentley seemed a dwarf perched on the shoulder of the giant Milton, attempting to speak his poem. It is well enough known that Bentley was seen by the Scriblerians as a leading representative of a modern scholasticism one of whose chief characteristics was an arrogant pride in its own creations and its own fictions. In the account of how Martinus Scriblerus 'became a great critic' the satire is accurately aimed at the editorial procedures of Bentley himself:

He conceiv'd, that ... *assembling parallel sounds*, either *syllables*, or *words*, might conduce to the Emendation and Correction of *Ancient Authors* ... He resolv'd to try first upon Virgil, Horace, and Terence; concluding, that if the *most correct* Authors could be so served with any reputation to the Critick, the amendment and alteration of *all the rest* wou'd easily follow; whereby a new, vast, nay boundless Field of Glory would be open'd to the true and *absolute Critick*.[41]

The constraining fences of authority once broken down, the critic's or editor's 'Field of Glory', of victory over the author, becomes a field of new creation, of speculation, of play. Bentley's rationale for his re-writing of *Paradise Lost* depends on a grandiose piece of self-liberating modern fictionalizing, the 'phantom editor'. Pope's Goddess Dulness, who 'ever loves a joke' (*Dunciad*, ii, 34), performs a parallel act of ludic creation, offering as a prize for the competing booksellers a phantom poet:

> All as a partridge plump, full-fed, and fair,
> She form'd this image of well-body'd air;
> With pert flat eyes she window'd well its head;
> A brain of feathers, and a heart of lead;
> And empty words she gave, and sounding strain,
> But senseless, lifeless! idol void and vain!
>
> (ii, 41–6)

Nor of course is the phantom poet the only such creation of the Scriblerians, who were always much given to ghost-writing. Martinus Scriblerus himself, epitome of false learning and a centrepiece of the Scriblerian creative imagination, was (in Pope's words) a 'Learned Phantome'.[42] Most famously he was a fictive editor of the *Dunciad Variorum*; Hare's Horace and Bentley's Terence were also attributed to him; and indeed, in a final ironic Scriblerian inversion, it was claimed that Bentley's Milton itself was the work of the phantom Martinus.[43] If Milton could be re-written, in Bentley's vision, by a ghostly editorial fiction, so too, it appeared, could Bentley.

The modern editor had become not merely an explicator and consumer but an inventor and producer of meaning. As that other great modern, William Wotton, put it, in one of the central works of the Ancients and Moderns controversy, a 'judicious Critic' is often raised 'much above the Author upon whom he tries his Skill':

> There are Thousands of Corrections and Censures upon Authors to be found in the Annotations of Modern Critics, which required more Fineness of Thought, and Happiness of Invention, than, perhaps, Twenty such Volumes as those were, upon which these very Criticisms were made.[44]

By the Moderns the editor had come to be valued not for judgement but for wit. The judicious critic turns out to be the critic capable of happy invention. (One should be reminded of Bentley's stated editorial policy of 'happy Conjecture'.) It is the critic's creative faculty that enables him to produce new readings by the thousand, and to surpass and supersede his original. The editor has become prolific, a revolutionary against the power of the author. One of the heroes of Dulness's revolution in the fourth Book of the *Dunciad* is Bentley the imperious critic, the man who had 'humbled Milton's strains' (IV, 212). In the following passage he tells how editors, in the service of the goddess Dulness, by their very productiveness hide and obscure original meaning:

> For thee explain a thing till all men doubt it,
> And write about it, Goddess, and about it:
> So spins the silk-worm small its slender store,
> And labours till it clouds itself all o'er.
>
> (IV, 251–4)

'Explain' has here a modern and ironic sense. The 'silk-worm' is of course a relation of the spider in the *Battle of the Books*, who is accused by Swift's bee of boasting 'of being obliged to no other Creature, but of drawing and spinning out all from yourself'. For the Scriblerians the modern subjectivist editor is a creature spider-like confined to itself and the little it knows, 'which by a lazy Contemplation of four Inches round; by an over-weening Pride, which feeding and engendering on it self, turns all into Excrement and Venom; producing nothing at last, but Fly-bane and a Cobweb'.[45]

Bentley, however, is a modern for us as well as for the

Scriblerians, and Roland Barthes tells us exactly why. This is Barthes's account of the traditional role of the critic as explicator of a classic 'work':

the *author* is always supposed to go from signified to signifier, from content to form, from idea to text, from passion to expression; and, in contrast, the *critic* goes in the other direction, works back from signifiers to signified. The *mastery of meaning*, a veritable semiurgism, is a divine attribute, once this meaning is defined as the discharge, the emanation, the spiritual effluvium overflowing from the signified toward the signifier; the *author* is a god (his place of origin is the signified); as for the critic, he is the priest whose task is to decipher the Writing of the God.[46]

The objective editor sees her task as the elucidation of the author-god's true meaning, the signified, from the signifiers, the sign-sequence, of the text. This is precisely what Bentley does not do. For Bentley the Milton of *Paradise Lost* has no theological or aletheological privilege; there is scarcely a real presence, in either sense, at all. For Milton, 'a good book is the precious life-blood of a master spirit'; the image is implicitly eucharistic, to consume a literary work is to enter into communion with its author. For a humanist, even secular works are due a pious respect, embodying an author's sacred meaning. For the scholastic, as Barthes puts it:

the Text...reads without the inscription of the Father...Hence no vital 'respect' is due to the Text: it can be *broken* (which is just what the Middle Ages did with two nevertheless authoritative texts – Holy Scripture and Aristotle).[47]

Bentley, as Pope well knew, was the 'great scholiast', properly at home in *The Dunciad*, a poem whose controlling image is monkish darkness, which is named for Duns Scotus. In *A Tale of a Tub* it is the '*Scholiastick* Midwifry' of 'numberless Commentators' that has delivered from dark writings 'Meanings, that the Authors themselves, perhaps, never conceived'; and it is Peter, 'the Scholastick Brother', whose hermeneutic ingenuity allows a more 'favourable Interpretation' of the Will and thereby undermines his 'Father's Authority' (the Father is here, explicitly and significantly, both God and Author).

Bentley treats *Paradise Lost*, not as a work or scripture, but as a text, from which the Author has been desacralized and removed. His contemporaries, by contrast, speak frequently of the reverence due to an author, and of the holy task of the editor. Though Alexander Pope held, as far as my argument is concerned, an awkwardly good private opinion of Bentley's Miltonic emendations,[48] and though he himself, in his edition of Shakespeare, was not entirely above practising the fashionable editorial art of conjecture, he none the less avowed, in significant terms, the high (if tedious) calling of the editor: 'I have discharg'd the dull duty of an Editor...with a religious abhorrence of all Innovation, and without indulgence to my private sense or conjecture.'[49] Pope here evinces the same reverence in interpreting Shakespeare as a humanist would in interpreting the Bible. Here at least he explicitly rejects 'conjecture', identifying it with the new subjectivism of the 'private sense' which the sectaries brought to reading Scripture. It is not an accident that he portrays Bentley as a Quaker in the *Dunciad* (iv, 208). It is this 'private sense', of course, which causes Jack in the *Tale of a Tub* not to follow the 'plain, easy Directions' of his Father's Will, but to turn the sacred book to his own uses. Whereas Martin the faithful interpreter seeks 'the true Intent and Meaning of his Father's Will', Jack the critic searches rather for significance, applying the holy writings to all the occasions, not equally sanctified, of his own life:

He had a Way of working it into any Shape he pleased; so that it served him for a Night-cap when he went to Bed, and for an Umbrello in rainy Weather. He would lap a Piece of it about a sore Toe, or when he had Fits, burn two Inches under his Nose.[50]

Bentley could readily be satirized as both scholastic and sectary; the Scriblerians associated with each extreme an interpretative scepticism which could become, as Jack and Peter do, indistinguishably crazy.

Here the assumptions and purposes of interpreters and textual editors are inevitably bound up. If a work is to be seen as the emanation of a divine or quasi-divine author, the particular text which embodies it must be seen as true, faithful, sacred. In the great religious controversies of the late

seventeenth century such Protestant apologists as John Tillotson, grounding their faith in Scripture, argued that written
texts are effective and reliable means for the transmission of
doctrine to succeeding ages, and that the holy writings were by
God's providence preserved in essentials incorrupt.[51] In *A Tale
of a Tub* Martin and Jack become free to arrive at a sound
reading of the plain easy directions of the Father's Will only
when they seize their chance to make a *copia vera*.[52] Bentley had
no such reverence for the inherited copy of *Paradise Lost*. His
first and necessary step in breaking the text (to use Barthes's
metaphor) was to argue that it was in so many ways, and for
so many reasons, defective. Naturally his opponents insisted
that an 'authentic copy', 'the Finish'd, the Genuine, the
Uncorrupted Work of *John Milton*' survived.[53]

Paradise Lost achieved a special status as holy writ before the
end of its own century. Patrick Hume's massively learned notes
on the poem are generically closest to late seventeenth- or early
eighteenth-century biblical commentaries.[54] Such works typically offered paraphrase of and annotations on their holy
original. These are two normal modes of Hume's work.
Frequently he gives straightforward explicatory paraphrase,
reverently eliciting sense and rarely making critical comment;
and he brings learning, commonly biblical and often patristic,
to bear on the text with an encyclopaedic copiousness generally
thought proper in sacred commentary. By the mid-eighteenth
century Milton was firmly established as a 'Divine Author' and
his great epic as a 'divine poem'.[55] For Thomas Newton, the
status of *Paradise Lost* was to be established by comparison with
Holy Writ: 'Whoever has any true taste and genius, we are
confident, will esteem this poem the best of modern productions, and the Scriptures the best of all ancient ones.'[56] The
view of the poem implicit in Patrick Hume's *Annotations* had
become both explicit and accepted.

Bentley's edition, which so signally failed to treat *Paradise
Lost* with the reverence due to Scripture, was greeted with a
sense of outrage which articulated itself in metaphors of
profanation. The *Weekly Register* insisted on the sanctity of
standard authors: 'The name of *Milton* was become as
venerable as *Homer* or *Virgil*; we deem'd it Sacrilege to treat his

Work irreverently.'[57] And the author of *Milton Restor'd, and Bentley Depos'd* similarly shuddered at the blasphemy of Bentley's conjectural method: 'this way of restoring, *i.e.* interpolating by Guess, is so sacralegious an intrusion, that, as it had its Rise, so it is to be hoped it will have its Fall with you' (p. viii). Bentley's opponents were not alone in their century in insisting on the priestly duty of the editor. Nor was Milton's the only text held sacred. As the eighteenth century discovered literary history and developed the practice of editing secular literary works, so it developed the concepts of the canonical and of the sacred in those texts. Thomas Edwards, who had 'exploded' Warburton's edition of Shakespeare in his *Canons of Criticism* (1748), replied to a friend, who had urged him to edit Spenser: 'I regret as much as you do that our Classic Authors have fallen into such unhallowed hands as they have of late been profaned by, but who am I that can prevent the sacrilege?'[58] The implied image here is of the Ark of the Covenant, untouchable container of the holy testimony of God (Exod. 25:16, 21).

Such eighteenth-century quarrels starkly enact the disagreement between those who believe it is our task 'to decipher the writing of the God', and those who would wrest meaning from the divine author for the creating reader. No doubt the terms of the debate have changed. Warning that the institutions of English must be rebuilt, Robert Scholes reminds us that 'nothing comes back as it was. That is the most fundamental lesson of history.'[59] Certainly few today could use without some self-consciousness the imagery employed by Pope or Edwards or the *Weekly Register*. A conversation between a reborn Bentley and Barthes in a Left Bank bar is particularly hard to imagine. But the other lesson of history is that some contraries have always been in opposition: text and scripture, scholiast and humanist, producer and devourer, Bentley and Pope, Barthes and Hirsch. Bentley is only the limit-case of a critical subjectivism that blankly refuses to interpret the code, to know the context, of the literary work. Such works as *Paradise Lost* come to us from a past which we do not inhabit, and which, in a Barthesian sense, we cannot *write*:

On the one hand, there is what it is possible to write, and on the other, what it is no longer possible to write: what is within the practice of the writer, and what has left it: which texts would I consent to write (to re-write), to desire, to put forth as a force in this world of mine?[60]

Milton's work remains, in Barthes's not Bentley's sense, classic. Bentley's project of writing, of re-writing, *Paradise Lost* six decades after Milton's death was inevitably doomed: 'things thought too long can be no longer thought'. None the less, *Paradise Lost* is not as precariously contemporaneous as Swift's hack's *Tale*, which 'will grow quite out of date and relish with the first shifting of the present Scene'.[61] If *Paradise Lost* can no longer be written, it can certainly still be *read*, interpreted. Jerome McGann argues that we can serve the present only by accurately interpreting the past, only by conceding its difference:

the special privilege of past human products, especially artistic ones, is that they come to us in finished and complete forms which, by their very finishedness, are able to judge the incompleteness of our present lives and works. They speak to the present precisely because they speak in other tongues, saying what we cannot say, and criticizing what we can. Literary works transcend their historical alienation by virtue of their definitive otherness, by their sharp and peculiar differentials with their later audiences, including our own.[62]

If we hope that the future may attend to our own writings, it might be well to accord a corresponding respect to the meaning of texts of earlier times. Swift's hack laments, to Prince Posterity, that Time has killed, almost at birth, the '*never-dying* Works' of modern writers.[63] The extreme Modern, in refusing to acknowledge what the past can tell him, or by denying its distinctive pastness, is in turn condemned to be ignored by succeeding Moderns. The perpetual temptation to smooth away the differences of the past, to make it fit the present, was especially strongly felt as Bentley's age attempted to classicize its literary inheritance. The same urge which led Dryden to tag Milton's points, Tate to make Shakespeare regular, and Watts to make David a Christian, led Bentley to re-write *Paradise Lost*. (None of these versions have lasted so well as their originals.)

Bentley's *Milton*, like these other modernizing revisions, offers the lesson that to ignore the difference of the past, to privilege the critic's quest for significance to himself over the interpreter's quest for author's meaning, is to run some risk of comparison of author's achievement with critic's achievement, not always to the advantage of the latter; and some risk of becoming, endlessly, the subject of essays like this one.

NOTES

1 Especially in *Validity in Interpretation* (New Haven, 1967); *The Aims of Interpretation* (Chicago, 1976).
2 *Validity*, p. 5.
3 'The Death of the Author', in *Image-Music-Text*, trans. Stephen Heath (London, 1977), p. 147.
4 *S/Z*, trans. Richard Miller (London, 1975), p. 5.
5 James Thorpe, *Principles of Textual Criticism* (San Marino, 1972), p. 79; Fredson Bowers, 'Remarks on Eclectic Texts', *Proof*, 4 (1975), 75.
6 'The Editorial Problem of Final Authorial Intention', *Studies in Bibliography*, 29 (1976), 169n.
7 'Editorial Problem', pp. 181, 183.
8 *Validity*, pp. 69–71.
9 *Ibid.*, pp. 238, 242.
10 *Ibid.*, p. 86.
11 'Editorial Problem', p. 179.
12 *Validity*, pp. 171–2n.
13 *Ibid.*, p. 8.
14 'Textual Study and Literary Judgement', *Papers of the Bibliographical Society of America*, 65 (1971), 113.
15 See Marcia Muelder Eaton, 'Good and Correct Interpretations of Literature', *Journal of Aesthetics and Art Criticism*, 29 (1970–1), 227–33; Michael Hancher, 'The Science of Interpretation, and the Art of Interpretation', *Modern Language Notes*, 85 (1970), 791–802. Swift was aware of this distinction, complaining in the Apology for *A Tale of a Tub* of readers 'who have neither Candor to suppose good Meanings, nor Palate to distinguish true Ones' (*A Tale of a Tub: to which is added The Battle of the Books*, ed. A.C. Guthkelch and D. Nichol Smith (Oxford, 1973), p. 5).
16 'Editorial Problem', p. 180n.
17 'What Do We Do When Two Texts Differ? *She Stoops to Conquer* and Textual Criticism', in *Evidence in Literary Scholarship: Essays in Memory of James Marshall Osborn*, ed. René Wellek and Alvaro

Ribeiro (Oxford, 1979), pp. 276, 277. A striking recent example of subjectivist editing is the modernizing of Shakespeare's text in the Oxford *Shakespeare*, ed. Gary Taylor and Stanley Wells.

18 'Recent Editorial Discussion and the Central Questions of Editing', *Studies in Bibliography*, 34 (1981), 57n.

19 'Shall these Bones Live?', in *The Beauty of Inflections* (Oxford, 1985), p. 91.

20 'The Monks and the Giants', *Textual Criticism and Literary Interpretation* (Chicago, 1985), p. 198. McGann's argument is presented at fullest length in his *Critique of Modern Textual Criticism* (Chicago, 1983).

21 'The Monks and the Giants', pp. 192–4.

22 *Ibid.*, p. 189.

23 'Shall these Bones Live?', p. 93.

24 *Ibid.*, pp. 93, 94.

25 Among the subscribers were Arbuthnot, Pope, Prior, Burlington, Bathurst, Coke of Holkham, Harley, Hervey, Kneller, Chandos, Thornhill, St. John, Isaac Newton, and Vanbrugh.

26 See Helen Darbishire's James Bryce Memorial Lecture, *Milton's 'Paradise Lost'* (London, 1951), pp. 31–2.

27 Mallet, *Of Verbal Criticism: an Epistle to Mr. Pope. Occasioned by Theobald's Shakespeare, and Bentley's Milton* (1733), p. 10n.; Johnson, Life of Milton, *Lives of the English Poets*, ed. G. Birkbeck Hill (3 vols., Oxford, 1905), I, 181.

28 One of the British Library copies (11626.h.6) of Bentley's edition contains marginal MS notes, transcribed out of the copy of the Tonson 1720 quarto edition of *Paradise Lost* from which Bentley had worked. These notes show that Bentley had an even greater number of changes originally in his mind.

29 All quotations from *Paradise Lost* in this essay are taken from Bentley's text.

30 *Explanatory Notes and Remarks on Milton's Paradise Lost* (1734), Preface, p. cxxxiv.

31 Fol. 1^r. See note 34 below.

32 See *Tale of a Tub*, ed. Guthkelch and Nichol Smith, p. 29 and n.

33 *Cf.* Bentley's similar objection to *Paradise Lost*, v, 708–10 ('[Satan's] count'nance...allur'd them; and with Lies/Drew after him the third part of Heaven's Host'): 'He is the *Father of Lies* indeed, if not his Tongue, but his Countenance spoke them. The Author gave it, *And his Lies.*' The 'Gentleman of Christ-Church College' who wrote *A Friendly Letter to Dr. Bentley, Occasion'd by his New Edition of Paradise Lost* (1732) ironically sides with Bentley in his note on *Paradise Lost*, II, 304: 'we know nothing of Metaphors and such stuff, nor don't allow of them...if an

Author, under cover of poetical License, shall fly out of our *Ken*,
with his *Figures*...we must clip his Wings, and clap a lead on his
Shoulders to keep him within the Sphere of our own Apprehensions'.

34 Part I (1732) offers remarks on *Paradise Lost*, I–IV; Part II (1732)
on V–VIII; and Part III (1733) on IX–XII.

35 Stillingfleet's notes are extremely copious for all of the first book
of *Paradise Lost*, thinner for the opening pages of the second book,
and peter out almost entirely thereafter. The MS, in Stillingfleet's
hand, is interleaved in a copy of Bentley's edition now in the
British Library (C.134.h.1). Interleaved with the Arguments
printed before the beginning of Book I is a long prefatory letter,
also in Stillingfleet's autograph, dated 27 April 1746, and
addressed to 'D—', that is, to Stillingfleet's friend Dr Thomas
Dampier. Stillingfleet's notes were nowhere mentioned or drawn
on in Thomas Newton's variorum edition of *Paradise Lost* (1749),
but they were selectively used in Henry John Todd's edition of the
Poetical Works of John Milton (6 vols., 1801).

36 Letter to Dampier, fol. 1^r.

37 Compare Pearce, who, in connection with this line of *Paradise Lost*
cites Servius' note on Virgil, *Georgics*, II, 182.

38 See Hirsch, *Validity*, p. 188.

39 The parallel with *Comus* had also been pointed out by Pearce.

40 *Some Versions of Pastoral* (London, 1935), p. 152.

41 *The Memoirs of the Extraordinary Life, Works, and Discoveries of
Martinus Scriblerus*, ed. Charles Kerby-Miller (New Haven, 1950),
p. 129.

42 In a letter from Pope to Arbuthnot, 2 September 1714. Pope,
Correspondence, ed. George Sherburn (5 vols., Oxford, 1956), I, 250.

43 *Martinus Scriblerus*, p. 129.

44 *Reflections upon Ancient and Modern Learning* (2nd edn, 1697), pp.
382–3.

45 *Tale of a Tub*, p. 232.

46 *S/Z*, p. 174.

47 'From Work to Text', in *Image-Music-Text*, p. 161.

48 Pope added in his own copy a number of marginal *bene*s, *recte*s, and
*pulchre*s against editorial suggestions by Bentley.

49 *The Works of Shakespeare*, ed. Pope (6 vols., 1725), I, p. xxii.

50 *Tale of a Tub*, pp. 136–7, 190.

51 See Tillotson, *The Rule of Faith*, in *Works* (6th edn, 1701), pp.
660–1; and compare Dryden, *Religio Laici* (1682), line 299.

52 Since lost, and now, in a wonderful irony, in the process of being
reconstructed by the 'elaborate conjectures' of Bentley himself
(*ed. cit.*, p. 121 and n.).

53 Thomas Newton (ed.), *Paradise Lost: A New Edition, with Notes of Various Authors* (2 vols., 1749), Preface a2^r; Richardson, *Explanatory Notes*, Preface, p. cxxxviii.
54 I discuss Hume's use of the methods of biblical paraphrase and commentary in 'Literary Annotation and Biblical Commentary; the Case of Patrick Hume's *Annotations* on *Paradise Lost*', *Milton Quarterly*, 22 (1988), 109–14.
55 Richardson, *Explanatory Notes*, Preface, p. cxxxvi; Newton (ed.), *Paradise Lost*, II, 431.
56 Newton, II, 432.
57 *Weekly Register*, Sat. 12 February 1732, quoted in *Gentleman's Magazine* 2 (February 1732), 601.
58 Letter to Philip Yorke, 5 April 1751, BL Add. MSS 35606, ff. 16^v–17^r. Quoted by Martin Battestin, 'A Rationale of Literary Annotation: The Example of Fielding's Novels', *Studies in Bibliography*, 34 (1981), 1.
59 *Textual Power: Literary Theory and the Teaching of English* (New Haven, 1985), p. 11.
60 *S/Z*, p. 4.
61 *Tale of a Tub*, pp. 23–4.
62 'Shall these Bones Live?', p. 107.
63 *Tale of a Tub*, p. 33.

CHAPTER 8

The editor as annotator as ideal reader

Ian Small

To use a metaphor now much in favour in some educational circles, textual editors and literary theorists have traditionally addressed different sectors of a very diverse market. Theory has been the sunrise industry of literary criticism because it has apparently concerned itself with the 'large' issues: the notion of literature, practices of reading, the construction of meanings, the ideology of literature, the relationships between discourses, and so forth. And, by contrast, it has often been supposed that textual editors occupy the drab, mechanical, and labour-intensive sector of the literary-critical economy. No large surveys of contemporary culture or grandiose claims about the nature of textuality here: no promises about the study of texts contributing 'to the strategic goal of human emancipation, the production of "better people" through the socialist trans-formation of society'.[1] Far from it: the collation of texts, the establishing of stemmata, the privileging of one textual variant over another – in general these have been taken to be laborious, crude, and naively historicist tasks which, when set against the more ambitious projects of theorists, seem to be not only unexciting but also unproblematic. In fact, such a charac-terization could scarcely be further from the truth; textual editors and annotators have confronted, but in an unsystematic and practical fashion, a great many of the problems recently identified by contemporary literary theorizing. As such, textual editors have been interested in some of the problems which have dogged literary theories. They have had to confront the problems of theory but, as it were, accidentally: so their concern has not been with theory *qua* theory, but with theory only in so far as it makes a practice explicit. The subject of this essay is the relationship of one aspect of recent theorizing – the concept of authorial intention – to editorial practice. In particular, I shall be examining whether rationales for annotation can ever be adequate without resorting to such a concept.

The introduction to this volume indicates the diversity of the problems encountered by text-editors; and in particular the way different demands made by different *kinds* of texts and works[2] has led to doubts about the possibility of a single, unified, and comprehensive theory of text-editing. The case which I wish to argue is that, in much the same manner, the sheer variety of problems which any annotator faces suggests that there can never be any single adequate theory of the practice of annotation. Explicit discussion of the theoretical issues involved in textual annotation is in fact surprisingly rare. Most recent editions of the works of major writers silently acknowledge this paucity of theorizing, but fail to recognize the profound nature of the problems of annotation. In fact, they simply ignore them. A number of recent editions have proposed for their contributing editors a set of prescriptions about annotation which – not to mince words – are intellectually naive. So it is not unusual to see general editors proposing a universal *fiat* to their contributors which requires the provision of annotation for allusions which a moderately well-educated, non-native speaker of English would not understand. The imperatives dictating such a *fiat* may be simple economic ones – after all, to continue with my financial metaphor, editions which can identify the widest possible *market*, rather than a cohesive or homogeneous *readership*, clearly stand the best chances of selling well. But there are some important theoretical consequences of such programmes. Generally speaking, the unstated aim of such editions is the reconstruction of the entire historical context in which a work was originally produced. The operations of what philosophical aesthetics has called the institutional elements involved in the production of a work of art constitute this context; hence it is these elements which must be made explicit by the annotator. With a work of literature, such institutional elements will include considerations such as the nature of an audience and an awareness of the fact that a work is produced via a set of relationships, and, on occasions, transactions, between author, publisher, and reader. Such annotation takes as its premise, then, that all literary works are produced within a cultural milieu: hence, the proposition that there can be a non-social literary artifact is a contradiction in terms. The general schemes for annotation which I referred to above, then, have as their (invariably unstated) aim an attempt to recover the role of the institutional elements (as Dickie understands them) involved in a work's production. In so doing they take as their criterion for annotation the recovery of those aspects of a cultural milieu which are deemed appropriate for a work's understanding.[3]

Martin C. Battestin, in what is perhaps the best-known attempt to determine a rationale for annotation, proposes an argument broadly in line with these observations.[4] He suggests that any annotator has to be aware of the character of her (modern) audience, of her own (subjective) interests, and of the precise nature of the work to be annotated. While he concedes that there can be no 'single rationale for literary annotation', and that an editor should distinguish between what he calls 'notes of recovery' and 'explanatory' notes, he also finally suggests that a work may be perfectly understood:

The purpose of literary annotation, whether of 'explanatory notes' or 'notes of recovery,' is to recover for the reader, as briefly and objectively as possible all essential information (and *only* essential information) necessary to render the author's meaning wholly intelligible, the 'author's meaning' being understood as not only the primary denotative significance of a passage but also, when appropriate, its full range of implicit associations, whether biographical, historical, or literary.[5]

Already some of the contradictions and problems implicit in the enterprise may be glimpsed. Thus the difficulties of ascertaining what constitutes the real import of terms such as 'essential information', 'the author's meaning', 'intelligible', the 'full range of implicit associations', are never properly addressed, let alone explained. The question which Battestin fails to discuss adequately is the one which motivates his whole rationale for annotation – namely, what constitutes the understanding of a literary work. These are general objections. A fairly trivial example from the work of Walter Pater will give them the force of a concrete problem. It will indicate the nature of the dilemma faced by most annotators, but it will also expose the limitations of the projects which envisage historical reconstruction as a remedy. Under the rubric usually proposed by general editors which I have described above, a phrase from Walter Pater's imaginary portrait, 'Emerald Uthwart' about Uthwart's schoolboy companion and hero, James Stokes, would have to be glossed for three kinds of audience. The phrase describes James Stokes as 'the prefect, his immediate superior'.[6] For a non-European reader the phrase might simply be meaningless. For a European reader it might have contradictory connotations: thus for French readers the term 'prefect' suggests particularly national forms of authority and is alarmingly similar to current French usage for the head of a police force. And for readers educated in some Catholic institutions the term designates a senior master (that is, a teacher) in a Jesuit school. So for all of these cases some modern general editors would require the elucidation of a term still in fairly wide usage in Britain, particularly among those Britons educated in public or grammar schools. What such editors have done is to presuppose a degree of ignorance based, in the first instance, upon assumptions about a limited knowledge of British culture. In these prescriptions the role that the individual editor is required to take is that of an ideal, perfectly knowledgeable, and perfectly competent reader, a reader for whom all textual allusions and all possible meanings are simultaneously available. Of course, the problem is not simply that no such reader exists. Rather, it is that no such reader can exist. In the first instance, changes in the significance of allusions are simply products of larger, historical changes. So even those contemporary British readers who know the meaning of the term 'prefect' (and who, given experience of prefect-systems in British schools, might perhaps be reminded of its current French usage) will not necessarily be in possession

of the changes in the significance of the term. It is precisely here
that the limitations of Battestin's programme can be seen.
Accounts of prefecture, and thus of authority, are never value-
free. Put crudely, the prefect-system in nineteenth-century
British public schools was varied, and is different from the
system that operates in some British schools today. Attitudes to
authority, to social hierarchies, to what some contemporary
American cultural historians have called 'male homosocial
bonding' – all these issues are susceptible to significant, but
silent, historical change as the values which give them force
change also. The ability of the commentator to reconstruct the
nature of those changes is both practically and theoretically
flawed.

In fact the general objections to the schemes for annotation
outlined above fall into three groups and may be ranged on a
spectrum, from the highly abstract to the severely practical; I
shall elaborate them in that order. The first set of objections has
to do with the basic rationale for any annotation – its aim of
enabling a prospective reader to 'understand', in whatever
way, the work before him. Annotation will by its very nature
validate some readings and attempt to disable others: such,
after all, is one of its undeclared purposes. And often
annotation, although rarely explicitly so, tends to point to *one*
reading to the exclusion of others. It tends, that is, to limit what
critics since the heyday of Roland Barthes have called the
plurality of the text. This tendency to assign priority to one
particular reading at the expense of others, to move in the
direction of an allegedly 'correct' reading, may not always be
the intention of the annotator, but it is a simple consequence of
selectivity or partiality. In so far as the annotation of any work
inevitably places limits on possible readings, the case for its
provision will be contested by a powerful group of contemporary critics, the most prominent of whom are decon-
structionists. Because a contemporary deconstructionist would
want to expose the contingent nature of these assumptions, she
would almost certainly want to adopt a position which would
entail the disabling of all such annotation. On its own terms,
such a view cannot be contested. As I shall suggest later, all

annotation *is* by its very nature contingent; moreover all annotators and all readings of texts obviously exist within an historical moment and within a particular culture. Thus no annotation will ever be able to acquit itself from the charge of being arbitrarily authoritative; and thus annotation willynilly, like all other texts (and, indeed, all human products), will bear witness to the specificity of the moment of its production. Clearly, then, there can be no congruence between the principles of explicatory textual annotation and those underlying the practices of deconstruction. Any attempt to bring the two together is a compromise of both parties, because there can be no grounds for an agreement, or even for a debate, between theorists of text-editing and theorists of deconstruction. There is no epistemological agreement about the nature of texts or works, about the existence of 'the literary', and finally no real agreement about the nature of knowledge, evidence, proof, and so forth. But if the deconstructionist's case cannot be adequately rebutted on its own terms, then it certainly can be met on other grounds.

The rationale for the production of scholarly editions of literary works is posited on two assumptions: first, on the existence of a concept of 'the literary' as a defining feature or characteristic or aspect of certain texts, and secondly, on the proposition that some texts are to be valued on that ground more than others. Today these views might need defending or justifying by literary critics, but textual scholars have always based their activities upon the assumption that the concept of literariness is unproblematic. The obvious examples are editions of Shakespeare. All editors and critics, with a few notable exceptions,[7] assume the distinction of Shakespeare's work rests primarily on literary grounds – insofar as the term 'literary' is generally understood. Although there are obviously cases where such grounds are less clear (including, for example, many minor Renaissance writers, and more pertinently, the letters of all major literary figures) this assumption remains unquestioned. However, invoking a concept of 'literariness', while it may be a justification for the production of scholarly editions of texts, cannot in itself be a justification for annotation.

The practice and problems of annotating (what I shall for the moment call) a self-evidently literary work are inevitably quite unrelated to the rationale for the selection of the work in the first place.

This distinction between the rationale for producing an edition and that for annotating an edition becomes a little clearer if I compare a literary work with a political or philosophical one. In the latter case there is no disjunction between the rationale for editing the work in the first place and the rationale for the provision of annotation: the reasons for choosing to produce a scholarly edition of a political or philosophical work are inseparable from its political or philosophical contexts. But the literary judgement involved in making a case for editing, say, a work by Shakespeare, has nothing initially to do with the kind of information which an annotator would invariably wish to provide in an edition – information about sources, about the work's social and political reference, and so forth; and perhaps only secondarily with information about the semantic shifts of individual lexical items, and so on. Such information is not strictly relevant to a literary judgement, insofar as a literary judgement is invoked as the principle reason for the editing of a work in the first place; it is, however, like notes about sources and reference, relevant to an understanding of a work's historical significance. But such information will not in the first place have any significant bearing upon a *contemporary* judgement about the literariness of an individual work, otherwise there would obviously be no need for the edition. Scholarly information is not usually a necessary precondition for the designation or attribution of literariness; rather it is appropriate *after* an initial judgement about a work's literariness has been made. To justify an edition of a work by arguing a need for contextualizing information (historical, social, and political) is to press the work's historical, not literary, significance. This qualification is one which underlies many critical objections to the notes provided in particular editions. Thus, for example, in the case of a nineteenth-century writer it is possible to provide a body of contextualizing information about the intellectual and intertextual reference of his work (although, as I shall suggest, in the case of a group of writers which includes Walter Pater and Oscar Wilde, even this practice can be problematic). However, this argument for the provision of annotation makes no distinction on literary grounds between works such as Wilde's *The Picture of Dorian Gray* and John Stuart Mill's *On Liberty*. The primary justification for an edition of Mill's work is its philosophical and political contexts, although of course there are other social or historical contexts which might be relevant and which a prospective editor might wish to address; however, no cultural contexts, in whatever way they may be defined, can provide an equivalent justification for producing an annotated edition of a literary work.

These observations are in fact far from new. The same issues surfaced in the 1880s when Frederick Furnivall set up the Browning Society in order to make the poet's work more accessible by annotating it. The rationale for this enterprise was Browning's acknowledged literary pre-eminence. So in his inaugural address to the Society in University College, London on 28 October 1881, the Reverend J. Kirkman argued that 'our *raison d'être*...is that Browning is undoubtedly the profoundest intellect, with widest range of sympathies, and with universal knowledge of men and things, that has arisen as a poet since Shakespeare...[H]is truly Shakespearean genius pre-eminently shines in his power to throw his whole intellect and sympathies into the most diverse individualities.'[8] The practical objective of the Society was to produce annotated and scholarly editions of Browning's work, and in his reply to Kirkman's introductory address Furnivall spoke of such a need. Indeed, a little later the first report of the Browning Society's committee noted that this objective had been met by the commissioning of 'extra books like...*primers*...lexicons of Browning's Allusions, and of Browning's Words and Phrases'.[9] However Furnivall's proposals did not meet with universal approval. In fact he was criticized by a variety of individuals and institutions; he was even enlisted to the ranks of distinguished figures mocked by the cartoonists of *Punch*. But the most famous of Furnivall's opponents was Algernon

Swinburne, an old adversary, who expressed the generally held view that the literary qualities of Browning's work were self-evident; or, if those qualities were not self-evident, no amount of annotation could or would demonstrate their existence. Swinburne was particularly dismissive of the usefulness of Furnivall's scholarship, pouring scorn on his 'monumental, his pyramidal, his Cyclopean, his Titanic, his superhuman and supernatural nescience of everything and of anything that could give him the faintest shadow of a moment's right to put forth the humblest whisper of a neophyte's suggestion on the simplest and most insignificant subject connected with the text'.[10] Wilde, as usual, was wittier but equally withering. He noted drily in 'The Critic As Artist' that 'The members of the Browning Society, like the theologians of the Broad Church Party...seem to me to spend their time in trying to explain their divinity away. Where one had hoped that Browning was a mystic, they have sought to show that he was simply inarticulate.'[11.]

These issues surfaced much more recently, but at a more theoretical level, in the early 1950s in an exchange between F.R. Leavis and F.W. Bateson in the pages of *Scrutiny* over the editorial programme announced by the then newly-founded *Essays in Criticism*. In *Scrutiny* Leavis had consistently maintained that the defining characteristics of literary texts were their *literary* qualities, and that it was the literary critic who was therefore uniquely qualified to elucidate them. The editorial of *Essays in Criticism*, however, explicitly opposed itself to this view, arguing that literary criticism so defined and so practised was inevitably far too subjective. In order to introduce what he described as a necessarily objective, and therefore scholarly, rigour into the discipline, Bateson proposed that texts should be read in the light of their 'social context'. And in so doing he was, of course, making exactly the kind of case assumed by most annotators today. Indeed Bateson went on to argue that 'correct' readings depended upon such contextual knowledge:

To discover their meaning [of the words of a whole poem] we have to ask what they meant to their author and his original readers, and if we are to recover their full meaning, the connotations as well as the denotations, we shall often find ourselves committed to precisely those stylistic, intellectual and social explorations that Dr Leavis now deplores. There is no alternative – *except to invent the meanings ourselves.* Dr Leavis is in fact opening the door to sheer subjectivism.[12]

Bateson's polarization of the issues into objective contextuality and 'sheer subjectivism' was of course, as he later conceded, plainly silly. But Leavis was none the less stung to an immediate response, and his reply addressed two issues, the methodological and the theoretical. His first objection was that in the absence of any *literary* criteria to establish the conditions of appropriateness, it was simply impossible to set limits to the investigation of a social context. The process and procedures of contextualization thus became an infinite regression, and so in practice it could only be a completely pointless task:

What *is* this 'complex of religious, political and economic factors that can be called the social context'...? How does one set to work to arrive at this final inclusive context...? Mr Bateson doesn't tell us, and doesn't begin to consider the problem...all he could do...would be to go on...[taking random notes from his historical reading] more voluminously and industriously. For the total 'social context' that he postulates is an illusion...'context', as something determinate, is, and can be, nothing but his postulate; the wider he goes in his ambition to construct it from his reading in the period, the more is it *his* construction (in so far as he produces anything more than a mass of heterogeneous information alleged to be relevant)...The student who sets out in quest of such a 'context'...will find that the kind of 'context' that expands indeterminately as he gets from his authorities what *can* be got contains curiously little significance – if significance is what, for a critic, illuminates a poem. And he may go on and on – indeterminately.[13]

While this criticism was debilitating, it is Leavis's theoretical objections which are more important for my argument. In the first place Leavis reiterated a familiar criticism of historicism, that any account of the past, because inevitably incomplete, will of necessity be a subjective construction of it. In the second place, he suggested that such a procedure anyway diverted the critic from his proper object of study, the 'literariness' of the literary work:

If you propose to place the importance of literary criticism in some non-literary-critical function, you betray your unbelief that literary criticism really matters. And, if you don't believe in literary criticism

then your belief that literature itself matters will have the support of
an honoured convention, but must be suspect of resting very much on
that. And if you don't see that literature matters for what really gives
it importance, then no account you offer...can be anything but
muddle and self-delusion.[14]

What Leavis recognized, and Bateson by default later
conceded, was that such an historicist project threatened to
abolish the only ground upon which the singularity of literary
criticism could be sustained: that is, it collapsed the 'literary'
into other categories, such as, in Bateson's programme, the
social, the political, or the economic. While Leavis was willing
to concede that literary judgements had social and political
dimensions, he none the less insisted (as he did throughout his
career) that their basis had to be criticism of a specifically
literary character:

> The special discipline of an English school is the literary-criti-
> cal...There is no more futile study than that which ends with mere
> knowledge *about* literature. If literature is worth study, then the test
> of its having been so will be the ability to read literature intelligently,
> and apart from this ability, an accumulation of knowledge is so much
> lumber. The study of a literary text about which the student cannot
> say...why it should be worth study is a self-stultifying occupation.[15]

Leavis had thus inadvertently identified, although with an
unerring correctness, precisely the issues involved in drawing
up a programme for annotation. He had recognized, that is,
that decisions about the provision of historical, social, or
biographical contextual information depend upon a *prior*
literary judgement; and that this provision therefore cannot in
any way contribute to a literary judgement. And secondly, that
any such contextual historical information is inevitably a
construction placed upon the past. In fact Leavis's objections
can be made in a stronger form. A familiar argument in
hermeneutics holds to the view that, if through the passage of
time a literary work has come to be culturally distant from the
modern reader, then there can be no guarantees that works (or
documents) taken from other discourses or disciplines will not
have also suffered from a similar process of hermeneutic
obfuscation: bluntly put, if the understanding of a literary work

has become 'corrupt' (in whatever way), then so too has the understanding of texts (or works) from all other discourses.

For the sake of my argument, however, I shall assume that all these qualifications and reservations concerning both the theoretical and practical limits to be placed on contextual information count for nothing: I shall take as given, that is, the notion of 'literariness', and I assume the theoretical possibility of the provision of appropriate annotation. Given these enormous concessions, then – given that we can in theory know why we need to annotate – the second problem becomes *how*, or for whom, in practice do we annotate. Unlike the first set of issues, which has generally been ignored, this second set has been addressed by editors; indeed, the notion of audience, however defined, is the most commonly invoked criterion of appropriateness for annotation. The most thoughtful pre-scriptions for annotations along such lines have been made by Ian Jack and Stephen Wall.[16] Broadly put, in their view, the *raison d'être* of annotation requires an editor to make explicit the cultural and literary knowledge which was implicit for contemporary readers; or to make explicit the cultural knowledge which a writer assumed was implicit in the cultural assumptions of his or her contemporary readers: to define, that is, in the language of Jauss and German reception theorists, the 'horizon of expectations' of a work. So Wall, quoting a well-known passage in *Dombey and Son*, argues that, as modern readers removed from the specific referents of Dickens's descriptions, and without adequate textual information, we are unable to decide whether Dickens is writing 'as a keen-eyed reporter of a verifiable contemporary scene, or whether he is transmuting it into Hogarthian hallucination'.[17] Wall goes on to suggest that one reason 'why classic English novels need annotation is that they often still feel close enough for us not to realise how far off they have become'.[18] Wall's case is that the task of the modern editor is to make explicit the knowledge (relevant to the work in question) which was implicit in nineteenth-century culture and which any author of the time knew his audience possessed. As I have indicated, the principles outlined by Wall have found a lot of agreement (although it is never made wholly explicit) among the general editors of many recent nineteenth- and early twentieth-century novels. In them, however, one crucial problem of editorial judgement remains vexed: the question of what contemporary cultural knowledge is deemed relevant for understanding a work. Leavis's point, expressed rather differently, about a constantly receding historical context remains unaddressed. Later in the same periodical Ian Jack took up Wall's proposals and enlarged upon them by describing how a similar set of principles had guided the intentions of the Clarendon editors of the novels of the Brontes:

> The conclusion is obvious that even an edition which has been well annotated is likely to require new notes a few decades later. There is always a new audience, with its new ignorance.
>
> The principal duty of an annotator is to attempt to enable his contemporaries to read a book as his original audience read it. This calls for the explanation of words which are unfamiliar or which have changed their meaning, the provision of information about social customs and historical events, and the identification of quotation and allusion.[19]

Jack's assertion here that a work requires a constant re-annotation (because, as he alleges, every audience has its 'new ignorance'), reveals the relevance of Leavis's strictures about the limitations of historical reconstruction. For, as Leavis suggested, all such reconstruction as 'something determinate, is, and can be, nothing but [the editor's] postulate'. If the original 'well-annotated' edition *necessarily* has a built-in obsolescence, then what is the point of the reconstruction of the original context of the book (even granted that such a context may be so reconstructed)? The 'original context', that is, can only be an illusion if it stands in need of such constant reconstruction and rediscovery. Jack wants to have his editorial cake and eat it too, for in his argument one of the duties of the annotator is to be aware of the constantly changing needs of a modern audience, while another is merely to recreate a contemporary historical context, defined without reference to any present-day demands. The latter programme has as its declared ambition a definitive annotation, while the former takes for granted the provisionality of any possible annotation.

If the notion of an audience is to be used as a criterion of appropriateness for annotation, then the question remains, is it possible to come to any fixed decisions about the nature of either a modern or a contemporary audience? To take the case of the modern audience first. It is obvious that the modern annotator of any work has to have a fairly clear working concept of the literary competence of her prospective (that is, modern) readership, even if that concept is nowhere made fully explicit. It is after all only such a concept which will allow an editor to determine what information still forms part of our own (that is, modern) culture and what information has ceased to do so; without such a concept all decisions about annotation will constantly encounter accusations of arbitrariness. Now it is probably true that in most cases all actual decisions about annotation will be strongly contested, for what is to count as knowledge of contemporary culture is not the simple matter it at first sight appears to be. Criticism of annotation very often picks up this point; and disputes about the level of shared cultural knowledge, as Wall and Jack noted, become more frequent the more recent the work. So the Shakespearean editor can be reasonably confident that Troilus' pledges to Cressida in Act ii of *Troilus and Cressida* require *some* form of annotation:

> As true as steel, as plantage to the moon,
> As sun to day, as turtle to her mate,
> As iron to adamant, as earth to th'centre...[20]

The annotator is unlikely to need reassurance that knowledge about the coinage of the word 'plantage', of the contemporary significance of the term 'adamant', and the proverbial fidelity of turtles does not form part of modern readers' cultural knowledge. But the case for glossing the reference to a 'Tantalus frame' in the stage directions of Act iii of Oscar Wilde's *Lady Windermere's Fan* is less clear. The editor may decide that knowledge about the use of such a frame is no longer part of most readers' general experience. And there will always be areas, as in the case of James Stokes's prefectship mentioned above, where annotation will reveal as much about the values and social experience of the annotator as it does about the work in question. The same is true of a veritable minefield of problems for the annotator of nineteenth-century society drama, the effect of which often depends upon very precise representation of nuances of late nineteenth-century etiquette, some of which survive to the present day in some circles of British society, but not necessarily in the domestic arrangements of provincial academic critics or editors. The general point concerns the modern editor's relationship to his audience. An annotator has to address a homogeneous audience, for she cannot provide information for a culturally (let alone nationally) diverse audience; yet the concept of a homogeneous and undifferentiated audience, which a prospective annotator can identify and address, clearly requires an accompanying concept of a homogeneous and undifferentiated culture and sub-culture. Today such cultures and sub-cultures manifestly do not exist. And even if homogeneous and identifiable cultures were to exist, they would, as Ian Jack notes, be subject to constant change through time.

There are difficulties, then, in establishing what is to count as literary competence in our own time, and hence what is to count as a common cultural knowledge among modern readers. Given this, how possibly can the modern editor set about establishing, as Bateson, Jack, Wall, and, to some extent, Battestin indicate, what counted as literary competence in a nineteenth-century readership, and so discover how an 'original' audience read, or might have read, the work in question? Some of the general objections to such a simple historicism have already been rehearsed, but if we assume for the moment that such objections may be overcome, and that the nature of past audiences may in theory be defined, then we are still left with a set of practical problems – the third of those general issues mentioned above – concerning the way in which an editor sets about his task. I shall keep to examples taken from the nineteenth century, for it is clear, as Jack and Wall note, that works from that period throw general editorial problems into sharp relief.

Now the social history of the nineteenth century is, among other things, the history of the growth of cultural pluralism.

Some literary historians of the later nineteenth century have gone further and have tended to characterize changes in late nineteenth-century culture in terms of the advent and growth of consumerism, economic changes which in their turn had profound consequences for the relationships between author, publisher, and audience or readership.[21] With the advent of consumerism, works became commodities; given contemporary developments in printing technologies, greater general literacy, a widening general readership, and the increasing influence of the popular press, popular writers tended to become personalities. All of this, if correct, has quite clear implications for the task of identifying and describing a contemporary audience. Thus although quite a lot of information about what social historians have awkwardly called the 'social addressees' of Victorian literature is available, and although, in some cases, as with West End theatre, those audiences can be characterized with a fair degree of precision, the concept of an author's original readership still needs to be handled with caution. (The distinctions which ought to be made, and to which I shall return, are between, as in the case of some late nineteenth-century theatre, actual addressees, and the class or category of potential addressees: broadly, as I have already suggested, the difference between a market and a readership.) One example of the problems inherent in the concept of readership occurs in *Wuthering Heights* (and, although in a less severe form, in D.H. Lawrence's early novels). Ian Jack discusses the need for a modern editor to gloss the dialect words in *Wuthering Heights*; the contributing editors to the Cambridge edition of the works of Lawrence follow a similar practice. It is not however immediately clear on what grounds such information should be provided. Jack's argument, that dialect should be glossed as part of the overall ambition of the editor to recover the ability 'to read a book as [the] original audience read it', certainly becomes an implausible one, because it is far from clear whether or not many contemporary readers *were* in fact in possession of such linguistic knowledge. (There is another explanation, to which I shall return, for the use of dialect in *Wuthering Heights*: the annotator should at least entertain the possibility that Emily Brontë *did not intend* dialect words to be understood.) In cases such as the supposed knowledge of dialect words, the possibility of discovering who an audience actually was, and thus of determining what exactly can be said to constitute a common cultural knowledge, is much more remote than at first sight it appeared to be. It is clear that such a task will not readily lend itself to empirical investigation; and even if it were possible to conduct such an investigation, where would its limits, practically and theoretically, be drawn? How in fact is it possible to count readers, as opposed to purchasers or potential purchasers of a book? Would readers of the second and successive editions count as 'original' readers? Would the editor discount, for the purposes of constructing the notional 'original' audience, Scottish, Welsh, Irish or, indeed, American readers, whose knowledge of English culture would necessarily be different from that of English readers? And – a qualification which substantially affects issues such as dialect words – in what senses does an 'English' audience constitute a homogeneous group? These examples may seem trivial, and in some cases involve splitting hairs; and certainly they seem far removed from the practical problems of annotation; but none the less they point to an important qualification. The concept of an 'original' (contemporary) audience is always, in some senses, going to be a conjecture or construction by the modern editor placed upon the past; and it thus renders itself liable to exactly the same kind of objections as Bateson's project for the construction of an historical context for literary works.

It could at this point be objected that the *actual* readers of a work form a too restricted notion of readership. It *is* possible to discover a great deal about the income, social background, and beliefs, and so forth, of the *category of potential readers* which might well have formed the actual readership of a nineteenth-century novel or play. And, as theatre historians such as Joseph Donohue and Russell Jackson have demonstrated,[22] in the case of some performances of plays, it is indeed possible to recover a great deal of this and similar information. However, in the case of readerships of novels, and of some poems, such an investigation would not be easy to undertake, and might not perhaps even be desirable, since, even if it could be intelligently and accurately characterized, the categories of *actual* or of *potential* readers will not tell us much about the category of *possible* readers, and it is this last category which is going to suggest to the modern editor what can be meaningfully understood as common or shared cultural knowledge. (It should be noted in passing that the concession that there are differences between dramatic and other forms of texts involves abandoning the project of a general theory of annotation, even if the limitations which I have noted above are discounted.) But the concept of a possible readership is also one fraught with difficulties and in the end turns out to be as problematic as the category of actual readers. Once more, the crucial question concerns the ways in which it should be restricted. Should it, for example, merely mean all those who could read, or those who could read and buy, rent, or borrow the work in question? Should it be in some sense related to the initial sales of the book, so that the characterization of the relatively small numbers of 'original' readers of the *Lyrical Ballads*, say, would have to be, on that ground alone, clearly different from the vast 'original' readership of a novel such as *Robert Elsmere*? Should a characterization of an 'original' readership be subject to historical limitations, to include only those who could form a possible readership within a set period after a book's publication? Every definition of 'original' readers in terms of actual readers or notional readers creates more problems than it solves: as a hypothesis it is either plausible but unworkable, or workable but implausible, a distinction to which I shall return.

There are, then, severe practical problems when the rationale for annotation depends upon any notion of audience. Such annotation has to presuppose the homogeneity of an audience, whether it is defined as actual readers, possible readers, or notional readers. This assumption leads to intractable problems with some late nineteenth-century novels where what an editor may surmise about the implicit addressees or actual readers leads to difficulty and contradiction. The difficulties arise from the fact that such a presupposition ignores the possibility that a novel might quite deliberately address several different and mutually exclusive audiences. So in novels such as Wilde's *The Picture of Dorian Gray*, Pater's *Marius the Epicurean*, or Henry James's *The Tragic Muse*, quotation, allusion, and reference – precisely those textual features which an editor would feel impelled to annotate – may be seen as devices to distinguish between audiences: to exclude, in the case of Pater, for example, the mass of readers in favour of a coterie.

Some examples taken from *Marius the Epicurean* will make this general point a little clearer. In that novel Pater uses a great number and a great variety of liturgical quotations. At two points in the work he quotes from a rubricated Mass and from a form of words from one of the prayers to be said during the celebration of high Mass found in fairly obscure liturgical settings:

Cum grandi affectu et compunctione dicatur: – says an ancient eucharistic order...
Adoramus te Christe, quia per crucem tuam redemisti mundum! – they cry together.[23]

Pater does not translate for the reader – as he does with some of his quotations – nor does he indicate a source. The evidence from the text, then, as far as it can be used in this way, is that Pater expects his readers, or some of them, to be familiar with what now is, and was then, recondite liturgical material. Despite this, and despite the scholarly publishing of liturgical material by bodies such as the Henry Bradshaw Society (whose publication of the material in hand was in fact twenty years after the novel's first publication[24]), it seems a very moot point whether or not many of Pater's original readers were in fact in possession of such knowledge. The editor must suppose, however, that Pater's 'original' readers were indeed widely read in classical and liturgical material and hence in possession of such information; she will therefore presumably gloss the material to make such information available to his modern, less widely-read audience. The editor has already made an assumption which is tending to qualify or to compromise the nature of the 'original' readership which was the criterion by which the provision for annotation was to be gauged, for in fact it is highly unlikely that many of Pater's readers would have known such a recondite source (the original of which is a manuscript of a rubricated Mass held in the Bodleian Library).

A second example of this problem occurs in some of the intertextual references in the novel. On many occasions in the novel Pater runs together quotations from diverse sources. A good example of this complex use of intertextuality can be found in Chapter 18, where the reader encounters the following string of allusion, citation, and quotation in a meditation by the Roman emperor Marcus Aurelius:

> Chance: or Providence! Chance: or Wisdom, one with nature and man, reaching from end to end, through all time and all existence orderly disposing all things, according to fixed periods, as he describes it, in terms like certain well-known words of the book of Wisdom... Yet one's choice in that speculative dilemma, as he [Aurelius] has found it, is on the whole a matter of will. – ''Tis in thy power', here too again, 'to think as thou wilt.' For his part he has asserted his will, and has the courage of his opinion. 'To the better of two things, if thou findest that, turn with thy whole heart: eat and drink ever of the best before thee.' 'Wisdom', says that other disciple of Sapiential philosophy, 'hath mingled Her wine, she hath also prepared herself a table'...'Partake ever of her best!'[25]

Passages such as these are richly eclectic. The first reference is to the Book of Wisdom in the Apocrypha, especially 6:12 to 8:1, where Wisdom is described as 'reaching from one end of the world to the other' and 'ordering all things well'. Aurelius' first quotation is taken from the *Meditations*, IV.3; and the reference to 'Sapiential philosophy' is of course to the 'Wisdom' books of the Bible, while the quotation itself is taken from Proverbs, 9:2. The last quotation is also from the *Meditations*, but from an earlier passage (III.6). What is important, though, is obviously *not* the origins of the quotations, but the fact that they come to the reader dislocated from their original contexts, with no qualification about the vastly different nature of their liturgical, biblical, or philosophical authority. Part of the effect of the passage exists in precisely that process of textual dislocation, the effect of which would not have been lost on an educated nineteenth-century reader, but might well have been on his more ignorant contemporary. By

supplying the original context to the quotation, the annotator
is ignoring the fact that the novel marks out for itself two quite
different types of audience: the learned and the ignorant. A
much more precise instance of Pater playing on the ignorance
of his readers occurs in Chapter 12, where he appears to be
quoting Homer:

> [T]hat well-worn sentence of Homer sufficeth,
>   to guard him against regret and fear:
>   Like the race of leaves
>   The race of man is.[26]

True, this *appears* to be translated quotation from Homer. But
as the following lines in the novel make clear to anyone who has
read the *Meditations*, Pater is quoting Marcus Aurelius quoting
Homer. Then, two sentences later, in a final test of knowledge
of his reader, Pater supplies the next lines from Homer, which
Aurelius omits, but in the original (and unattributed) Greek.
The difficulty of annotating passages such as these lies not in
the location or attribution of quotations, but rather in the
complexity of their usage. They seem designed to differentiate
between sorts of reader, and the editor has to choose which sort
he will annotate for. Now if, as I have suggested, appeals to an
'original' readership will not help, for not only must there have
been in fact very diverse kinds of readers, but the novel itself
seems to discriminate *between* kinds of readers, then the
annotator's only recourse is to appeal to a notion of authorial
intention.

The annotator thus confronts quite squarely, as I indicated
at the beginning of this essay, the concept of intention.
Intentionality provides a way in which the notion of audience
can be defined, but it scarcely needs to be said that the
assumptions upon which it is posited have been questioned.
The annotator, by attempting to identify the implicit addressees
of a specific work (or text, even) necessarily has to invoke some
form of intention, since those addressees form the category of
readers which the author had, or could have had, in mind.
Such intentionalist theories have been subject to objections too
well-known and too numerous to list here. But there have also
been vigorous defences of the concept of intentionality, and a

group of philosophers of aesthetics have suggested that it might be useful for literary critics to talk of varieties of intentionality with regard to literary texts.[27] The debate about the rationale for the use of intentionality as a principle for annotation, then, is not as clear-cut as Wimsatt and Beardsley have led a generation of critics to believe.[28] There is, moreover, a larger point at issue. If, as I have indicated, there are no formulae or readily applicable tests which will allow decisions about annotation to be determined in advance, the crucial questions involve how, and on what grounds, annotators come to make the decisions which they do make. The idea of intention is once again helpful here; indeed, some examples of intertextual *jouissance*, such as Pater's citing of Homer via the work of Marcus Aurelius, become impossible to understand without the assistance of some notion of intentionality. Annotators and editors should only be concerned with theories in so far as they elucidate practice, or make the principles of a practice explicit; and, as a matter of practice, most editions rely (and have to rely) on a concept of authorial intention. And that for one simple, and very good, reason: that is more useful – in the sense that it does more work – than any other theory.

NOTES

This essay develops some ideas which I originally broached in 'Critical Opinion: Annotating "Hard" Nineteenth Century Novels', *Essays in Criticism*, 36 (1986), 281–93, and in 'Editing Pater', *English Literature in Transition*, 30 (1987), 213–18. Reviewers of the first essay suggested that I should elaborate some of my arguments, which I have attempted here. I have consequently reiterated some of the points made in the earlier essays. I have discussed the relationship between problems of editing and problems of annotation in 'Editing and Annotating Pater', in *Pater in the 1990s*, ed. Laurel Brake and Ian Small (Greensboro, N.C., 1991), pp. 33–42.

1 Terry Eagleton, *Literary Theory: An Introduction* (Oxford, 1985), pp. 210–11.

2 The terms 'texts' and 'works' are used interchangeably by many critics. In this essay I abide by the distinction made by textual critics: that texts may embody, but not exhaust a work. Hence there is one work called *The Importance of Being Earnest*, of which there are many texts.

3 For an account of institutional theories of art, see George Dickie, *Art and the Aesthetic: An Institutional Analysis* (London, 1974); for a critique of his argument, see Robert McGregor, 'Dickie's Institutionalized Aesthetic', *British Journal of Aesthetics*, 17 (1977), 3–13. Probably the most fruitful application of institutional analyses of art has been by reception theorists. See, for example, Hans-Robert Jauss, *Towards an Aesthetic of Reception* (Manchester, 1985).

4 Martin C. Battestin, 'A Rationale of Literary Annotation: The Example of Fielding's Novels', *Studies in Bibliography*, 34 (1981), 1–22.

5 *Ibid.*, pp. 19–20.

6 Walter Pater, 'Emerald Uthwart', in *Miscellaneous Studies* (London, 1900), p. 184.

7 Terence Hawkes is the most notable exception. So in a televised conversation with Kenneth Baker, the then Minister for Education, he confessed that in his view: 'There's another sense of culture... what ordinary people get up to in their lives, and how they make their lives meaningful... *Making Out* [is]...a programme... about women in our society, which I think is one of the finest dramatic confrontations that I've ever seen, far more interesting than Shakespeare' (*The Late Show with Clive James*: Terence Hawkes, Fiona Shaw, Kenneth Baker. BBC2 TV, 20 January 1989).

8 Revd J. Kirkman, 'Introductory Address to the Browning Society', *Browning Society Papers*, 1 (1881–4), 172.

9 Furnivall's reply is summarized in 'Browning Society: Monthly Abstract of Proceedings,' *Browning Society Papers, ibid.*, pp. 13–16; see also 'First Report of the Browning Society's Committee', *Browning Society Papers, ibid.*, p. iii.

10 Quoted in Claude K. Hyder, *Swinburne: The Critical Heritage* (London, 1970), p. xxxiv. Swinburne was writing here of Furnivall's Shakespearean scholarship. In his essay on George Chapman he wrote in a similar way of Browning, arguing that he was 'too brilliant and subtle for the ready reader of a ready writer to follow with any certainty the track of an intelligence which moves with such incessant rapidity' (Hyder, *Swinburne*, p. 157).

11 Oscar Wilde, 'The Critic As Artist', *Intentions*, in *The Oxford Standard Authors: Oscar Wilde*, ed. Isobel Murray (Oxford, 1989), p. 244.

12 F.W. Bateson, 'The Responsible Critic: A Reply', *Scrutiny*, 19 (1953), 320.

13 F.R. Leavis, 'The Responsible Critic', *Scrutiny, ibid.*, pp. 173–4.

14 *Ibid.*, p. 180.

15 F.R. Leavis, *Education and the University* (London, 1943), pp. 59 and 68.
16 See Stephen Wall, 'Annotated English Novels?', *Essays in Criticism*, 32 (1982), 1–14; and Ian Jack, 'Novels and those "Necessary Evils": Annotating the Brontës', *Essays in Criticism*, 32 (1982), 320–30.
17 Wall, 'Annotated English Novels?', p. 2.
18 *Ibid.*, p. 6.
19 Jack, 'Novels and those "Necessary Evils"', p. 323.
20 *Troilus and Cressida*, III.ii.175–7.
21 The first critic to suggest this way of regarding late nineteenth-century culture was Raymond Williams in *Culture and Society* (London, 1958); the most recent is Regenia A. Gagnier in *Idylls of the Marketplace: Oscar Wilde and the Victorian Public* (London, 1987). I have attempted to assess the significance of the changes in intellectual authority for a wide range of nineteenth-century disciplines of knowledge, and in particular of literary criticism, in my *Conditions for Criticism* (Oxford, 1991).
22 See Joseph W. Donohue, Jr, 'The First Production of *The Importance of Being Earnest*: A Proposal for a Reconstructive Study', in *Essays on Nineteenth Century British Drama*, ed. Kenneth Richards and Peter Thomson (London, 1971), pp. 125–43; and Russell Jackson (ed.), *Victorian Theatre* (London, 1989), pp. 9–76.
23 Walter Pater, *Marius the Epicurean*, ed. Ian Small (Oxford, 1986), pp. 216 and 219.
24 See 'Alphabetum Sacerdotum', Douce 14, in *Tracts on the Mass, Henry Bradshaw Society*, vol. XXVII, 1904.
25 Pater, *Marius*, p. 168.
26 *Ibid.*, p. 116.
27 The work of John Searle is of immediate relevance here. Apart from discussions of the exchange between Searle and Derrida in *Glyph*, Searle's account of intentionality has not been given much attention by literary critics. More importantly, its relevance for textual annotation has not been noticed. See John Searle, *Intentionality: An Essay on the Philosophy of Mind* (Cambridge, 1983).
28 See W.K. Wimsatt, and Monroe C. Beardsley, 'The Intentional Fallacy' (1946), in *The Verbal Icon: Studies in the Meaning of Poetry* (Lexington, Ky., 1954).

James T. Boulton: publications 1951–1991

1951

'An Unpublished Letter from Paine to Burke', *Durham University Journal*, 12, 49–55.

1953

'The *Reflections*: Burke's Preliminary Drafts and Methods of Composition', *Durham University Journal*, 14, 114–19.

1954

'Charles Knight and Charles Dickens: *Knowledge is Power* and *Hard Times*', *The Dickensian*, 50 (March 1954), 57–63.

1956

'The Use of Original Sources for the Development of a Theme: Eliot in *Murder in the Cathedral*', *English*, 11, 2–8. Partly reprinted in *Twentieth-Century Interpretations of Murder in the Cathedral*, ed. David R. Clark (Englewood Cliffs, N.J.: Prentice-Hall, 1971), pp. 74–9.

1957

'A Baconian Error', *Notes and Queries*, n.s. 4, 378.

1958

(ed.) Edmund Burke, *A Philosophical Enquiry into the Origin of our Ideas of the Sublime and Beautiful* (London: Routledge and Kegan Paul). (Second edition, 1968.)

'Exposition and Proof: The Apostrophe in Burke's *Reflections*', *Renaissance and Modern Studies* (Nottingham: University of Nottingham) 2, 38–69.

1960

(ed.) C.F.G. Masterman, *The Condition of England* (London: Methuen).

1962

'The Letters of Junius', *Durham University Journal*, 23, 63–9.
'Mrs Elizabeth Montagu (1720–1800)', *The Burke Newsletter*, 3, 96–8.
'James Barry (1741–1806)', *The Burke Newsletter*, 3, 144–8.
'David Garrick (1717–1779)', *The Burke Newsletter*, 4, 171–4.
'Literature and Politics: I. Tom Paine and the Vulgar Style', *Essays in Criticism*, 12, 18–33. Reprinted in *The Burke–Paine Controversy: Texts and Criticism*, ed. Ray B. Browne (New York: Harcourt, Brace, and World, 1963).

1963

The Language of Politics in the Age of Wilkes and Burke (London: Routledge and Kegan Paul). (Second edition, 1965.)
'Harold Pinter: *The Caretaker* and Other Plays', *Modern Drama*, 6, 131–40. Reprinted in *Harold Pinter: Twentieth-Century Views* (Englewood Cliffs, N.J.: Prentice-Hall, 1972).

1964

(ed.) John Dryden, *Of Dramatick Poesie: An Essay* (Oxford: Oxford University Press). (Second edition, 1971.)

1965

(ed.) Daniel Defoe, *Selected Writings* (London: Batsford).

1966

(with James Kingsley) *English Satiric Poetry: Dryden to Byron* (London: Edward Arnold).
'Edmund Burke's *Letter to a Noble Lord*: Apologia and Manifesto', in *Renaissance and Modern Essays Presented to Vivian de Sola Pinto*, ed. G.R. Hibbard (London: Routledge and Kegan Paul).
'The Letters of Edmund Burke: "Manly Liberty of Speech"', in *The Familiar Letter in the Eighteenth Century*, ed. Howard Anderson, Philip B. Daghlian, and Irvin Ehrenpreis (Lawrence: Kansas University Press).

1967

'Arbitrary Power: An Eighteenth-Century Obsession' (Inaugural Lecture, the University of Nottingham).

1968

Lawrence in Love: Letters from D.H. Lawrence to Louie Burrows (Nottingham: University of Nottingham). (Second edition, 1969; Japanese edition, 1972.)
'Arbitrary Power: An Eighteenth-Century Obsession', repr. in *Studies in Burke and his Time*, 9, 905–26.
'The Criticism of Rhetoric and the Art of Communication', in *Essays on Rhetorical Criticism*, ed. Thomas R. Nilsen (New York: Random House), pp. 29–49.

1969

'D.H. Lawrence's Odour of Chrysanthemums: An Early Version', *Renaissance and Modern Studies*, 13, 5–38.

1970

Introduction to Daniel Defoe, *Memoirs of an English Officer*, ed. M. Seymour-Smith (London: Gollancz).

1971

(ed.) *Samuel Johnson: The Critical Heritage* (London: Routledge and Kegan Paul).
Introduction to D.H. Lawrence, *Movements in European History* (London: Oxford University Press). (Revised edition, 1981.)
(with S.T. Bindoff) *Research in Progress in English and Historical Studies in the Universities of the British Isles*, 1 (London and Chicago: St. James's Press).
'A Note on an Unpublished Story by Jessie Chambers', *Renaissance and Modern Studies*, 15, 5–6.

1972

(ed.) Daniel Defoe, *Memoirs of a Cavalier* (London: Oxford University Press).
'Burke and the French Revolution', *The Listener* (27 February), 110–11.

1973

The Letters of D.H. Lawrence: Prospectus and Notes for Volume Editors (Cambridge: Cambridge University Press).

1974

'A Note on an Uncollected Article by W.H. Roberts', *Renaissance and Modern Studies*, 18, 5–6.
'E.M. Forster: "Three Generations"', *Notes and Queries*, n.s. 21, 376–7.

1975

(ed.) *Daniel Defoe, Selected Writings* (second edn. Cambridge: Cambridge University Press).

1976

(with S.T. Bindoff) *Research in Progress in English and History in Britain, Ireland, Canada, Australia and New Zealand*, II (London and Chicago: St. James's Press).

1977

'James Mackintosh: *Vindiciae Gallicae*', *Renaissance and Modern Studies*, 21, 106–18.

1978

'Letters That Reveal a Life: The Letters of D.H. Lawrence', *Times Higher Education Supplement* (10 November), 10–11.
(with Warren Roberts) *The Cambridge Edition of the Works of D.H. Lawrence: Prospectus and Notes for Volume Editors* (Cambridge: Cambridge University Press).

1979

(ed.) *The Letters of D.H. Lawrence: Volume I, 1901–13* (Cambridge: Cambridge University Press).

1980

'The Cambridge University Press Edition of Lawrence's Letters', in *D.H. Lawrence: The Man Who Lived: Papers Delivered at the D.H. Lawrence Conference at Southern Illinois University, Carbondale, April*

1979, ed. Robert J. Partlow and Harry T. Moore (Carbondale: Southern Illinois University Press).

1981

(ed., with George Zytaruk) *The Letters of D.H. Lawrence: Volume II, 1913–16* (Cambridge: Cambridge University Press).

1983

Introduction to Thomas Paine, *The Last Crisis No. XIII* (Birmingham: The Hayloft Press).

1984

(ed., with Andrew Robertson) *The Letters of D.H. Lawrence: Volume III, 1916–21* (Cambridge: Cambridge University Press).

1985

(ed.) *D.H. Lawrence, 1885–1930: First Centenary 1885–1985*, *Renaissance and Modern Studies*, 29.

'D.H. Lawrence: Letter-Writer', *Renaissance and Modern Studies*, 29, 86–100.

1987

(ed., with Warren Roberts and Elizabeth Mansfield) *The Letters of D.H. Lawrence: Volume IV, 1921–24* (Cambridge: Cambridge University Press).

(ed.) Edmund Burke, *A Philosophical Enquiry into the Origin of our Ideas of the Sublime and Beautiful* (rev. edn, Oxford: Basil Blackwell).

'"On the Brink of the Unknown": An Address in Honour of D.H. Lawrence' (Birmingham: Hayloft Press).

1989

(ed., with Lindeth Vasey) *The Letters of D.H. Lawrence: Volume V, 1924–27* (Cambridge: Cambridge University Press).

'"Quand je vous écris...": D.H. Lawrence à travers sa correspondance', in *L'Herne D.H. Lawrence*, ed. Ginette Katz-Roy and Myriam Librach (Paris: L'Herne), 43–8.

'D.H. Lawrence as a Letter-Writer', *Studies in English Language and Literature* (Seinan Gakuin University, Fukuoka, Japan), 3, 1–11.

Introduction to *D.H. Lawrence in the Modern World*, ed. P. Preston and
P. Hoare (London: Macmillan), pp. 1–6.

1991

(ed.), Daniel Defoe, *Memoirs of a Cavalier* (London: Oxford University
Press, World's Classics).
(ed., with Margaret H. Boulton and Gerald M. Lacey) *The Letters of
D.H. Lawrence: Volume VI, 1927–28* (Cambridge: Cambridge
University Press).

FORTHCOMING

(ed., with Keith Sagar) *The Letters of D.H. Lawrence: Volume VII,
1928–30* (Cambridge: Cambridge University Press).
(ed., with T.O. McLachlan) *The Writings and Speeches of Edmund
Burke: Volume I, Literary Writings* (Oxford: Oxford University
Press).
Selected Letters of D.H. Lawrence (Cambridge: Cambridge University
Press).

Index

Abrams, M. H., 8, 10
Addison, Joseph, 65; *Spectator*, 166
addressees of fiction, 200–1; *see also*
   audience
aesthetic criteria in editorial
   judgements, 36–48
Alexander, Peter, 127, 129
Ancients and Moderns, 174
annotation, 8, 186–207; and audience,
   197–200; and contextual
   knowledge, 9–11, 193–9; rationale
   for, 188–90; theory of, 187
Aristotle, 100, 113, 138, 177
art, institutional theories of, 187–8
audiences, 192; historical understanding
   of, 196–206; kinds of, 187, 189–90,
   199–200, 201–2; and market, 187;
   for nineteenth-century theatre,
   199; *see also* annotation
Austen, Jane, 68
author, death of, 157
authority, 1

Badaracco, Claire, 6, 8, 11
Bailey, Nathan, *Universal Etymological
   Dictionary*, 44; *Dictionarium
   Britannicum*, 44
Baker, George, 87
Baker, Kenneth, 208
Baker, Thomas, *Reflections Upon Learning*,
   57
Balderson, Katherine C., 60
Baldwin, T. W., 139
Barthes, Roland, 68, 157, 161, 177, 180,
   181, 190
Barton, John, 131
Bateson, F. W., 194–6; *Essays in
   Criticism*, 194
Battestin, Martin C., 188, 190, 200

Bayle, Pierre, 50
Beardsley, Monroe C., 208
Bentley, Richard, 10, 12, 157–85 *passim*
Bevington, David, 125, 127, 129, 130,
   135, 137
Bible, 10; and scholarship on, 7;
   Authorized Version of, 172; books
   of: Genesis, 7; Exodus, 171, 173,
   180; Job, 172; Proverbs, 205; 1
   Corinthians, 171, 172; Ephesians,
   172; Hebrews, 172; 'Wisdom'
   books, 205
Black, Michael, 34
Blayney, Peter, 96
Bloom, Harold, 10
Boccalini, 167
Bodleian Library, 205
Boothby, Hill, 61
Boulton, James T., 1, 5, 11, 32, 33;
   *Prospectus and Notes for Volume
   Editors of The Letters of D. H.
   Lawrence*, 5, 11
Bowdler, Thomas, 146; *Family
   Shakespeare*, 146
bowdlerization, 27
Bowers, Fredson, 4, 7, 23, 35, 39, 138,
   158
Bristol, Michael D., 142
British culture, audience's knowledge of,
   188–9
British Library, 54, 58
Brockbank, Philip, 131
Brontë, Emily, *Wuthering Heights*, 201–2
Brook, Peter, 108
Browning, Robert, 51, 194
Browning Society, 193
Bunyan, John, *Pilgrim's Progress*, 42
Burden, Denis, 162
Burlowe, Henry Behnes, 83

216

Butler, Charles, *Feminine Monarchie*, 173
Buxtorf, Johann, 50
Byron, George Gordon Lord, 67, 86

cabbala, 10
CD–ROM, 54; 100–1; *see also* interactive video disc; *see also* WORM
Chambers, Ephraim, 50
Chesterfield, Philip Dormer Stanhope, Earl of, 5, 65
Chilcott, Tim, 88
Clare, John, 1, 5, 62–89; *Child Harold*, 62, 86; *Don Juan*, 62; 'Farewell & Defiance to Love', 78; letters of, 1, 7; *The Midsummer Cushion*, 65; 'Prison Amusements', 86; *The Rural Muse*, 65; *Shepherd's Calendar*, 63, 64, 77; 'The Sleep of Spring', 86–7; 'The Village Ministrel', 63, 79
Clarke, Thomas, 85
Clayton, Douglas, 23, 31
Cohen, Murray, 60
Coleridge, Samuel Taylor, 69, 161; 'Conversation Poems', 69
Collier, John Payne, 142–3
Collins, John Churton, 152
Cooper, Lane, 60
Cooper, William, 67
Coulthard, Malcolm, 60
Cowden-Clarke, Charles, 143
Cowden-Clarke, Mary, 149
Crabbe, George, 72
Craig, Hardin, 125
Crane, Stephen, 23; *The Red Badge of Courage*, 23
Criticism, the New, 9
Culler, Jonathan, 69, 79
cultures, 200; *see also* audience
Cunningham, J. S., 129, 140

Dampier, Dr Thomas, 184
Daniels, Ron, 137
Darbishire, Helen, 158, 164
Davis, Tom, 13, 160
Davis, Walter R., 141
Davison, Peter, 93
De Maria, Robert, 51
deconstruction, 190–1
Derrida, Jacques, 10, 157
Dewey, John, 36
Dickens, Charles, 14, 22, 6–7, 197; *Dombey and Son*, 14, 22, 197

Dickie, George, 188
Dickinson, Emily, 63
discourse colony, 48–52
Dodsworth, Martin, 89
Dollimore, Jonathan, 156
Don Quixote, 167
Donato, Eugenio, 68–9
Donohue, Joseph W. Jr, 208
Dorsch, T. S., 126, 129, 135, 137, 140
Douglas, Lord Alfred, 5
Drakard, John, 83
Drury, Edward, 63, 72, 81
Dryden, John, 162, 167, 181; *Religio Laici*, 184; *The State of Innocence and the Fall of Man*, 167
Dudley, Dean, 87
Duppa, Bryan, *Holy Rules and Helps to Devotion*, 47

Eagleton, Terry, 207
Eaton, Marcia Muelder, 182
editing: conjectural, 164–5, 176; of dictionaries, 5, 7, 35–61; documentary, 6; historical, 6; humanist, 10; of letters, 6, 62–89; literary, 6–7; and metrics, 126–7; and original context, 159, 173; popular, 142–6; purposes of, 8; scholarly editing, assumptions of, 191; for schools, 146–55; subjective, 160; and value, 6; *see also* aesthetic criteria
editions: and character criticism, 148–50; expurgated, 145–6; moral and social purposes of, 143–6; and school exercises, 146–8
editorial conjecture, 127–9
editorial judgements, 48
Edwards, Philip, 92, 94
Edwards, Thomas, *Canons of Criticism*, 180
Eichhorn, J. G., 7
Encyclopaedia Britannica, 50
Erasmus, 12
Evans, Maurice, 141

facsimiles, 54, 66
Farmer, David, 33
Farmer, Fanny, 36
Fish, Stanley, 9, 10
Fleeman, David, 53, 55
Fleming, Lindsay, 47
Flower, C. E., 115, 145–6

Foakes, R. A., 129, 135
Fogarty, L. C., 154, 155
Foucault, Michel, 68
Fowler, Alastair, 162, 169, 170
Furness, Horace Howard, *New Variorum Shakespeare*, 146
Furnival, F. J., 143, 193; New Shakspere Society, 143

Gabler, Hans Walter, 14
Gagnier, Regenia A., 208
Galileo, *Siderius Nuncius*, 170
Ganzel, Dewey, 142
Gardner, Dame Helen, 9
Garnett, Edward, 25–8
Garnett, Mrs, 51
Gaskell, Philip, 11
gemara, 10
Gibbon, Edward, *Decline and Fall of the Roman Empire*, 42
Gilderoy, James, 78
Gower, William, *Confessio Amantis*, 118
Graff, Gerald, 9
Gray, Thomas, 65, 67
Greene, Donald, 47–8
Greg, W. W., 4, 35, 111, 122, 137
Gurr, Andrew, 137

Haight, Gordon S., 60
Hall, Sir Peter, 108
Hall, S. C., 81–2
Halsband, Robert, 11, 65
Hamlyn, Susan, 160
Hancher, Michael, 182
Hanmer, Sir Thomas, 135
Hardy, Thomas, 67
Hawkes, Terence, 156, 208
Henry Bradshaw Society, 204
Hercules Furens, 104
hermeneutics, 196–8
Hill, John, *History of the Materia Medica*, 44
Hinnant, Charles, 52
Hirsch, E. D. Jr, 38–43, 69, 157–60, 167, 174, 180
historicism, 194–5
Hoey, Michael, 48–51
Holland, Revd Isaiah Knowles, 72, 80
Homer, 10, 126, 138, 162, 179, 206
Hone, William, 78
Honigmann, Richard, 91
Hooker, Richard, 57
Horace, 167–8, 175

Horsman, Alan, 22
Howard-Hill, T. H., 136, 138
Howitt, Mary, 86
Hudson, Henry N., 153
Hume, Patrick, 163, 170, 179
Hyder, Claude K., 208

intention, authorial, 1, 37–46, 156–62; and dictionaries, 43–8
interactive video disc, 91, 99; *see also* CD–ROM; *see also* WORM
Iser, Wolfgang, 88

Jack, Ian, 50, 197–8, 199, 200, 201
James, Henry, 15–16, 204; *The Tragic muse*, 204
Jauss, Hans-Robert, 2, 197
John Rylands Library, Manchester, 53
Johnson, Dr Maurice, 84
Johnson, Samuel, 3, 65, 115–16, 135, 164, 170; *Dictionary*, 3, 35–61 *passim*, 129; *Irene*, 47; *Preface to Shakespeare*, 139, 166
Jones, William Arthur, 87
Jowett, John, 138
Joyce, James, 25; *Ulysses*, 14
Junius, Francis, 44

Kane, George, 12
Keast, William R., 60
Keats, John, 67, 68
Kemble, John Philip, 131, 136
Kernan, Alvin, 43
Kestner, Joseph, 68, 69
Keynes, Sir Geoffrey, 85
Kirkman, Revd J., 193
Knight, Charles, 143, 145
Knight, William, 86
Kolb, Gwin J., 43, 53
Komisarjevsky, Theodor, 117, 122

La Bruyère, Jean de, 167
Lachmann, Karl, 12
Lamb, Charles, 72
Lamb, Charles and Mary, *Tales from Shakespeare*, 146
Lawrence, D. H., 1, 3, 5, 6, 8, 14–33, 201; Cambridge edition of, 29, 32, 201; *Aaron's Rod*, 23, 4; *Amores*, 16; *The Boy in the Bush*, 23, 24; *Collected Poems*, 16, 18; *Delilah and Mr Bircumshaw*, 28, 32; *Fantasia of the Unconscious*, 23, 24; *Lady Chatterley's*

Lover, 23, 24; letters of, 129; *Love Among the Haystacks*, 32; *Mr Noon*, 23, 24; *New Eve and Old Adam*, 19; *The Prussian Officer and Other Stories*, 24; 'The Shades of Spring', 23; *Sons and Lovers*, 25; 'Virgin Youth', 15–16; *Women in Love*, 13, 17–22, 23, 24
Lawrence, Frieda, 17–19, 22, 28
Leavis, F. R., 194–6, 198; *Scrutiny*, 194
letters: and implied reader, 62, 66–7; and dating of, 79–87; *see also* editing
Levin, Harry, 129
Lewis, C. S., 136, 141
Lichfield, 45
literariness, 1, 3–4, 35–43, 191–7; and politics, 196; and economics, 197
literature, theories of, 186–7
Lloyd, Phyllida, 125, 136, 138, 139
Locke, John, *Paraphrase and Notes on the Epistles of St Paul*, 46
Locrine, 104
Lodge, Thomas, 143; *Rosalynde*, 143
Longhurst, Derek, 156
Lyde, Lionel W., 147, 151
Lyrical Ballads, 203

MacLeish, Archibald, 108
Mallet, David, 164, 166; *Of Verbal Criticism*, 166–7
Malone, Edmond, 129
Marcus Aurelius, 205–6; *Meditations*, 205–6
Marder, Louis, 156
Marshall, Revd F., 148, 149
Martin, Frederick, 80
Marvell, Andrew, 78
McCabe, Richard, 107
McCracken, David, 59
McGann, Jerome, J., 8, 161–2, 163, 164, 181
McKenzie, D. F., 138
McKerrow, R. B., 91, 122
meaning, determinacy of, 46, 157
meaning, distinguished from significance, 159–60
Meisel, Martin, 156
Messing, S., 81
microfiche, 66
Mill, John Stuart, 36, 68; *On Liberty*, 193

Miller, Philip, 44; *Gardener's Dictionary*, 44
Milton, John, 8, 10, 57, 158–85 *passim*; 'Lycidas', 9; *Comus*, 174, 184; *Il Penserososo*, 174; *Paradise Lost*, 9, 158–85 *passim*; *Paradise Regained*, 174
Milton Restor'd, and Bentley Depos'd, 166, 180
Minnis, Alistair, 4
Minor, Mark, 79
Montagu, Lady Mary Wortley, 65
Montaigne, Michel, 104
Montgomery, James, 86
Montgomery, William, 138
Morley, Henry, 143–4, 145, 151
Mozart, Wolfgang Amadeus, 115
Muir, Kenneth, 100
Murray, Isobel, 208

New Critics, 157
New English Dictionary, 45
New Grove Dictionary, 50
Newton, Isaac, 183
Newton, Thomas, 179, 184
Nicoll, Allardyce, 100
Noble, Adrian, 120, 136
Northampton General Lunatic Asylum, 62
Noyes, Gertrude E., 60
Nunn, Trevor, 108, 136

Ong, Walter, 69
Oxford English Dictionary, 43

Page, Thomas, 148
Parker, Hershel, 11
Pater, Walter, 5, 189, 193, 204; 'Emerald Uthwart', 189; *Marius the Epicurean*, 204–6
Pearce, Zachary, 162, 171–3, 184
Peckham, Morse, 36–8
Peele, George, 139; *The Old Wife's Tale*, 113
Pembroke, Countess of, 141
performance texts, 107–41 *passim*
Plato, 112, 113
Plautus, 118–25 *passim*, 139; *Amphritruo*, 115; *Curculio*, 140; *Menaechmi*, 115, 140; *Miles Gloriosus*, 139
Pliny, 173
Poel, William, 154
political and philosophical works, editions of, 192

Pope, Alexander, 5, 65, 76, 125, 128,
146, 165, 178, 183; *Dunciad*, 175,
176–7, 178, 180; *Epistle to Dr
Arbuthnot*, 165
Powell, David, 62
Prior, Matthew, 183
Punch, 193

quotation, 204–6

readership, 201–3; kinds of, 203;
modern, 206–7; original, 203; *see
also* audience
readings, 'good' and 'correct', 160,
165–6
reception-theory, 197
Reddick, Allan, 61
Reed, Joseph W. Jr, 60
Reynolds, Frederick, 115
Reynolds, Sir Joshua, 53
Richards, I. A., *Practical Criticism*, 9
Richards, Kenneth, 208
Richardson, Jonathan, 166
Richardson, Samuel, *Clarissa*, 44
Ricks, Christopher, 162
Robert Elsmere, 203
Roberts, Gareth, 140
Roberts, Warren, 33
Robinson, Eric, 62, 64
Ross, Charles L., 14
Ross, Robert, 5
Rousseau, J.-J., 151
Rowell, Rosie, 134
Rowse, A. L., 134
Rugby School, 150

Sagar, Keith, 26
Salgado, Gamini, 139
Saussure, Ferdinand de, 160
Scapula, Johannes, 50
Scholes, Robert, 180
Schorer, Mark, 26
Scotus, Duns, 177
Scriblerus, Martinus, 174–5
Searle, John, 208
Servius, 184
Shakespeare, 36, 46, 107–41, 191, 193,
199; texts of, 132–3; Cambridge
edition of, 96–9; Oxford edition of,
96; 1623 folio of, 111; folios and
quartos, 94, 104–5; performance
texts of, 3; *As You Like It*, 109,
142–55; *Comedy of Errors*, 107–41

passim; *Coriolanus*,57; *Cymbeline*, 114,
121; *Hamlet*, 91, 94, 132, 133;
Love's Labour's Lost, 102, 122;
Measure for Measure, 122; *Merchant
of Venice*, 122; *Merry Wives of
Windsor*, 122; *A Midsummer Night's
Dream*, 102, 107, 122; *Much Ado
About Nothing*, 122; *Pericles*, 112,
113, 114, 121, 132, 133; *Richard
III*, 93, 137; *Tempest*, 117, 122;
Timon of Athens, 105; *Troilus and
Cressida*, 199; *Twelfth Night*, 112,
114; *Two Gentlemen of Verona*, 122;
Winter's Tale, 113
Shakespeare, editions of, colonial, 151
Shakespeare Newsletter, 100
Sharp, William, 81–2
Shaw, Fiona, 208
She Stoops to Conquer, 160
Sher, Antony, 137
Sherbo, Arthur, 61
Sheridan, Thomas, 44
Shillingsburg, Peter, 39, 41, 55
Sidney, Sir Philip, 141; *Arcadia*, 141
Sinfield, Alan, 156
Skinner, Stephen, 44
Sledd, James, 43
Smart, Christopher, 1, 5; *Poetical Works*, 1
Smith, J. C., 152
Southey, Robert, 67
Spenser, Edmund, 180
Sprague, A. C., 156
Starnes, De Witt T., 60
Stavisky, Aaron Y., 156
Steele, Sir Richard, 65
Steiner, George, 10
Stenberg, Theodore, 60
Stenson, Joseph, 86, 87
Stevenson, O. J., 154
Stillingfleet, Benjamin, 166, 173–4
structuralism, 157
subjectivism, 194
Summerfield, Geoffrey, 64
Swift, Jonathan, 98, 167; *Battle of the
Books*, 176; *Gulliver's Travels*, 99,
105; *Tale of a Tub*, 167, 177–9,
181, 182
Swinburne, A. C., 194

Tale of Gamelyn, 144
Tanselle, G. Thomas, 3, 4, 5, 6, 12, 32,
38, 39–42, 72, 65–6, 138, 158–61,
164, 165–6

Tate, Frank, 151
Tate, Nahum, 167, 181
Taylor, Gary, 127, 129, 130–1, 133,
    132, 136, 138, 141, 142, 156; and
    Warren, Michael, 33; and Wells,
    Stanley, 183
Taylor, John, 67, 72–5, 77, 79–80, 88
Taylor, Dr John (friend of Samuel
    Johnson), 50
Taylor, John (publisher of John Clare),
    62–89 *passim*
Teale, Owen, 131
Tedlock, E. W., 34
Tennyson, Alfred Lord, 67
Terence, 175
Tetzeli von Rosador, Kurt, 129, 137
text: appearance of, 93–4; as
    differentiated from work, 157–8; as
    scripture, 177–80; originary
    moment of, 161
text-editing and pedantry, 90
texts: 'correct', 14, 21; data retrieval
    in, 101–3; definitive, 14; generic
    diversity of, 2; 'mobile', 96–7;
    modernization of, 11; multiple,
    14–33, 133; and performance,
    92–3, 95; physical embodiments of,
    2; private and public, 3–4, 66;
    transmission of, 94
textual instability, 91–2
Theobald, Lewis, 128
Thomson, Peter, 208
Thornton, R. K. R., 65
Thorpe, James, 158
Thyestes, 104
Tibble, Anne, 65, 70–1, 79
Tibble, J. W., 70–1, 79
Tillotson, John, 179, 184
Todd, John Henry, 184
Todorov, Tzvetan, 68
Townsend, Chauncey Hare, 79
Tuppenny, Revd Richard, 80

University College, London, 193

Vasey, Lindeth, 24, 33
Verity, A. W., 152
Virgil, 163, 170, 175, 179; *Aeneid*, 170;
    Eclogues, 170; *Georgics*, 170, 184

Walker, John, 44
Wall, Stephen, 197, 199, 200
Walpole, Horace, 65
Warburton, William, 180
Warner, Deborah, 137
Warren, Michael, 138
Warton, Joseph, 'Ode to Fancy', 85
Watts, Isaac, *Psalms of David Imitated*,
    167, 181
Webster, Daniel, 45
Wells, Stanley, 92, 95, 129, 134, 135,
    136, 138; and Taylor, Gary, 13,
    122, 140
Werstine, Paul, 122, 138
Widdowson, Peter, 156
Wiffen, Jeremiah, 86
Wilde, Oscar, 193, 194; *Works*, 1, 5, 8;
    'The Critic as Artist', 194; *De
    Profundis*, 5; *The Importance of Being
    Earnest*, 208; *Lady Windermere's Fan*,
    199; *The Picture of Dorian Gray*, 2,
    193, 204
William IV, 83
Williams, Raymond, 208
Williamson, Karina, 13
Wilson, John Dover, 123, 129, 136
Wimsatt, M. H., 60
Wimsatt, W. K., 60, 139, 208
Winbolt, S. E., 151
Womersley, David, 59
Wood, Stanley, 148, 149
works, versions of, 55–7
WORM, 100–1, *see also* interactive
    video disc; *see also* CD–ROM
Worthen, John, 33
Wotton, William, 175–6
Wright, William Aldis, 126, 152

Zeller, Hans, 55